FREE AND FEMALE is now. . . .

"The proper study of womankind is by woman—and this book is an important step toward honesty in the study of female sexuality."

—Gloria Steinem

"FRANK, FORTHRIGHT, EXPLICIT."

—Publishers Weekly

"I hope soon all women will be liberated enough to be 'free and female' in Barbara Seaman's sense—to explore and affirm honestly their own sexuality as subject, not object, and to experience a fully human sexual relationship with men."

—Betty Friedan

"REALLY ANSWERS ALL THE QUESTIONS WOMEN HAVE WANTED TO ASK ABOUT SEX BUT NEVER DARED."

—Chicago Sun-Times Showcase

"Barbara Seaman has written what every woman needs to know in the process of finding her inner identity and realizing her full sexual potential."

—Nena and George O'Neill,
authors of "Open Marriage"

FREE AND FEMALE tells all. . . .

"Compassionate, personal. . . . for women—and men—who want real food rather than cotton candy."

—Newsweek

"INTELLIGENT AND OPTIMISTIC."

—Kirkus Reviews

"Debunks the old mottos, amends the new ones, comes out sounding sensible and sensual. . . . This book is not a tract. It is humorous, open, and pointed toward all women who are looking for straight information about themselves."

—Boston Globe

"AN EXCELLENT BOOK."

—The New York Times

"Finally, a sex book that skips the old clichés. . . . It is recommended to any woman who felt 'The Sensuous Woman' was really a slave girl's guide to happiness."

—Houston Post

FREE AND FEMALE

by Barbara Seaman

A FAWCETT CREST BOOK

Fawcett Publications, Inc., Greenwich, Conn.

FREE AND FEMALE

A Fawcett Crest Book reprinted by arrangement with
Coward-McCann & Geoghegan, Inc.

Copyright © 1972 by Barbara Seaman

Library of Congress Catalog Card Number: 70-172633

Alternate Selection of the Doubleday Book Club

Printed in the United States of America
August 1973

Auerback, Alfred, "Roundtable: How Can Sex Be More Pleasure-
able?" *Medical Aspects of Human Sexuality*. Copyright © 1971 by
Hospital Publications, Inc. Reprinted by permission of the author.

Barnett, Joseph, "Sex and the Obsessive-Compulsive Person,"
Medical Aspects of Human Sexuality. Copyright © 1971 by Hospital Publications, Inc. Reprinted by permission of the publisher.

Brecher, Edward, "With a Life at Stake," *McCall's*. Copyright ©
1967 McCall's. Reprinted with permission of the author and publisher.

Bunker, John P., "Surgical Manpower," *New England Journal of
Medicine*. Copyright © 1970 by Massachusetts Medical Society. Reprinted by permission of author and publisher.

Connor, Lynn, "Male Dominance, the Nitty-Gritty of Oppression," *It Ain't Me Babe*. Copyright © 1971. Reprinted by permission of the publisher.

Davis, Hugh, *Intrauterine Devices for Contraception*. Baltimore, The Williams & Wilkins Co., Copyright © 1971. Reprinted by permission of the author and the publisher.

Friedman, Lawrence J., "Art Versus Violence," *Arts in Society*, Vol. 8, No. 1, 1971. Madison, University Extension, The University of Wisconsin. Reprinted by permission of the publisher.

Hoffman, Lois, Unpublished letter to David L. Murray. Reprinted by permission of the author.

Marshall, Donald S., and Suggs, Robert C., eds., *Human Sexual Behavior*. New York, Basic Books, Inc. Copyright © 1971. Reprinted by permission of the publisher.

Mead, Margaret, *Male and Female*. New York, William Morrow & Co., Copyright © 1949 by Margaret Mead. Reprinted by permission of the publisher.

Morehead, Mildred; Donaldson, Rose S.; and others, *A Study of the Quality of Hospital Care Secured by a Sample of Teamster Family Members in New York City*. New York, Columbia University, School of Public Health and Administrative Medicine, 1964. Reprinted by permission of the author.

Morehead, Mildred; Trussell, Ray E.; Ehrlich, June; and others, *The Quantity, Quality and Costs of Medical and Hospital Care Secured by a Sample of Teamster Families in the New York Area*. New York, Columbia University, School of Public Health and Administrative Medicine, 1962. Reprinted by permission of the author.

Parker, Dorothy, "Resume," from *Enough Rope* by Dorothy Parker, also in *The Portable Dorothy Parker*. New York, The Viking Press, Inc. Copyright 1926, renewed 1954 by Dorothy Parker. Reprinted by permission of the publisher.

Sexton, Ann, "The Ballad of the Lonely Masturbator," from *Love Poems* by Ann Sexton. Boston, Mass., Houghton Mifflin Co. Copyright © 1967, 1968, 1969 by Ann Sexton. Reprinted by permission of the publisher.

Sherfey, Mary Jane, *The Nature and Evolution of Female Sexuality*. New York, Random House, Inc. Copyright © 1966 by Mary Jane Sherfey. Reprinted by permission of the publisher.

Shuman, Mort, and Ragovoy, Jerry, "Get It While You Can." New York, Hill and Range Songs, Inc. Copyright © 1967 Hill and Range Songs, Inc. and Ragmar Music Corp. Reprinted by permission of the publisher.

Vidal, Gore, "In Another Country," *New York Review of Books*. Copyright © 1971 by Nyrev Inc. Reprinted by permission of the author and the publisher.

Wright, Helena B., *More About the Sex Factor in Marriage*. London, Ernest Benn, Ltd. Copyright © 1947 by Helena B. Wright. Reprinted by permission of the publisher.

This book is for my father, Henry J. Rosner, who may not agree with it but whose unfailing confidence in me enabled me to write it

CONTENTS

ACKNOWLEDGMENTS

—To my C.R. sisters, Pat Curtis, Mallen De Santis, Nancy Holmes, Barbara Lewis, Susan Moore, Lorna Sloane, Brenda Soloff, and the others, and to my familial sisters, Jeri Drucker and Elaine Rosner.

—To Betty Friedan and Dr. Natalie Shainess for introducing me to feminism, and to Margaret Fiedler, Alice Wolfson and the Women's Liberation Chapter at City College for introducing me to more radical feminism. I particularly wish to thank the anonymous undergraduate at City College who asked me, "If the pill had been a drug for men, would they ever have approved it with so little testing?"

—To Shirley Fisher, for introducing me to Peggy Brooks.

—To the gynecologists and other doctors who radicalized me by demonstrating, in the endless debates following my previous book, that they don't always do their "homework."

—To Beatrice Buckler and Ann Faraday for help with the title.

—To Carolyn Kone, Leon Savage, Diane Lobenfeld, Carol Milano, Andrew Nadel, Ann O'Shea and Ann Wilson for help with research, interviews, and preparing the manuscript; to Beatrice Martel for help with the questionnaires.

—To the 103 women who participated in the sex survey.

—To Dr. Sandor Lorand, Patrick M. McGrady, Jr., Dr. Alice Rossi, Dr. Doris Silverberg, Dr. William Simon, and Barbara Yuncker for reviewing portions of the manuscript and making valuable suggestions. Any remaining errors are entirely my own.

—To the dozens of experts who so patiently explained technical matters, especially Dr. Hugh Davis, Congresswoman Martha Griffiths, Dr. John Money, Dr. Christopher Tietze, attorneys Roy Lucas, Paul Rheingold, and Robert Veit Sherwin; to my grammar school classmate Dr. Charles Debrovner, with whom I always disagree but who always answers my questions honestly and knowledgeably, and to my almost equally long-standing adviser, Dr. Jean Pakter; to all who constitute the "sane fringe" among sex researchers—they know who they are.

—To Gideon, Noah, Elana and Shira Seaman, and also to Sylvia and Bill.

. . . when [a woman's] status and ultimate position do not depend greatly on her husband, she need not be so cautious. Her sexual activity may now be a pleasure to be enjoyed more nearly for its own sake, without regard for its loss in value through promiscuity and loss of "reputation." Her sexual activity is not so much a commodity by which she establishes her ultimate social position, and she need no longer withhold it for exchange purposes. She becomes more like the male in this regard, having less reason to maintain her sexual activity as a scarce good in a market, more reason to consume it for its direct enjoyment.

James Coleman
American Journal of Sociology
September, 1966

INTRODUCTION

Today many Women recognize that they were forced to become what Men wanted them to be. They are understandably angry as they search for a new identity. Some new feminists have rejected men altogether. Others are trying to copy the sexual feelings and behavior of men.

As, I think, all women should, I feel greatly indebted to these militant feminists. In toppling age-old customs and assumptions, they are giving us all a new chance to become happy, healthy, fully functioning human beings. However, women *are* different from men. Our sexuality is both less and more: less in that it is easily suppressed and more in that the limits of our potential almost defy measurement.

Also, we are different reproductively. The male's capacity for erotic experience is bound to and limited by his ejaculate. Normally, he must ejaculate to reach orgasm, and he must reach orgasm to ejaculate. When his seminal fluid exhausts itself, desire does also.

The female's erotic experience is only distantly connected to ovulation,[1] and yet, in every act of coitus, it is the woman who risks pregnancy and the subsequent pains or pleasures of childbirth and nursing. As Niles Newton, a Northwestern University psychologist, likes to point out, "The full understanding of female sexuality cannot come from concentrating on only those parts of the reproductive role that are of interest to adult men."

Some of the women who discover feminism go through a period of intense anger toward men. A few, such as Ann Leffler, a brilliant young sociologist, opt to stay with this feeling. Miss Leffler wears two buttons on her lapel. The first says, "Make War Not Love." The second says, "Feminists Demand Immediate Withdrawal."

She is perfectly serious. "Don't talk to me about love and equality between the sexes. Who needs it?" she said to an audience of psychiatrists recently. "No revolution of the oppressed has ever produced parity, and I don't want parity now. Come back in two thousand years when the first requisite for success is no longer a prick, and we'll argue about love and equality some more."

Some blacks need the likes of Rap Brown to help keep their heads high and spirits up, and some women need the likes of Ann Leffler or Kate Millett.

And yet Miss Leffler's statement is misleading because most feminists want love and equality very much indeed.

Jesus was not a typical Christian. Stalin was not a typi-

[1] As a consequence of fluctuations in hormones, many women feel more or less sexy at different points in the menstrual cycle. Some feel sexiest just prior to their periods, while others feel sexiest at mid-cycle. Some women achieve multiple orgasms during certain portions of the cycle but not at other times. The frequency of erotic dreams and fantasies also appears to vary with the menstrual cycle. However, when these differences occur, they are differences of degree only. Given proper stimulation, woman can reach orgasm at any time.

Another very tentative connection between ovulation and eroticism has been suggested by Masters and Johnson. They have found that under conditions of intense sexual stimulation, some women may ovulate out of their normal cycle.

cal Communist, Nader is not a typical consumer, Brown is not a typical black, and Leffler is not a typical feminist. Unfortunately, it is difficult for many persons to grasp that the revolutionaries who define and dramatize a position or movement are not the same as the ordinary people who typify it.

The typical feminist goes through an initial period of indecision. She says to her friends, "Well, they're right about some things, but they make such a spectacle of themselves, and they take such extreme positions. I agree that if you're a 32A, you don't need a bra, but what if you're a generous 36C—like me?"

Eventually, she realizes that bra burning is only a symbolic issue. And then she starts to burn on another level. A shy Midwestern nurse told me:

"I make thirteen thousand dollars a year, which is good pay for a nurse, but the doctor I work for usually clears more than a hundred thousand dollars. It isn't right because my hours are longer. I do most of the nighttime deliveries, since he has trouble getting himself up and getting to the hospital. I can't handle surgery or other special problems, but I preside at most of the ordinary deliveries. The pay differential is just too much."

The typical feminist is merely a girl or woman who is giving up the masochism that, subtly passed on from mother to daughter, has so long characterized women of the Western world.

Now she wants to be happy and free. She wants to exercise her mind, and her body, joyfully.

This book deals with the body issues.

I hope that it will help women to appreciate how exquisitely formed and beautiful their natural bodies are and what great instruments of pleasure these bodies can be.

I do not know why women should suffer from such shameful feelings about their own bodies. It is easy enough to blame modern commercialism. The sellers of bras and girdles, depilatories, wigs, cosmetics, estrogen pills and (at last—the ultimate insult) feminine hygiene deodorants have much to gain from exploiting our fears and doubts, as they, indeed, do with a vengeance.[2] And yet the roots are surely deeper and go farther back into history. Witness how harshly the Bible deals with menstruation or the fact that a venerable medical term for the female external genitalia, *pudendum,* is derived from the Latin *pudendus*—"that of which one ought to be ashamed."

The more one gives it thought, the more one inclines to believe that Robert Graves may be right after all.[3] Per-

[2]Feminine hygiene deodorants are unnecessary. (Soap and water is as good or better.) They cause irritations in some users. Doctors complain that they are often at a loss to treat patients who have reactions to feminine deodorants, because the ingredients are not contained on the labels (see *Medical Aspects of Human Sexuality,* July 1971, Dr. Bernard Kaye).

In July, 1971, Carol Milano and I wrote to the Food and Drug Administration, asking why it had not required the manufacturers of these products to prove efficacy and safety before placing them on the market and why there is no ingredient labeling. In his reply to our letter, M. J. Ryan, director of the FDA's Office of Legislative Services, explained:

"The Food and Drug Administration does not have the power to require manufacturers of feminine hygiene products to prove the efficacy and safety of these products. These products are classified as cosmetics and, unfortunately, the current law governing the safety of cosmetics only authorizes the Food and Drug Administration to take action against potentially dangerous cosmetics when it can prove the presence of a 'poisonous or deleterious substance.' There is no authority to require the ingredient labeling of known irritants nor even cautionary labeling, except in hair dyes. . . .

"The Food and Drug Administration is concerned with the safety of cosmetics. Particular concern is currently being placed on feminine hygiene sprays.

"You may be interested to know that the Federal Trade Commission also is currently concerned with the potential hazards posed by these sprays. . . ."

Vaginal deodorant sprays are "the success story of the decade," according to the *American Druggist* for June 28, 1971. They constitute "the fastest-growing category in the proprietary drug field." One estimate puts the total market figure for 1971 at $53,000,000.

[3]Some of the worst male chauvinists I have ever encountered were women, and some of the most sensitive feminists were men. Feminism is a state of mind.

haps there was once a Great Mother cult which the patriarchs deliberately destroyed. Surely the basic family unit was once mother and child, and surely, to primitive people, the ability to give birth must have seemed a far greater miracle than the mere possession of an observable, push-me, pull-me, shrink-and-grow penis, however interesting and even worthwhile this organ may be. If you doubt this, consider how small children respond to pets or farm animals. They may or may not notice (upon seeing an erection) that the male possesses something obvious (and often a little awkward-looking actually) which females lack. But should a small child have the opportunity to watch an animal giving birth, he or she, regardless of gender, is positively awestruck. If you have ever had the opportunity to watch a child watch an animal give birth, you will recognize that primitive humans must have held the female body in higher regard than the body of the male. Somewhere along the way, perhaps for political or economic reasons—we shall never know for certain—a deliberate effort must have been made to shift the balance of respect for bodies.

I personally do not think there is any want of scientific evidence that the female body *is* superior, more complex,

---

Robert Graves is certainly a feminist compared to Helene Deutsch. She was a follower of Freud who, in her influential work *The Psychology of Women* (New York, Grune & Stratton, 1944) carried his theory of penis envy further than he had ever dared. The clitoris actually is an "inferior organ," she wrote, and normal girls and women *should* feel inferior because the clitoris lacks the "forward thrusting, penetrating qualities of the penis."

Perhaps it is wise to maintain a high index of suspicion toward all males who claim to be feminists since some of them *are* using the woman issue for their own purposes. I am thinking, for example, of men who have been active in the abortion movement, *not* because they sincerely believe that women have the right to control their own bodies, but, rather, out of concern for population control.

Nonetheless, I plan to cite some male scholarship and research in this book. I have been favored with a generous father, a patient husband and a sweet son, and I cannot despise or dissociate myself from all men.

more economically designed, and even stronger. But, perhaps this is beside the point. For now, if most of us can merely come to respect and enjoy our bodies as much as most men do theirs, we will truly have come "a long way, baby," out of the artificialities of our recent past and into a world that is more natural and more human.

We will almost surely become more creative in the bargain. Anyone who has ever attempted to paint a painting, pen a poem or strum an electric guitar knows that erotic and creative impulses are intimately connected. Freud held that creativity is a result of *sublimated* eroticism. Perhaps he was correct and perhaps not. In any case, one can hardly sublimate an eroticism which has been so thoroughly repressed that one feels no stirrings of it at all. As we shall see in this book, absolute sexual repression has been the fate of many women, but few men. (Those women who have made major contributions to literature and the arts were often exceptionally sexual, perhaps through some permissive quirk in their upbringing.) Actually, Freud (whose own sex life was incomplete, by his own admission) was quite ambivalent and confused on the subject of eroticism vis-à-vis sexuality. He admitted as much, but some of his followers made dogma out of his most tentative suggestions. In any case, Freud stated over and over that the artist needed to enjoy a certain amount of direct sexual gratification. As he commented in the essay *"Civilized" Sexual Morality and Modern Nervousness:*

An abstinent artist is scarcely conceivable. . . . on the whole I have not gained the impression that sexual abstinence helps to shape energetic, self-reliant men of action, nor original thinkers, bold pioneers and reformers; far more often it produces "good" weaklings who later become lost in the crowd that tends to follow painfully the initiative of strong characters. . . . A man who has shown determination in possessing himself of his love-object has our confidence in his success in regard to his other aims as well. On the other hand, a man who abstains, for whatever reasons, from satisfying his strong sexual instinct, will also assume a conciliatory and resigned attitude in other paths of life.

When certain followers of Freud such as Ernest Kris (who was himself a distinguished art historian) and Annie Reich made a study of gifted adolescents they were led to conclude:[4]

> . . . talented people, especially those gifted in the field of art, are characterized by a particular nearness to the instinctual life; that they are, one might say, "more alive" than other people. . . . Such aliveness has to do with a special state of libidinal excitement. . . .

All in all, the best and most lucid of the Freudians *have* equated creativity with a certain amount of *active* eroticism, while failing to resolve the question of where this leaves woman, for whom they recommend a passive eroticism.[5]

The Kinsey studies of women also reveal (to those sufficiently untainted by prejudice to seek out such information) a rather startling connection between female sexuality and intellectual or creative development. Those American women who go farthest in their intellectual, academic or professional development tend to have had their first orgasms at far earlier ages than the norm. (That is to say, the norm for American females; males, of course, have their first orgasms rather earlier.) Dr. William Simon, a former Kinsey Institute researcher, summed up the findings like this: "Most girls are raised to believe that they have a time-bomb between their legs. They are en-

[4] *The Psychoanalytic Study of the child,* XIII (New York, 1958), p. 60.

[5] For further behavioral-science insights into significantly creative females see *The Vanguard Artist* by Drs. Bernard Rosenberg and Norris Fliegel (Chicago, Quadrangle Books, 1965).

couraged to devote much of their creative energy toward preventing this time-bomb from going off. The women who manage to *escape devoting their energies to repression* seem to be the ones who have the most energy left for mental activities, and who also enjoy the most active sex lives."

In the United States, there is a direct correlation (in women) between age of first orgasm and contribution to society. To put it another way, most of the women listed in *Who's Who* and subsidiary volumes had their first orgasms at an earlier age and continue to have orgasms more frequently than the women who are listed in the roster of your local garden club.

There is nothing really new or revolutionary in this information. If you will examine Chaucer's women, you will see that, so many hundreds of years ago, he recognized all these connections. (Perhaps Chaucer and others might really have been females in drag, as Anne Richardson Roiphe fantasizes in *Up the Sandbox!)*

The last vestiges of belief that good sex and good achievement—even in males—might be contradictory has been expressed, in recent years, by certain athletic coaches in the United States who advise their performers to abstain. Recent psychological research establishes that these coaches are antiproductive. Even in sports, it is the independent, self-actualized, rather erotic personalities (Joe Namath, Billie Jean King) who, expressing themselves, manage to bypass their advisers, reach the highest levels of physical accomplishment and become stars.

Today the woman-as-mother is being devalued by the population controllers. The woman who fills the years of her life by raising a large brood of children will become an increasing rarity, for the social pressures are all against it now. Inevitably, woman will rediscover the same outlets that men have long reserved unto themselves—creative work and sex.

And women will be whores no more.

When Ann Landers says to teen-age girls, "If you play around, no nice boy will marry you," she is endorsing prostitution, *polite* prostitution, to be sure.

Professor James Coleman explained why in restrained and sober language (indeed, one might almost say jargon) in the *American Journal of Sociology:*[6]

> . . . the female's principal good-in-exchange by which she can locate herself favorably in society is her sexual activity . . . if this good is to remain valuable it must be carefully guarded and conserved. In contrast, when her status and ultimate position do not depend greatly upon her husband, she need not be so cautious. Her sexual activity may now be a pleasure to be enjoyed more nearly for its own sake, without regard for its loss in value through promiscuity and loss of "reputation." Her sexual activity is not so much a commodity by which she establishes her ultimate social position, and she need no longer withhold it for exchange purposes. She becomes more like the male in this regard, having less reason to maintain her sexual activity as a scarce good in a market, more reason to consume it for its direct enjoyment.

CHAPTER ONE

IS WOMAN INSATIABLE?

Did Eve come out of Adam, or did Adam come out of Eve? Which sex is primary? At first glance, this may appear to be a trivial enough question. Who cares, actually, particularly in these times when few of us take the Bible literally?

And yet the myth of creation continues to shape our lives. It is still generally assumed that the male is somehow primary, the female *his* helpmeet, *his* companion. And sexually, many women are still made to feel that men got there first with the most. We have a womb, of course, and we can grow babies, but that is a separate function, or so it seems. As far as the more strictly sexual apparatus go, it is so easy to think of ourselves as possessing "miniature" structures, derived from the male, but humbler and less magnificent. (And perhaps, the implication goes, also less responsive and less enjoyable.)

In some stunning research which had been going on for the previous fifteen years and which came to full flowering in 1957–58, embryologists established, beyond any doubt, that *all mammalian embryos are innately female*. Female development is basic and autonomous; male development is a deviation triggered by hormones. In the beginning, we were all created female.

Genetic sex is established at fertilization, of course, but during the first five or six weeks of fetal life, the influence of the sex genes have no bearing. Then, if the fetus is a normal male, his genes somehow trigger off an "androgen bath," which gradually converts his basically female structures into male structures. Should something go wrong, as occasionally happens, and the "androgen bath" not occur, or should the baby's mother be given anti-androgens, the baby, while genetically male, will look like a female at birth.[1] Only the male embryo is required to undergo a transformation of his sexual anatomy. Without androgens this cannot be achieved. The female embryo needs no such transformation. Hence, male development is now considered a *deviation* from the basic female pattern.

Dr. John Money, a Johns Hopkins University researcher, puts it like this: "Nature simply uses the rule, add androgen and get a male; do nothing and get a female."

Not surprisingly, modern biologists have recorded these facts with little fanfare or comment. It took a woman psychiatrist, Mary Jane Sherfey, to draw the logical conclusion:

"Embryologically speaking, it is correct to say that the penis is an exaggerated clitoris, the scrotum is derived from the labia majora, the original libido is feminine, etc. The reverse is true only for the reptiles. For all the mammals, modern embryology calls for an Adam-out-of-Eve myth!"[2]

It is also well established through medical statistics that the human male is far more vulnerable to a variety of dis-

[1] Anti-androgens are biochemical compounds, related to progestins. They are being used experimentally to treat sex criminals. They wipe out the effect of natural androgens.

[2] Mary Jane Sherfey, "The Evolution and Nature of Female Sexuality in Relation to Psychoanalytic Theory," *Journal of the American Psychoanalytic Association*, 14:50 (1966).

eases than is the female. Indeed, the male is "in trouble," or "endangered," comparatively speaking, from the moment he is conceived, for more males than females die in the womb, in the birth canal, and at every subsequent step along the way. It is now believed, although the whys and wherefores are not yet clear, that the greater vulnerability of the male may be related to the fact that his embryonic development is less autonomous and more chancy. There are more opportunities for things to go wrong—in his body and in the male circuits of his brain. . . . The male may be larger, on the average, and better able to lift weights, but let us not allow appearances to deceive us any longer. In many respects, including staying power, we must correctly be called the first and the stronger sex.

One writer enumerated some of the female's biological advantages: ". . . more efficient metabolism, the more specialized organs, the greater resistance to disease, the built-in immunity to certain specific ailments, the extra X chromosome, the more convoluted brain, the stronger heart, the longer life. In nature's plan, the male is but a 'glorified gonad.' The female is the species."[3]

Modern research also indicates that females are emotionally less "vulnerable" than males. Dr. Nancy Bayley, a recipient of the American Psychological Association's Distinguished Scientist Award, began a study of seventy-four babies in 1929. Dr. Bayley is still in touch with fifty-four of them, still testing and interviewing. She found that girls are more "resilient" and less susceptible to the ups and downs of the environment, perhaps because of the pattern of genes that makes one female. (We don't have different genes from men, but we have more of them because the male Y chromosome is an incomplete X.)

Dr. Bayley explained at the American Psychological Association's annual meeting in September, 1966, "The female of the species tends to return somehow to an innate

[3] Elizabeth Gould Davis, *The First Sex* (New York, G. P. Putnam's Sons, 1971), p. 329.

potential. A boy's mental growth depends a good deal on his mother's treatment of him, but the only thing we could find to correlate with the I.Q.s of girls was the intelligence of their mothers."

Woman's sexual, reproductive and excretory organs are also better differentiated than the male's and therefore more elegant and more advanced. For example, men possess only one canal for the emission of both seminal fluid and urine, while women have separate orifices for ovum and urine. In lesser animals, a single cavity, the cloaca, is the opening for the intestinal, generative and urinary canals.

In sexual potential, as well as the other features mentioned, *woman* now appears to hold the anatomical edge. Freud called the clitoris a "stunted penis." He maintained that many of woman's sexual difficulties stemmed from the fact that her clitoris is rudimentary, vestigial, a feeble imitation of the superior male organ.[4]

But Freud was wrong on this, or certainly "superficial." For the fact is that the clitoris is merely the visible tip of a vast and complicated internal system of highly responsive sexual tissue. When you compare the penis to the entire *clitoral system,* which is hidden from the eye but which, biologically, is what the penis should be compared to, you find that woman is *more* richly endowed. During sexual excitement, the blood vessel engorgement of the male is obvious. (It's what creates his erection.) The blood vessel

---

[4] As a consequence of her genital inferiority, Freud believed, woman is also morally inferior. He reasoned as follows: When the girl child discovers that she does not possess a penis, she inevitably becomes envious of the male. She rejects her mother, who also has no penis, and therefore she cannot resolve her Oedipal complex (through identification with her own sex) as successfully as her brothers can. The resolution of the Oedipal complex, in Freud's system, is necessary for the development of a sturdy conscience or superego. Because she lacks a penis, woman possesses an inadequate sense of justice, a predisposition to envy, weaker social interests and a lesser capacity for sublimation. She is also, normally and inevitably—masochistic and passive.

engorgement of the female is less obvious, being mainly subterranean, but it is probably greater. This may explain why woman takes longer to prepare for her orgasm. In Dr. Sherfey's words, ". . . the female undergoes a more generalized pelvic vasocongestive process . . . which simply takes longer to develop fully. . . . Women have a larger volume capacity of venous networks to maintain in the engorged state. . . ."[5]

It's sort of like this: It takes more furniture to fill up a large apartment than a small one. Well, we, not they, have the larger apartment. Contrary to what may meet the eye, we have *more* sexy tissues. Furthermore, *our* apartment keeps growing. The male's sexual capacity peaks in his late teens and thereafter diminishes. But in woman, sexual experience (and also pregnancy) increases her "venous bed capacity." Provided she is sexually active, her "sexy tissues" continue to enlarge and grow.

This is all so contrary to what we have been taught about "masculinity" (very sexy) and "femininity" (reserved, shy, feeble) that the mind can hardly absorb it. Nonetheless, the latest scientific evidence indicates that, sexually, the male is but a pale imitation—of *us*.

His capacity, which, compared to ours, was not much to start with, peaks at a ridiculously early age, and after that, it's downhill all the way. Our capacity continues to grow throughout much of our adult lifetime, *if* the world we inhabit and the men we consort with do not cruelly abort it.

Psychosexually, you may be entirely different from your own sister or your best friend, much more different from her than your husband is apt to be from *his* brother or *his* best friend. For, as anthropologist Lee Rainwater has written:

"Men only rarely say they are indifferent to or uninterested in sexual relations. But women present the gamut of

---

[5]Sherfey, *op. cit.*, p. 91.

responses, from 'If God made anything better, He kept it to Himself' to 'I would be happy if I never had to do that again; it's disgusting.' "[6]

As a twentieth-century woman, sex may be the most important thing in your life, or it may be one of the least important. Whatever it is, it's your secret. Women who are very sexy walk and talk and look like other women. And so do women who are very frigid.

You cannot tell a sexy woman by her pointy breasts, her mini-skirts, or the way she may or may not undulate her hips.

For in some cultures, and in many American subcultures, girls and women are encouraged to *look* seductive, without *feeling* sexy.

Moreover, consciously or unconsciously, many men *do not want* passionate wives. They fear that if they stimulate and please a woman, "she might get to like it too much," and then, presumably, she might be unfaithful. (Or she might be distracted from cooking and washing socks.)

Rainwater tells us that the lower-class males—in the United States, in England, in Mexico and Puerto Rico—still hold openly to the *macho* concept of masculinity where the man is insistent on taking his own pleasure without reference to the woman's needs. Sure, he may try to stimulate her when he is first courting her, but after that —no.[7]

[6]Donald S. Marshall and Robert C. Suggs, ed., *Human Sexual Behavior* (New York, Basic Books, Inc., 1971), p. 188.

[7]It is better for men if their partners are responsive. They will enjoy sex more frequently, and they will not be made victims in the kinds of punitive power games that sexually frustrated women are wont to play.

In my opinion, men have to be taught *early* through subtleties of precept probably, more than through words, that women are sexual creatures, too. The commitment to satisfy a woman must be made a very basic part of their egos or sense of sportsmanship or else they will not satisfy most of their partners, on most occasions. The model of an *obedient* wife, who never refuses sex, but who enjoys it only for the pleasure she gives her husband, has much to recommend it from the male perspective. One thinks of

In cultures where the men expect their wives to enjoy sex, they do, they do! as we shall see. In cultures where the men do not expect their women to enjoy sex, the women usually don't. Of course we cannot make any generalizations about our twentieth-century American males because our culture is so complex (and so confused and contradictory about sex) that our men's expectations probably run the gamut. To some, their partner's satisfaction is almost as important as their own, while to others, it hardly matters or might even *frighten* them.

Now let us look at a happy Polynesian island, Mangaia, where no woman is frigid. Dr. Donald S. Marshall, an anthropologist, has made three field trips there and has reported his findings in two books:[8]

> The Mangaian male lover aims to have his partner achieve orgasm (mene) two or three times to his once. . . . His responsibility in this matter is so ingrained into the Mangaian male that upon hearing that some American or European women cannot or do not achieve a climax, the Mangaian immediately asks (with real con-

---

the classic story of the Victorian bride who, on her wedding day, asked her mother for sex information. "Well, dear," her mother replied, "I've always found it helpful to lie back and think of England." No doubt this bride made an estimable wife, in her husband's view. He never dreamed that her chronic backache and fatigue or her annoying attempts to reform and refine him were probably a product of bitterness and sexual frustration.

Some British and American physicians still (as a joke!) define woman as "a constipated biped with lower back pains."

Today, in our supposedly sexy society, it has become rather common for women to fake orgasms. The woman who finds herself "faking it" is probably responding to the signals of a man who is ambivalent about feminine sexuality. He wants her to moan and groan because *Playboy* has assured him that's part of the procedure. But if her satisfaction is genuinely important to him, why isn't he taking the trouble to find out what *she* really likes? I think the reason is that he doesn't want a woman who is truly responding.

[8]Marshall and Suggs, "Sexual Behavior of Mangaia," *op. cit.*, Chapter 5. Also Donald S. Marshall, *Ra'ivavae: an Expedition to the Most Fascinating and Mysterious Island in Polynesia* (New York, Doubleday, 1961).

cern) whether this inability will not injure the married woman's health.

The seriousness which Mangaians pay to the sex education of their adolescent boys could be a lesson to us except it is difficult to imagine that even the most progressive school or family in the United States would be willing to experiment with a similar program.

First of all, in Marshall's words, ". . . the average Mangaian youth has fully as detailed a knowledge—perhaps more—of the gross anatomy of the penis and the vagina as does a European physician." He, the Mangaian youth, also has a *better* vocabulary, simply because a better vocabulary is available. To some extent, you can measure the importance which a certain people give to an activity just from the richness of the vocabulary they have developed to describe it. In the English and European languages we note, merely, that clitorises come in different sizes and shapes. But in Mangaia, they have specific modifying terms for different kinds of clitorises. That means, presumably, that the men pay more attention to them. Clitorises are classified by their degree of sharpness or bluntness and are also described as "projecting," "erecting" or "protruding." (The Mangaian male is equally expert on the size, shape and consistency of the mons veneris.)

The serious sex education of a Mangaian youth begins when he is circumcised, early in adolescence. The skin is cut, and the penis has "no hat," as the local expression goes.

The reason for this procedure is that the Mangaian male would not want a malodorous penis. Indeed, to suggest that he has one is practically the worst insult an enemy could deliver.

After his circumcision, the youth runs into the sea, proclaiming, just as Jewish boys do at their Bar Mitzvahs, "Now I am really a man."

But here the similarity ends. The Bar Mitzvah boy must

prove that he knows Hebrew. The boy in Mangaia must establish other skills:

> . . . more important than the physiological treatment . . . is the knowledge of sexual matters and the training in sexual behavior given to the youth by the circumcision expert. Not only does this detailed information concern techniques of coitus but . . . the expert teaches the youth (as the elderly woman instructs the young female) about such techniques as cunnilingus, the kissing and sucking of breasts, and a means of achieving simultaneous mutual climax, as well as how to bring the woman to climax several times before the male partner permits himself to achieve the goal. Some of this instruction is by straightforward precept, some by the use of figurative stories.

> The period of formal instruction is followed by a "practical exercise" in copulation. . . . The intercourse, often arranged by an expert, must be with an experienced woman . . . of significance to the youth is the coaching he receives in the techniques he has learned from the expert. The woman teaches him to hold back until he can achieve orgasm in unison with his partner; she teaches him the techniques involved in carrying out various acts and positions about which the expert has advised him—especially the matter of timing . . . the last day . . . is marked by a feast given for both the boy and his mentor. . . . This feast is the signal for the boy to be called a man by his people.

In Mangaia, then, a boy is a man when he has proved he can satisfy a woman. The Mangaians believe that "the orgasm must be 'learned' by a woman and that this learning process can be achieved through the efforts of 'the good young man.'" A boy is not unleashed on young girls until he has proved his skills. Should he seduce a virgin and should she not reach orgasm, he has a solemn obligation to continue "visiting her" until she does.

"There is considerable technique involved in Mangaian

foreplay," Marshall reports, but performance during intercourse is considered more important.

> Once penetration has been made, the male realizes that his action must be continuously kept up in order to bring his partner to climax . . . a "good man" will be able to continue his actions for fifteen to thirty minutes or more . . . the ultimate and invariable goal of the two lovers is to so match their reactions that when the male finally does permit himself to reach climax it is achieved simultaneously with the peak of his partner's pleasure . . . the really important aspect of sexual intercourse . . . is to give pleasure to his wife or woman or girl. . . . Supposedly this is what gives the male partner his own pleasure and a special thrill. . . .

In contrast, consider nineteenth-century England, where William Acton, the leading authority of his time, could declare it a "vile aspersion" to even suggest that woman has any sexual nature.[9] "The majority of women (happily for society) are not very much troubled with sexual feelings of any kind," he wrote.

Did Victorian women conform to Acton's view of them? As best we know, most of them did. Dr. Marie Nyswander tells the following story about a late friend of hers, a liberated woman in some respects (a very successful physician) who married, happily, in 1904, and reared five children. This woman had only one orgasm in her lifetime, and it was not a welcome event. When she married, the mantle of Victorianism was still very much upon her, and so although she was deeply in love with her husband, she was totally frigid. After the birth of her third child, she

[9]Acton, a London urologist (1813–1875), was sort of the Dr. David Reuben of his day. Acton's highly influential book, published in 1857, bore the catchy title *The Functions and Disorders of the Reproductive Organs, in Childhood, Youth, Adult Age, and Advanced Life, Considered in Their Physiological, Social and Moral Relations* (London, J. Churchill, 1857).

confessed to Dr. Nyswander, she started to experience some feelings of pleasure during intercourse. Now she had her fourth child, and intercourse was interrupted for several months. Upon resumption, the pleasure had increased enormously, and on the second time, she had a profound orgasm. Alas, Dr. Nyswander relates, her friend was very consciously frightened and very consciously ashamed. She decided never to let the experience repeat itself and was entirely successful in her resolution. Not until years later, after her husband had died, did this woman physician, who, for her time, must have been exceptionally sophisticated and knowledgeable, recognize the tragedy of her decision.[10]

Occasionally, a male from one sort of culture encounters a female from the other sort, and the outcome, if successful for the woman, is perplexing for the man. John C. Messenger, who has been performing field studies in a small and isolated Irish folk community, recently reported:

> There is much evidence to indicate that the female orgasm is unknown—or at least doubted, or considered a deviant response. One middle-aged bachelor, who considers himself wise in the ways of the outside world, and has a reputation for making love to willing tourists, described one girl's violent bodily reactions to his fondling and asked for an explanation; when told the "facts of life" of what was obviously an orgasm, he admitted not realizing that women also could achieve a climax, although he was aware that some of them enjoyed kissing and being handled.[11]

The male orgasm is nowhere unknown, or doubted, or considered a deviant response. With rare exceptions (which are pathological), a sexually mature male must

[10]Marie N. Robinson (Nyswander), *The Power of Sexual Surrender* (New York, Doubleday, 1959).

[11]Marshall and Suggs, "Sex and Repression in an Irish Folk Community," *op. cit.*, Chap. One.

have an orgasm to deposit sperm. He cannot perform his part in reproduction without sexual pleasure. By contrast, a woman can and often does. She can ovulate monthly, get pregnant yearly, can live and die, and leave behind a huge family, without ever having an orgasm or dreaming that it is possible. Reproductively, the female orgasm is a luxury, the male orgasm a necessity.[12]

But precisely because orgasm and sperm production are intertwined, there is a natural ceiling, as well as a floor, to the number of orgasms a man can have. Women have no such limitation, which brings us to the "unmentionable" finding of modern sex research, the finding which no one likes to talk about.

In her extraordinary study, entitled *The Evolution and Nature of Female Sexuality in Relation to Psychoanalytic Theory,* Dr. Mary Jane Sherfey, recognizing the "extreme importance of cutting across the compartmentalization of knowledge," has undertaken a vast integrative effort, which explains female sexuality in terms of "physiology, anatomy, comparative embryology, endocrinology, gynecology, paleontology, evolutionary biology, population genetics, primatology, and ethology—not to mention anthropology and psychiatry, the central foci upon which the rest converge."[13] She concludes that—potentially—women may well have an insatiable sex drive, like the sex drive of certain female primates who have an anatomy much like ours:

[12]This all too evident fact of life has been widely construed to mean that the male, exclusively, is and should be the initiator of sexual relations. But at the 1971 annual meeting of the American Psychological Association, Dr. Eleanor Maccoby, a professor at Stanford and editor of the highly regarded book *The Development of Sex Differences,* pointed out that, in fact, throughout the mammalian kingdom it is usually the female who initiates sex relations. The male, as it were, is always prepared, and sex relations ensue when the female signals that *she* is available. In many species, sex relations only occur at certain times in the female cycle.

Rape is exclusive to human beings.

[13]Sherfey, *op. cit.,* p. 30.

Having no cultural restrictions, these primate females will perform coitus from twenty to fifty times a day during the peak week of estrus, usually with several series of copulation in rapid succession. If necessary, they flirt, solicit, present and stimulate the male in order to obtain successive coitions. They will "consort" with one male for several days until he is exhausted, then take up with another. They emerge from estrus totally exhausted, often with wounds from spent males who have repulsed them. I suggest that something akin to this behavior could be paralleled by the human female if her civilization allowed it.

Why hasn't civilization allowed it? Dr. Sherfey suggests that:

The human mating system, with its permanent family and kinship ties, was absolutely essential to man's becoming—and remaining—man. . . . The forceful suppression of woman's inordinate sexual drive was a prerequisite to the dawn of every modern civilization and almost every living culture. Primitive sexual drive was too strong, too susceptible to the fluctuating extremes of an impelling, aggressive eroticism to withstand the disciplined requirements of a settled family life. . . . It could well be that the "oversexed" woman is actually exhibiting a normal sexuality—although because of it her integration into her society may leave much to be desired . . . this hypothesis will come as no great shock to many women who consciously realize or intuitively sense their lack of satiation.

In sedate, scientific language, Dr. Sherfey predicts that all hell could break loose as more and more modern women come to recognize—even to dare suspect—what a vast sexual capacity they have. "The magnitude of the psychological and social problems facing mankind is difficult to contemplate," she observes.

Woman, it appears, has a plastic sex drive which both is

and isn't designed for monogamy. At the lower limits, it can be turned off almost completely. Woman can live virtually without sexual expression if she and her lovers were reared to expect that she requires none. But sex may well be addictive in woman, and once she starts letting herself enjoy it, there may be no upper limit short of her own exhaustion.

An orgasmic woman can be emotionally satisfied with an average sex life of several copulations per week, and sometimes she can *will* herself to believe that she is physically satisfied as well. But if Dr. Sherfey is correct, such a woman is never sated—as her husband or lover is sated. At some primitive level of her being, she desires a much higher frequency than does her mate. Recent sex research suggests that the female orgasm may increase pelvic vasocongestion, which sparks a taste for further orgasm. *The more a woman does, the more she can, and the more she can, the more she wants to.* Masters and Johnson claim that they have observed females experiencing six or more orgasms during intercourse and up to fifty or more during masturbation with a vibrator.

Dr. Sherfey, who maintains that the nymphomaniac may actually be the most normal and natural of women, practices psychiatry and psychoanalysis in New York City. As an undergraduate, she studied with Dr. Alfred Kinsey at Indiana University. She received her MD degree in 1943.

Dr. Sherfey points out with some bitterness that nearly all anatomy books were written by men who tend to regard the human female as "sexually inadequate or inferior" and the clitoris as a pale imitation of the penis. Quite to the contrary, however, the external clitoris is merely the tip of the iceberg or (more accurately) the volcano. Conventional anatomy books usually ignore the internal clitoral system, as distinct from the clitoris itself.

Surprisingly, Dr. Sherfey is a Freudian. While on a superficial level she appears to disagree violently with

Freud's thoughts on orgasms and female sexuality, she actually views his theories as flexible, and feels that he might have agreed with her biological updating. She quotes from his famous book *Behind the Pleasure Principle,* which was published in 1920:

> Biology is truly a land of unlimited possibilities. We may expect it to give us the most surprising information, and we cannot guess what answers it will return in a few dozen years to the questions we have put to it. They may be of a kind which will blow away the whole of our artificial structure of hypotheses.

Freud recognized that the twentieth century would bring many scientific advances. Now, as we have seen or shall see:

—Embryologists have established that females are the first sex and that the male sexual structures are merely a variation on the structures of the female.

—Sex researchers, especially Masters and Johnson, have established that the female has a sexual capacity which is at least as great as the male, and probably greater.

—Anthropologists have clarified that in some cultures, even today, the vast sexual capacity of the female is taken for granted. Their field work in primitive cultures lends extremely convincing support to the historical thesis that the forced suppression of female sexuality was somehow necessary for the development of "higher civilizations."

Does all this mean that women (under ideal conditions) actually enjoy sex more than men?

There may never be an answer because sexual experience remains so subjective and even mystical. It is one thing to take measurements in a laboratory and quite another to describe the meaning of an act. It appears that most people's most tenderly remembered sexual experiences have little to do with number of contractions, length of orgasm, or anything else of the sort. A reunion with a beloved person is, obviously, far more significant than a blast-off which is merely technically terrific.

Nonetheless, the mystical appeal of sex, crucial as it is, has been too often used in a fashion that disserves women and encourages selfish or lazy men. (Good women only care about the "closeness" and "don't really mind" if they aren't brought to climax; that sort of thing.) Therefore, if only to redress this imbalance, it should be stated here that we just might be able to have better orgasms than men. At least, we are reported to have more erogenous zones, throughout the body, and more sexy tissue in and around the pelvis. Our orgasms are longer and perhaps more complex, occupying "three stages," in Masters-Johnson terms, while the male orgasm exhausts itself in only two. Also, if a male is low on seminal fluid, his orgasms are usually less enjoyable, whereas the female has no such limitation. For whatever it's worth, she can have many more orgasms in a short period of time, and the second or third may be even better than the first. (Some males under thirty, and relatively few thereafter, can climax several times within ten or fifteen minutes. The quality invariably diminishes. But many females can climax even more times in the same period.)

Also, what the Mangaians call "knockout" orgasm and Masters and Johnson call *status orgasmus* has been observed—in islands under the sun and in sex laboratories both—in females only. This is an orgasm that seems to go on and on, the heart beating at an inordinately rapid rate.

Well, then, if women have all this sexy tissue (which grows richer and sexier with pregnancy and experience, rather as a well-chewed piece of bubble gum gets more expansive) and if we also have this impressive capacity to keep having more, and even better, orgasms, for as many minutes or hours as good stimulation abides, and if we also occasionally demonstrate a capacity for a "knockout" orgasm, which is apparently rather beyond anything the male experiences, then why do so many women not know how sexy they are?

Sherfey, as mentioned earlier, believes that males have forcibly suppressed the vast and virtually insatiable erotic potential of females. She goes so far as to suggest that "the suppression by cultural forces of woman's inordinately high sexual drive and orgasmic capacity" has been a "major preoccupation of practically every civilization." (Dr. William Simon, a former Kinsey Institute researcher, agrees with Sherfey and carries her thinking one step further. "The suppression of female sexuality has not been easily achieved," he comments. "Societies have had to work very hard at it. A similar investment in males would have paid off easier.")

Dr. Sherfey accepts J. J. Bachofen's theory of human history, which was first published in 1861. From his analysis of myths and early artifacts, Bachofen concluded that until about 8000 B.C. human societies were ruled by women.

Sherfey writes:

There are many indications from the prehistory studies in the Near East that it took perhaps 5,000 years or longer for the subjugation of women to take place. All relevant data from the 12,000 to 8000 B.C. period indicates that the precivilized woman enjoyed full sexual freedom and was often totally incapable of controlling her sexual drive. Therefore, I propose that one of the reasons for the long delay between the earliest development of agriculture (c. 12,000 B.C.) and the rise of urban life and the beginning of recorded knowledge (c. 8000-5000 B.C.) was the ungovernable cyclic sexual drive of women. Not until these drives were gradually brought under control by rigidly enforced social codes could family life become the stabilizing and creative crucible from which modern man could emerge.

To this day, the Bachofen thesis attracts interesting and eloquent advocates. Yet most conventional historians reject it. This does not at all disturb Sherfey, for, as she points out, most conventional historians are also conventional males.

Men, however scholarly, are usually quite loath to concede any area of female equality, much less superiority, until the evidence becomes overwhelming.

Earlier we noted that there are two ways of comparing clitoris to penis. One can examine and dissect the externals only, in which case the laurels go to the penis. If, however, one adds up external *and* internal anatomy, the laurels go to the clitoris, for a more complicated and responsive venous system underlies it.

By the end of the nineteenth century dissections and studies of human anatomy were well enough advanced so that any scientist working in this area could and should have been able to note that the female clitoral system was rather impressive. Yet this anatomical evidence was given so little importance that it even failed to come to Freud's attention. Apparently, the only nineteenth-century physician who made any fuss over it was Elizabeth Blackwell (1821–1910), a staunch feminist who was the first woman to be graduated from any United States medical school.[14]

[14]Dr. Blackwell, a proper Victorian, held typically repressive attitudes toward sexuality in both the female and the male. However, she hated to see the female belittled, and so she wrote:

"The chief structures of the male are external, but they are internal in the female . . . failure to recognize the equivalent value of internal with external structure has led to such crude fallacy as a comparison of the penis with such a vestige as the clitoris, whilst failing to recognize the vast amount of erectile tissue, mostly internal, which is the direct seat of special sexual spasm."

In the United States, Dr. Blackwell is best known for pioneering medical education for women and for founding the New York Infirmary for Women and Children and the Women's Medical College of the New York Infirmary. However, after returning to her native England in 1869, Blackwell wrote many books and pamphlets on sex and sex education. These were collected and published in 1902 in a three-volume book entitled *Essays in Medical Sociology* (London, E. Bell).

The historical evidence may still be shrouded in fog, but the scientific and anthropologic evidence has become overwhelming. Woman, while having a plastic sex drive which can be repressed more completely than the sexuality of the male, has, under optimum or natural conditions, as good as and probably a *better* sexual potential than the male. It is clear that in many cultures some social process has taken place which has curbed or muted female sexuality or—sometimes—eliminated it.

We can assume that in prehistoric days the basic family unit was probably mother and child and that it must have been a genius, let alone a "wise child," who knew his own father. Women may have sensed a glimmering of immortality, through their children, and men must have envied it.

It seems only common sense to suppose that in the interests of establishing paternity, an orderly family life, the descent of property, and so on, it was necessary to curb woman's sex drive and encourage her to be monogamous. And surely one way to do this was to make sex unsatisfactory for her. After all, we know that sex, even today, is more or less addictive in women, and the-more-she-gets-the-more-she-wants. We know that there are sound biological reasons for this, for as she enjoys sex, the sexy tissues get more sexy, their vascularity increasing, and the muscles of orgasmic response being strengthened. We know that the male, whose sexual capacity peaks in his teens, is not likely to keep up with his wife's growing needs, as they mature together. And finally, we know that males in most civilized cultures have long feared sexy women, drawing a sharp division (which may be justified)

Blackwell recognized that women, as well as men, have orgasms or "sexual spasms," and somewhat unlike other Victorian sexologists, she held to a single standard of sexual behavior, urging men, as well as women, to save themselves for higher things.

She suspected the motives of male gynecologists, who, she suggested, did altogether too much unnecessary poking around with their speculums. ". . . this custom is a real and growing evil," she asserted.

between the chaste and sexless "good" woman and the unreliable woman who *likes* sex. Even today, as sophisticated as we think we are, in many of our subcultures the males deliberately refrain from using their best erotic techniques on their wives, in fear that their wives might get to like it. These men possess something of a sexual "repertoire" to borrow Margaret Mead's phrase, but they deliberately withhold it.

On the other hand, it seems to me implausible that it was *men only* who set out to cool and restrain the natural passions of women. A pregnant woman, a woman in labor, or a mother with a nursling at her breast is vulnerable. She cannot run as fast or as far, nor can she hunt and gather food so efficiently, nor can she hide from an emeny as quietly or as well. Surely, under primitive conditions, the survival chances of a mother and her babies were improved if she had protectors. Thus, I think we must consider the possibility that it was adaptive for woman herself to curb her own sexuality. The children of a mother who was capable of forming ties with one male probably stood a better chance of growing up. The "plastic" woman who smothered her own sexuality lost something, but gained something, too.[15]

[15]On reviewing all that is presently known (1971) about biologically based differences between the sexes, Eleanor Maccoby finds three essentials:
1 Males have greater physical strength, of the sort that allows them to fend off an attacker or beat up a wife.
2 Males are more aggressive, although not necessarily more active and certainly not smarter.
3 The childbearing and nursing functions of the female have made her dependent on men.
Today, Dr. Maccoby adds, the greater muscular strength and aggressiveness of the male are no longer assets. He need not fend off wild animals. Even in the business world, the old captains of industry who pounded the table and terrified employees have gone out of style. Today managerial decisions are made by teams and committees, and the overly aggressive executive is *unlikely* to succeed.
Woman's biological dependence on the male is also obsolete, for she is no longer pregnant or nursing throughout most of her

Sherfey concludes that the ruthless suppression of female sexuality was a historical necessity:

> Although then (and now) couched in superstitions, religious and rationalized terms, behind the subjugation of woman's sexuality lay the inexorable economics of cultural evolution which finally forced men to impose it and women to endure it. If that suppression has been, at times, unduly oppressive or cruel, I suggest the reason has been neither man's sadistic, selfish infliction of servitude upon helpless women nor women's weakness or inborn masochism. The strength of the drive determines the force required to suppress it.

But even sexy women can learn, as Sherfey points out, to *will* satisfaction. And so the wives of Mangaia, who are surely very stimulated and who, by middle age, want more sex than their husbands, nonetheless stay with their husbands because of economic and affectionate bonds. The same was true, by and large, of the sexy American women in a study I made in the spring of 1971. As one said, "When we have sex, I always want to do it again, immediately or sooner, but he can't. So I adjust to it. I'm horny the first twelve hours, but then I feel fine. The strange thing is that when we are apart from each other, he misses it more than I do. He needs sex every three days or so. I can turn off completely when there's no stimulation around, or when I am stimulated, I could just go on and on. Well, obviously I've had to adjust to his pattern. But I'm not complaining because he's good, very good."

Men may or may not have suppressed our sexuality more brutally than was necessary. On the one hand, as Sherfey points out:

---

adult life. "Let's be realistic," Dr. Maccoby urges, "about the kinds of lives most women led until quite recently. They were pregnant or nursing most of the time, and this fostered a state of dependence which is not functional in the modern world."

Each orgasm is followed promptly by refilling of the venous erectile chambers; distention creates engorgement and edema, which creates more tissue tension, etc. The supply of blood and edema fluid to the pelvis is inexhaustible. . . . *To all intents and purposes, the human female is sexually insatiable in the presence of the highest degrees of sexual satiation.*

On the other hand, as Sherfey also allows:

I must stress that this condition does not mean that a woman is always consciously unsatisfied. There is a great difference between satisfaction and satiation. A woman may be emotionally satisfied to the full in the absence of *any* orgasmic expression (although such a state would rarely persist through years of frequent arousal and coitus without some kind of physical or emotional reaction formation . . .).

The man *is* satisfied. The woman *usually wills herself* to be satisfied because she is simply unaware of the extent of her orgasmic capacity. However, I predict that this hypothesis will come as no great shock to many women who consciously realize, or intuitively sense, their lack of satiation.

Has woman's inherent drive abated in all these years? Sherfey thinks not. She believes that every girl born has the capacity to become a veritable nymphomaniac.

Even if she is right, however, I think that most of the women who opt for marriage and family life will continue, sedately and perhaps a little sadly at times, to "will themselves" satisfied. A mother's attachment to her young is very strong and not easily jeopardized.

On the other hand, there is no question that a new lifestyle is emerging for educated women in civilized countries. The world is pretty well filled up, and the men who rule it are coming to view babies as a threat to their own survival. The pressures on women to marry and reproduce are rapidly diminishing, at the same time as their solo economic position is improving.[16]

[16]The first steps, at least, have been taken. Thanks to Congresswoman Martha Griffiths, the Civil Rights Act of 1964 prohibits job discrimination based on sex. At first the men who were charged with enforcing this law tried to make a joke of it. They wasted their time arguing over specious issues like: Would Playboy Clubs be required to hire male bunnies?

Recently, however, groups of women who were barred from job promotions because of their sex have been bringing class suits against their employers and have been winning these cases. Employers have been held liable for hefty amounts of back pay.

But overall the situation is still dismal. Teresa Levitin, of the University of Michigan's Survey Research Center, recently analyzed the income of working women. She reports: "Although we expected to discover that a woman received fewer occupational rewards than a man with equal scores on the achievement predictors, we were hardly prepared for the size of the discrepancy between observed and expected annual income. *The average woman actually received $3,358 less than she should have received.*" In other words, it costs you an average of $3,358 a year to be a woman. Your income would have to be increased by *71 percent* to bring it to the level of a man with precisely comparable qualifications.

Such discrimination is apparent in traditionally "feminine" fields, such as teaching, as well as traditionally "masculine" fields. It is true that entering female teachers receive the same salaries as males, but after that, less competent men are normally promoted to higher-paying administrative jobs, over the heads of more competent and better-qualified women, according to Dr. Neal Gross of the Harvard School of Education.

It appears that few women recognize what a bargain they are to employers. Levitin notes that only 7.9 percent of the women in her sample (most of whom were, in fact, grossly underpaid) said that they *felt* discriminated against.

It is curious how job discrimination is so taken for granted in our society since, in a sense, it is economic discrimination against all groups *except* bachelors. Married men, as well as single and married women, are hurt by it since the more a wife earns, the more secure is her husband's economic position. Martha Griffiths tells the story of a friend of hers, a married man, who was unhappy in his job. Reviewing his problems with the Griffithses, he suddenly brightened. "I'll quit," he announced. "Harriet is making fifteen thousand dollars a year, and we won't starve while I look for another job." Where Harriet isn't making $15,000 a year, Mrs. Griffiths points out, her husband does not enjoy the same freedom.

Men and women alike may be afraid that marriage and family life will deteriorate if women gain too much economic indepen-

A certain group of educated, independent single women in my study were sexually active beyond the wildest dreams of most wives. They didn't look like nymphomaniacs or prostitutes or loose women. Indeed, as a rule they *appeared* rather prim and ladylike.

There is no doubt that such women will increase, for, to complicate matters further, we may be very close to the day when scientists (male) will be able to grow babies in test tubes, thereby proving themselves equal to Eve and leaving woman even freer to indulge her own sexuality.

As the woman as mother becomes obsolete, perhaps packs of ravenously sexy, rapacious women will roam the world, as in some grim work of science fiction. But sufficient unto the day is the evil thereof. For now it is problem enough convincing our husbands and lovers that we have sexual appetites, too, which may have a different rhythm from theirs but which are every bit as normal and (in an aroused woman) every bit as urgent.

There are those who deplore feminism and the "melting of the sexes," but it is difficult not to be hopeful about the situation when currently so few people are happy or sexually satisfied. As Dr. Alfred Auerback, clinical professor of psychiatry at the University of California School of Medicine in San Francisco, pointed out recently:

> . . . the pattern of rearing children in this country is designed to make the male and female incompatible in terms of later intimate relationships. Boys are brought up not to show their feelings. They are not supposed to cry. They are supposed to be little men. The emphasis is on being emotionally detached, playing it cool. Sexual activity is heralded as a form of conquest. It's an activity in which you don't get emotionally involved. So the pressures are toward making the male predatory, certainly not romantic or involved.

---

dence. I have heard brilliant and capable women express fear that if they started to earn more than their husbands, it might ruin their marriages.

Girls in our society are brought up to be narcissistic. They are supposed to look pretty and hence to be eventually marriageable. There is increasing pressure on them to be sexually alluring and coquettish but at the same time to hold back their feelings, not to get physically involved. They are taught to be careful about sex, to be ladylike, to protect themselves from exploitation by the male. Their attention is focused on romance, falling in love, being a wife, having children, raising a family.

In the so-called primitive societies, children are educated in the skills of pleasurable sexual activity through erotic teachings, pictures, and puberty rites. Yet in our Western culture, we have subdued overt eroticism. We imply that the biological drive is sufficient unto itself. Therefore, it is no wonder that most men assume that inserting the penis into the vagina after minimal sexual foreplay is all that is required to satisfy a female partner.

The Kinsey studies of some 20 years ago found that about 75% of men ejaculate in less than 2 minutes, many within 10 or 20 seconds after entrance into the vagina. Obviously, it's over before it's begun, and there isn't much in it for the female partner.[17]

[17]Dr. Alfred Auerback, moderator, "Roundtable: How Can Sex Be More Pleasurable?" *Medical Aspects of Human Sexuality*, Vol. v, No. 9 (September, 1971).

CHAPTER TWO
THE LIBERATED ORGASM

If there is going to be a breakthrough in human sexuality —and I think that such a breakthrough might be in the wind—it is going to occur because *women* will start taking charge of their own sex lives. It is going to occur because women will stop believing that sex is for men and that men (their fathers, their doctors, their lovers and husbands, their popes and kings and scientists) should call the shots. We need only study a little anthropology or history to understand that the sexuality of women is incredibly elastic and rather easily repressed. In fact, it is almost true that there are no frigid women—only frightened or foolish men. Years ago Margaret Mead told us, "The human female's capacity for orgasm is to be viewed . . . as a potentiality that may or may not be developed by a given culture."

But what precisely is this female orgasm (which may or may not be developed by a given culture) and *where* does it take place? A woman knows when she's had one (if she doubts it, she hasn't), but since her orgasm is not punctuated by the sure sign of ejaculation, men have felt free to develop lunatic theories about it, and women have retaliated with some lunatic theories of their own.

You've heard about the current orgasm controversy with Norman Mailer and some militant Freudians on one side (the vaginal) versus Kate Millett and some militant feminists in the other, or clitoral, position.

Masters and Johnson are not what you would call lucid communicators, so if Kate Millett misunderstood them, I'm not blaming her. However, the clitoral militance of Miss Millett and others is apparently based on a misunderstanding of the Masters and Johnson finding that even though there is no direct contact between penis and clitoris during sexual intercourse, the thrusting of the penis into the vagina does produce *clitoral stimulation.*

A woman's external sex organs consist of labia majora, or outer lips; labia minora, or inner lips; and the highly eroticized clitoris, the only organ known to man or woman whose sole purpose is to receive and transmit sexual pleasure. The hood of the clitoris is attached to the labia minora, which *are* directly affected by penile thrusting. Thus, intercourse causes the labia to exert traction on the clitoral hood, producing rhythmic friction between it and the clitoris itself.

Get that? Masters and Johnson have proved—or believe they have proved (their work has not yet been replicated)—that virtually all feminine orgasms, however vaginal some of them may *seem,* do include indirect clitoral stimulation, the labia minora being the agent of mediation.

Miss Millett *el al.* appear to assume that this makes the vagina a mere funnel for sperm and babies and not an organ of sexual pleasure. "Vaginal orgasm is a myth" has become a rather popular phrase.

It's catchy, but is it true?

Well, this much is true. Some Freudian analysts have long maintained that vaginal orgasms are entirely distinct from clitoral orgasms and are, indeed, the hallmark of a sexually mature woman. If clitoral stimulation, whether direct or transmitted through the labia, occurs in all orgasms, then their distinction is invalid. So is the complicated mystique attached to it. Vaginal women have been said to be mature, feminine, loving and happy, while clitoral women have had all the opposite traits ascribed to them.

However, if I read Masters and Johnson correctly, they never intended to put the vagina out of the sex business. Clitoral stimulation may occur in orgasm, but orgasm does not chiefly occur in the clitoris.

To the contrary, orgasm, which is a total body response, is always marked by vaginal contractions. No specific physiologic response in the clitoris has yet been recorded.

Let us review the physiology of the female sex cycle:

Stage One: *Excitement*. Within ten to thirty seconds after erotic stimulation starts, the vaginal lining is moistened with a lubricating fluid. Nipples erect, and the breasts begin to swell, increasing in size by one-fifth to one-quarter in women who have not nursed a baby. (Breasts that have been suckled do not enlarge as much.) Other changes start to occur in the clitoris, labia and vagina, as vasocongestion (the engorgement of vessels and organs with blood) and muscular tension start to build. Late in the excitement phase, some women may start to develop a measleslike rash, or sex flush, across their bodies. (Seventy-five percent of the women evaluated by Masters and Johnson showed this response on *some* occasions.)

Stage Two: *Plateau*. The tissue surrounding the outer third of the vagina engorges and swells, creating an "orgasmic platform." The deeper portion of the vagina balloons out to form a cavity. The uterus enlarges. The swelling of the outer third of the vagina reduces its diameter, allowing it to grip the penis better. The clitoris retracts, making it more difficult to locate.

Just prior to the orgasmic phase, the labia minora undergo a marked color change called the sex skin reaction. In the woman who has not had children, the labia minora turn pink or bright red. In the mother, they turn bright red or deep wine (presumably because she has a greater number of varicosities). This coloration remains throughout orgasm, but disappears ten to fifteen seconds afterwards. Once a woman develops sex skin she is almost certain to go on to orgasm. Women who are aroused to plateau levels but not brought to orgasm experience a prolonged and sometimes uncomfortable ebbing away of vasocongestion and muscular tension.

Stage Three: *Orgasm*. The typical orgasm lasts only ten or fifteen seconds, if that long. Changes occur throughout the body. Muscles of the abdomen, buttocks, neck, arms and legs may contract; pulse and breathing are more rapid; and blood pressure climbs. The woman experiences a series of rhythmic muscular contractions in the outer third of the vagina and the tissues surrounding it and in the uterus. These contractions, each taking about four-fifths of a second, serve to discharge the accumulated vasocongestion and tension which have been brought on by sexual stimulation. A mild orgasm usually involves three to five contractions; an intense one, as many as fifteen.

From time to time a woman may experience what the Mangaians called the "knockout" orgasm, and Masters and Johnson *status orgasmus*. Masters and Johnson suspect, but are not certain, that the woman is probably having rapidly connected multiple orgasms, over a time period of sixty seconds or so.

The male orgasm is briefer in duration, and afterward, woman's tensions ebb more slowly, so on occasion she can be restimulated. In prolonged intercourse a woman may have three, four or five separate orgasms, and in a few primitive cultures, where all men have good control of themselves, multiple female orgasms are apparently the norm.[1] Some masturbating women can have up to fifty successive orgasms, according to observers.

Stage Four: *Resolution.* Blood vessels emptied and muscular tensions relieved, the various parts and organs return to their normal condition, some rapidly and some slowly. One woman in three develops a film of perspiration across her body.

The Masters and Johnson orgasm is clitoral, vaginal and more. The clitoris contributes mightily to the buildup of sexual tensions, but orgasm itself is more correctly described as centering in the vagina. Tensions established, it is vaginal contractions that bring relief by emptying engorged organs and vessels. Masters and Johnson call these vaginal contractions "the visible manifestations of female orgasmic experience."

Yes, even for those lucky women who can fantasy to orgasm, the clitoris serves as receptor and transformer of sexual stimuli, while vaginal contractions always punctuate the orgasm itself.[2]

[1]Here is the latest bulletin on timing from Dr. Paul Gebhard, director of the Kinsey Institute. If a woman has at least twenty minutes of *effective* foreplay, she has a 95 percent chance of reaching orgasm. If her lover can maintain penile thrusting for fifteen minutes or more, her odds of reaching climax are also very, very high.

Multiple orgasms are most apt to occur when intercourse is prolonged. Thus, while the much vaunted "mutual orgasm" has some very nice features, it also has some drawbacks from the woman's point of view. Or to put it another way, there is no need for a woman to hold back deliberately, for the Mangaians are right in their belief that if the male can maintain effective thrusting for a long enough period, the woman will have several preliminary orgasms and, quite possibly, another when he reaches his.

[2]Women who do not possess a clitoris are capable of orgasm. Dr. Michael Daly, a Philadelphia gynecologist, reports that he has studied in depth two patients in whom the total clitoris was removed, because of cancer. Both continued to have orgasms, and both said that their sexual responsiveness after surgery was as great as before.

There are also established cases of women in whom an artificial

Thus, it is false to say "vaginal orgasm is a myth," and we need not worry that our vaginas will atrophy. We could hardly have proper orgasms without them.[3]

But even if the vagina is necessary for sexual release, does it contribute to sexual arousal, or is it anesthetic, as some sex researchers, most notably Kinsey, and some women have thought? Granted that the vagina lives, does it feel?

Yes, it does, or at least it can. Vaginal sensations are believed to be "proprioceptive," which means they contain messages about our own bodies, not the outside world.

Close your eyes and lift one leg, or extend an arm and bend it at the elbow. If you can describe the position of your leg or arm, if you know whether it is bent or straight, you are receiving and using proprioceptive information. Ordinarily, we do not pay much conscious attention to our proprioceptive intelligence, but it is valuable, for without it we would not even be able to walk.

The vagina is most apt to develop proprioceptive abilities during states of sexual arousal and distention. In unaroused states, as, for example, when a gynecologist inserts a speculum into it, it may be quite unresponsive.

In *The Sex Researchers,* Edward M. Brecher[4] cites studies in which veterinarians have found certain free nerve endings in the genital tissue of domestic animals. These are "deeply enough embedded so that they might be re-

---

vagina had to be created, because they were born without any. These women are also capable of reaching orgasm.

Apparently, it is lucky for us that most of our sexy tissue is internal and can be stimulated by an almost infinite variety of methods.

[3]Some people talk as if the vagina may soon start to atrophy, since babies are out and the clitoris is in. "Who needs a vagina?" you can almost hear people say. "Besides, if women want babies, they can have them in test tubes."

But according to many of the 103 women in my survey (see next chapter), the vagina is still a dear and treasured part.

[4]Edward M. Brecher, *The Sex Researchers* (Boston, Little, Brown and Company, Inc., 1969), p. 121.

sponsive during coitus, but not responsive to a light touch or gentle pressure with the tissues in a nonengorged condition."

Some women, as we shall see, swear that for a first-rate orgasm, they require a penis or other object within the vagina. Other women are indifferent. Perhaps their vaginal nerve endings are sparser, if, indeed, human females do have free nerve endings like cows or cats. Or perhaps their vaginal musculature is so constructed that they have less need of something firm to squeeze against during the contractions of orgasm. Perhaps they are merely less interested in their vaginas and less receptive to information derived therefrom. No doubt there are many psychological as well as anatomical variations which might influence a woman's perceived degree of vaginal sensitivity.

Analysts are undoubtedly telling us the truth when they report that they have "converted" thousands of women to vaginally experienced orgasms. The point is merely that for some women at least, the strong desire to notice vaginal sensations make them more noticeable. If Masters and Johnson are correct, all orgasms are essentially the same and quite sensibly involve all the pertinent parts God gave us.

But if all orgasms are similar, why do women not recognize it? Are we hopelessly stupid or recalcitrant?

No, for there is a crucial distinction between motor experience (what's happening) and sensory experience (what we're aware of). Masters and Johnson do not always draw this distinction as sharply as many psychologists (and women) might wish.[5]

Some orgasms *seem* to be experienced vaginally or deep in the vagina, while others *seem* to be in the clitoris. Some orgasms occur while direct clitoral stimulation is taking

[5]The Yale psychologist Kenneth Keniston accuses Masters and Johnson of committing what he calls "the physiological fallacy." In his opinion, they reduce all human sexuality to physical response, and they fail to draw a sufficiently clear distinction between orgasm as *felt* and orgasm as registered on laboratory equipment.

place, while others occur only with vaginal stimulation. The experts who have been discussing us have never even defined the terms "vaginal" and "clitoral" orgasm, and women could hardly be sure whether a clitoral orgasm meant an orgasm that was induced by clitoral stimulation, an orgasm that seemed to be experienced in the clitoris or both.

The same woman may, at different times, experience orgasms in different locations or from different types of stimulation. Women know this, but as a rule men appear to have difficulty comprehending it. In 1968, Drs. Jules Glenn and Eugene Kaplan accused their fellow psychoanalysts of assuming, incorrectly, that clitorally stimulated orgasms are necessarily *experienced* clitorally, while vaginally stimulated orgasms are necessarily experienced vaginally.[6] They described a patient who, following a fleeting touch to the clitoris, experienced intense orgasms localized deep within the vagina which did not involve any conscious clitoral sensations at all. Glenn and Kaplan classify such orgasms as "clitorally stimulated, but vaginally experienced."

They go on to say that their patients have reported a great variation in the location of the experienced orgasm. Occasionally, sites other than the vagina and clitoris (the abdomen, the anus) seem to be the focus of feeling. The area in which the orgasm is experienced need not be the area of stimulation, and there is great variation in the area or areas stimulated, as well as in the area or areas where orgasm is felt. The terms "vaginal" and "clitoral" orgasm, they conclude, "are widely used but ill-defined."

My esteemed friend Betty Friedan has questioned whether women should "compare orgasms." I think they should. Feminine sexuality is so easily bruised and buried in the myths and medical models of the prevailing culture

---

[6]J. Glenn, and E. H. Kaplan, "Types of Orgasm in Woman," *Journal of the American Psychoanalytic Association,* 16:549 (1968).

that the self-awareness needed for liberation will be difficult to achieve unless women support each other in exploring their own true sexual feelings and needs.

Today we know that all female orgasms are similar physiologically, which is an interesting medical fact but should not be a revolutionary one. Did the public go into paroxysms when some nineteenth-century doctor discovered that all dinners are digested the same way? No, because the public *knew* that all dinners do not taste the same and that a feast of Boeuf Bourguignonne or Homard en Coquille is an entirely different *experience* from a hasty meal of brown bread and water.[7]

But women—especially women—have been afraid to think for themselves about their own sexual tastes and pleasures. They have tried to model their own preferences after the prevailing views of normality. They have been exceedingly shy about telling their lovers what they want. They have feared it would be unwomanly to do other than let the male take the lead, however ineptly.

The modern sex manuals are filled with misinformation, such as the standard advice to men that they should flail away at the sensitive clitoris. But even when their suggestions are applicable to some women, in some moods, they

[7]Some of the anatomical details Masters and Johnson unearthed are interesting and useful to know, certainly for gynecologists and prehaps for women. And yet the interest we express in their work is, above all, a testament to the abysmal limits of our own timidity.
ITEM: "During the six-hour observation period (in which a woman was stimulated but not brought to orgasm) venous engorgement of the external and internal genitalia persisted—so much so, in fact, that the woman was irritable, emotionally disturbed, and could not sleep. She complained of pelvic fullness, pressure, cramping, moments of true pain, and a persistent severe low backache."
Certain marriage counselors have long maintained that a loving wife is content merely to satisfy her husband and that it need be of no great consequence if she fails to achieve satisfaction herself. We have Masters and Johnson to thank for convincing them that sexual frustration can even give a *woman* cramps and headache. But how sad it is that we had to wait for sex researchers to demonstrate it. Didn't we know it all the time?

are rarely applicable to all women, all the time, and they foster a certain technical rigidity that is antithetical to really good sex.[8]

[8]The charge of technical rigidity is frequently leveled against not only the writers of certain types of sex manuals, but also modern sex researchers, such as Kinsey and Masters and Johnson. I have always found most sex researchers a bit grim and humorless, but perhaps this is a pose they feel they must adapt.

There is a great deal that can be said against Masters and Johnson, and some of it *has* been said prettily and publicly. In an *Esquire* article entitled "The Calculus of Sex" (May, 1966) Colette Dowling and Patricia Fahey comment: "Now, thanks to Science, a woman can tell finally and conclusively, beyond the shadow of a doubt, whether what she's having is Authentic. . . . The Panjandrum of Sexologists is a man at Washington University, in St. Louis, a Dr. William Masters. Dr. Masters has been studying sex, particularly female sex, for twelve years now, and he has made some notable discoveries. . . . The word from Dr. Masters is that to achieve The Quality the body must go through four phases (Excitement, Plateau, Orgasm, and Resolution), and that it undergoes notable changes from one phase to the next. If the woman knows what to look for and makes regular spot checks, she's got it made. She must look, for example, to the labia minora. It will change from "bright pink" to "burgundy" as the Big "O" becomes imminent. . . . A woman need only keep a stopwatch, calipers and a bottle of vintage burgundy at bedside to know within a hairbreadth whether her orgasm qualifies as "The Quality."

In scientific journals the debate also rages. We have noted that Keniston (among others) has commented on their "physiological fallacy." He has also suggested that their research techniques would "raise the eyebrows, if not the hackles, of many other researchers." He is quite right about this, for any kind of human experimentation can get very sticky and poses many ethical problems. Should women be *paid* to bed down with sexually inadequate males, as Masters and Johnson have done? (It's been observed that there's another word for this, and it's not "science.")

Among the many eloquent critics of Masters and Johnson, Keniston has observed that they are, although unintentionally, "helping to perpetuate rather than to remedy some of the more prevalent ills of our time—the confusion of human sexuality with the physiology of sexual excitement, naïveté with regard to the psychological meaning of the sexual act, and an inability to confront the ethical implications of sex." He also points out how little they have revealed of their actual laboratory procedures and remarks that "Masters and Johnson repeatedly reduce human sexuality to physical responses."

Dr. Rollo May observes that "Masters and Johnson's research

Outside or in, we are in no way as standardized as Hugh Hefner's airbrushed and silicated playmates. For example, fourteen women in my survey complained that their lovers do not engage in enough physical foreplay; eight others complained that they do not engage in enough verbal foreplay, pillow talk or conversation.

---

represents the incursion of technology into that most personal of all things—sexual relations between a man and a woman. Such research leads people to assume that sex is related to how much they practice, how much they've done, what they've learned. . . . Actually, . . . sex depends on the relationship between the man and the woman. . . . The distinguishing characteristic of a machine is that it can go through all the motions but it never feels. . . . The more sex becomes mechanical, the more pleasure decreases."

Dr. Natalie Shainess considers the Masters and Johnson view one in which "sex seems little more than a stimulus-response reflex cycle, devoid of intrapsychic or interpersonal meaning. . . . What is the attitude toward sex in a researcher who says, 'Masturbating women concentrate on their own sexual demand without the *distraction* of a coital partner.' Distraction! Is that the meaning of a partner in sex? This points to a dehumanizing view even as it is necessary to consider the effect on an individual of giving command sexual performances in the presence of others. May it not be ego-damaging, and therefore destructive eventually, if not immediately?"

Significant questions have also been raised about the quality of the records Masters and Johnson keep. They did not make a record of the *number* of orgasms which occurred in their laboratory, and they admit that some of the case histories in their books are "composites," rather than based on individuals. They are so vague about laboratory procedures that one doubts another scientist could replicate their work. Their vagueness has sometimes made it difficult for them to get research support from the usual sources, and so, back to back with their solemn pronouncements favoring women's liberation, they accept support from Hugh Hefner's Playboy Foundation and from International Flavors and Fragrances, and the hormone and drug manufacturers, Ayerst Laboratories and G. D. Searle & Co.

But with all this (and even if their number of patients or exact techniques and safeguards were not exactly what they claim) the fact remains that they have recorded some sexual response cycles in women and done it in a way that could help clarify many issues for us. If we use their findings in a self-destructive way, it is we who are choosing to do so. It is probably too much to ask that they be great humanitarians and love advisers, as well as intrepid researchers.

But two respondents take the opposite position. They like to get down to the main business of sex more swiftly than their lovers. One observed: "I find foreplay detrimental. When I really get into rubbing up against him, the feelings become sensuous, not sensual. Sex is more direct —from the inside out."

So that is how one woman feels, and it is her body and her privilege. She is sexually active and well realized, and she agrees with Janis Joplin, whom she quotes:

> I say get it while you can
> Don't you turn your sweet back on love.

The second woman asks wryly: "I have very little interest in foreplay. Is that an inhibition or a total lack of it?"

Or consider the question of the handsome stranger, an alleged apparition in the dreams of younger females. Most of the women in my survey dislike sex with strangers. Over and over they emphasized the importance (to them) of warmth, intimacy, trust, tenderness. For example, "I appreciate kindliness in a man—and one who appreciates and loves women (*i.e.* me.). Too many people use sex as an outlet—it should be a mutual experience of lovingness. . . ."

Why, one of the "swingers" in my survey even boasts, "I have been a part of so-called 'group sex' before it was a common term; . . . *but the participants have always been extremely close friends.*"

Yet, undeniably, for some women, intimacy breeds boredom or contempt. One girl admitted, "I can only be uninhibited in sex with people (men) I do not know very well."

Women are so varied in their sexuality that even those who are very similar are different. Let us contrast two whom I shall call Marie and Antoinette.

Both women are sexually informed and active, and both

have given considerable thought to their sexual needs. To achieve orgasms, both require direct clitoral stimulation.

They are not militant clitorists, for neither doubts that some women obtain orgasms via vaginal stimulation, but it doesn't work for them. Marie says, "I know that lots of girls do *not* need as much direct stimulation as me—but I think this is because they have larger and better placed clitorises." Antoinette says, "I don't know what percentage of women have orgasms during intercourse. It would seem to depend on individual anatomy and placement of the clitoris."

It is not yet clear whether these interpretations might be correct. While clitorises are highly variable, in size as well as placement, Masters and Johnson say that in eleven years of research they found no evidence to support the belief that differences in clitoral anatomy can influence sexual response. This, however, must be viewed as a highly tentative finding since they were unable to observe any clitorises during orgasm. Masters and Johnson think that certain *vaginal* conditions can operate to prevent the thrusting penis from exercising traction on the labia and clitoral hood, as it would ordinarily. So perhaps idiosyncrasies of the vagina, rather than the clitoris, better explain the anatomical need for direct stimulation. One hopes that Marie and Antoinette know that direct clitoral stimulation can be obtained in sexual intercourse, provided the woman is on top or the couple is side by side, and the pubic bones of the man and woman are touching.

What, in the experience of Marie and Antoinette, is the most common lovemaking "error" that men make?

Marie: "Not enough direct manipulation of clitoris."

Antoinette: "Many men don't realize that the clitoris is source of orgasms."

Two peas in a pod. Of all the women in my survey, there were no two who were more similar. . . . And yet Marie loves sexual intercourse, while Antoinette finds it dull!

Marie: "Intercourse to me is very exciting! I get depressed if a sexual contact doesn't include penetration, and a man doesn't come inside me."

Antoinette: "How a man performs intercourse is unimportant to me—since I never have and never expect to achieve orgasm during coitus. The faster, the better."

Should we then just lie back and wait for our lovers to push the right button? I think not. It isn't fair to us or to them. Women must discover and express their own sexuality, without shame and without inhibition. And instead of slavishly following sex manuals, men must learn to seek and receive signals from the women they love.

This is more easily said than accomplished, for until recently most women in our cultures were terribly inhibited. One woman confessed, "It was thirty years before I worked up the courage to tell my husband what I liked. Thirty wasted years!"

A fifty-five-year-old judge's wife, a woman who is deeply loved and admired in her community, told me:

"I was born too early and too late. Unlike my mother, I recognized that I too had sexual desires, but unlike my daughter, I considered it unthinkable to vocalize them. In the early years of my marriage I suffered unbearable frustration because I couldn't bring myself to tell my husband what he was doing wrong. By the time I worked up the courage he had lost most of his interest in sex. I've learned how to satisfy myself with an electric massager, but it's lonely. Some women are very sexy, and it's cruel to all concerned that delicacy prevents them from expressing it. I've had a good life but I hope my granddaughter will have an even better one. That's why I joined NOW—for her."

Indeed, if you read between the lines of Masters' and Johnson's second book, *Human Sexual Inadequacy,* you will see that a failure to communicate was the main problem afflicting most of the frigid wives they treated. And Dr. Masters says, "Communication was the whole core of our therapy—for our chances of success are negligible unless full, free and effective communication is established."

Sherfey provides us with a valuable historical insight into the history of analytic thought on the superiority of vaginal orgasms:

Almost seventy years ago, in Freud's *Three Essays on the Theory of Sexuality* (1905), the master postulated that females are endowed with two independent erotogenic centers. During development they must transfer the "infantile" sensitivity of the clitoris to the "mature" sensitivity of the vagina. This "clitoral-vaginal transfer theory" was held essentially unchanged by psychoanalysts and psychiatrists, despite the following objections to it:

—The infrequency of "vaginal" orgasms in apparently normal women.

—The lack of discernible sensory nerve endings in the main body of the vagina.

—The confusion many women report over the kind of orgasm they might be experiencing.

—The seeming absence of vaginal orgasm in subhuman animals.

In 1953 a female analyst, Marie Bonaparte, attempted to modify the theory slightly. She suggested that there were "four gradations" of orgasmic experience:

—the "infantile" clitoral orgasm alone

—the clitorial orgasm with some vaginal sensations

—the vaginal orgasm requiring prior clitoral stimulation

—infrequently, but best, in Dr. Bonaparte's view—the "complete vaginal orgasm" with clitoral participation being unnecessary or irritating. This orgasm is the "peak of mature femininity."

The next year, 1954, a male analyst, Dr. Judd Marmor, also raised his voice in dissent. He suggested that orgasm is "always initially clitoral," but that a woman who is emotionally prepared can *think* her way into a vaginal orgasm by transferring impulses from the clitoris onto the vaginal wall. This theory, as Dr. Sherfey points out, is based on no acceptable neurological or anatomical evidence, but it does seem to describe what some women say has actually happened to them.

Finally, in 1960, a (comparatively) major break or development occurred. At a panel discussion on frigidity, two of the leading female authorities on orgasm expressed a willingness to modify their earlier views. Dr. Theresa Benedek conceded that "female sexuality cannot fit into the *male model* [italics mine] of sexual maturity upon which psychoanalytic concepts are based" and that "the expectation that clitoral sensation should be transferred to the vagina is inconsistent with the distribution of the sensory cells responsible for the perception of orgasm."

Dr. Helene Deutsch, previously a leading defender of the vaginal orgasm (in two influential books on female psychology, published in 1944), admitted that she was "shocked by the high incidence of so-called frigidity in women" (vaginal frigidity, she meant) and "disappointed in the results of psychoanalytic treatment for it." She even questioned whether "the vagina was really created for the sexual function we assume and demand for it." Indeed, Dr. Deutsch announced herself ready to reverse the burning question from "Why are women frigid?" to "Why and how are some women endowed with vaginal orgasms?"

Unfortunately, Dr. Deutsch's earlier writings continue to carry more influence than her later doubts. This was so, even though she pointed out, at the panel discussion, that no form of psychotherapy or analysis has been singularly successful in the treatment of "clitoral fixation" and even though she and Dr. Benedek agreed that vaginal frigidity has not decreased with the increased freedom in the upbringing of girls, but rather "clitoral eroticism and fixation" seem to have increased.

At this point, I would like to interject an interpretation

of my own. In our survey of 103 relatively independent and sexually oriented contemporary women, all but 6 regularly achieved some sort of orgasm with relative ease. This is substantially higher than the figure for women in general in our society, especially when you consider that about one-third of the women in my survey were under twenty-five. (From the Kinsey report and other recent investigations, we know that while the majority of our women do achieve orgasms sooner or later, for many it is *later*. It often takes years or even decades of work.)

So, by an ordinary woman's definition, mine was a singularly unfrigid group. Yet, by a strict Freudian definition, this group was quite "frigid" because very close to half of the women stated that they could not usually achieve orgasm without direct clitoral stimulation. (Orthodox Freudians consider clitorism the most dangerous frigidity of all. The woman merely *thinks* she is being satisfied, in this view, but the orgasm does nothing for her.)

There was a group of women in my survey who said that they could not comment on clitoral versus vaginal at all and that to them personally the whole debate seemed meaningless. These women simply did not experience their orgasms in one place more than the other. But, omitting this group, there were, at the two extremes, many women who stated a preference for, or more frequent experience of, one type or the other. That is to say, regardless of the actual physiology of the event, they *felt* most of their orgasms in either the vagina or the clitoris.

Comparing these two groups, the women with a strong preference for either vaginal or clitoral orgasms, my research assistant, Carol Milano, and I did think we found certain differences in their returns. These differences were by no means 100 percent consistent, and indeed, some of the clitoral women gave what appeared to be very sound anatomical explanations of their preference. Example: "Before the birth of my son, who weighed over nine pounds and had an inordinately large head, I used to reach orgasm without needing to have my clitoris massaged. I don't believe that my vagina was repaired properly after childbirth. I think it must have gotten stretched out of shape because my same husband, with the same penis (and to whom I feel closer than ever) cannot bring me to orgasm so easily by his thrusting alone. I enjoy sex more than ever. My desire, if anything, has increased. But something is different about *me,* and if my understanding of Masters and Johnson is correct, I believe that the difference is that my vagina was slightly damaged, so that my husband's thrusting no longer provides as much traction on my clitoris."

This woman, incidentally, is a physician, and from *my* understanding of Masters and Johnson, she could very well be correct.

So, allowing for the probability that there *are* anatomical differences which may have a strong bearing, at least in some cases, what were the social differences between "vaginal" and "clitoral" women?

The general difference which Carol and I thought we spotted was simply this: There were more women in the vaginal group whose early experience with *men* had been favorable and who had not had to struggle to learn to enjoy sex. These women, perhaps because they were more "trusting" or, perhaps, more simply, because their earliest lovers were better controlled and had stimulated them, vaginally, for long enough periods to bring them to orgasm by that route, had somehow learned (often, but not always, quite early on) to experience "feeling" in their vaginas and to let themselves come to orgasms through vaginal stimulation alone. In short, the woman whose first orgasm—or first orgasm with a man—had occurred during intercourse appeared more likely to be a "vaginal" type.

The "clitoral" types had generally been exposed to more

selfish or fumbling lovers, particularly in their early experiences. Some, of course, had themselves insisted on the practice of merely "petting to climax" in order to preserve a token virginity during their premarital years.

It appears that the male lover who wishes to teach his young partner to enjoy vaginally experienced orgasm must be skilled at two levels. First, he must be sensitive at arousing her and getting her "ready" during foreplay. Second, he must be skilled at penile thrusting and well enough controlled to continue it for fifteen minutes or longer, if necessary. Of course his anatomy and hers and how well they mesh together—whether his penis is the right size and shape to provide traction on her labia and thereby on her clitoris—are additional factors, but these are beyond the conscious control of the couple. I believe that it is only in relatively rare cases, certainly a minority, that these anatomical factors make a crucial difference.

Yet they should certainly not be discounted. Some women noted a difference in their response to vaginal stimulation after childbirth. Several other women noted that they first experienced "vaginal" orgasm—that is, orgasm without direct clitoral stimulation—during intercourse with men who could either sustain vaginal thrusting for an exceptionally long period of time (compared to other lovers) or who had organs which seemed exceptionally large and "filling." One woman also noted a most interesting difference in male "sex rhythms":

> I have now had fourteen different lovers, most of them pretty skilled, and only one of them a one-night stand. My pattern, ever since college, has been to get intensely involved with one guy from anywhere from a few months to a few years. (I am now 38.) My parents had a very unhappy marriage, and I have no desire to repeat it. I recognized quite young that I prefer the single life, and hence my affairs usually break up when the man starts pressuring me to marry. (I have been involved with a

few married men. I don't believe in it, and it isn't fair to the wife. Also, I prefer to be monogamous for as long as a relationship lasts.) I am hoping that as I get into my forties, or certainly my fifties, I will find some agreeable widower or bachelor or divorcé who feels as I do about marriage and sharing a household but with whom I can work out a nice, enduring "arrangement," European-style, to serve us through our declining years, so we will not have to be "on the make" or lonely.

However, with some of my lovers, I need my clitoris fondled to reach orgasm, and with others I don't. I find that every man has his own individual sex rhythm and way of thrusting. This is something a man cannot control, no matter how much he may wish to. Some men make short, rapid, jerky thrusts, and other men make longer, deeper thrusts, which I like better. With a man who takes the longer thrusts, I can have orgasms without clitoral manipulation, and with a man who takes jerky thrusts I can't. This is oversimplifying of course, because every one of my fourteen lovers had his own unique sex rhythm, and I more or less enjoyed them all, even though some required that the man use his finger in supplementation. I believe that I could recognize most of my lovers blindfolded, just on the basis of their own unique sex rhythm. This, to me, is one of the most fascinating differences in men.

The liberated orgasm is any orgasm *you* like, under any circumstances *you* find comfortable. (The only qualification is that liberated persons don't exploit each other; that's just for masters and slaves.)

We know that all orgasms are similar, on a motor level, and all orgasms are different, on a sensory level.

We know also that there is no "ideal" or "norm" except in our own imaginations. Take multiple orgasms. Women who don't have them may fear that they are missing something, but women who do have them often report that these are not their most pleasurable experiences. "If I've had a *great* orgasm, I can't bear to go on," one such woman explained.

Or take this mysterious thing called "orgasmic intensity," which is measured, principally, in number of contractions. Masters and Johnson maintain that females have the most intense orgasms when they are free to please themselves only—"Without the distraction of a partner." But they do qualify it. "A woman might tell me that she had a delightful experience with the machine," Dr. Masters commented at the New York Academy of Medicine in 1968, "but the next night with her husband might have been even better, in her opinion, although we registered fewer orgasmic contractions."

While it is true that vibrators have become very popular, there is little imminent danger that they will replace sexual intercourse. In one recent survey of vibrator users only four women out of several hundred came to prefer these gadgets to their human partners.

A word of caution about vibrators might be inserted here. A girl of our acquaintance took hers on a Bermuda vacation, with her lover. He kindly allowed her to "finish up" with it at night, although her sessions were occasionally so prolonged that they interrupted his sleep. On the return trip, as they were clearing customs, the young woman's suitcase was severely bumped, causing the vibrator to go off. Fearing that it might be a bomb, the entire customs staff gathered around to investigate. At this point her lover vanished and has not telephoned since. We conclude from this that, if your companions are easily embarrassed, it might be inadvisable to travel with your vibrator, unless of course it is a plug-in model. (If you are embarrassed to buy a vibrator, there are other ways. A woman in my C.R. group achieved her first orgasm, at the age of thirty-four, by means of an electric toothbrush.)

Other women are turning to homosexuality, and they claim they are happy:

There are four advantages to lesbianism. First, a woman understands another woman's body so much better than a man can. Other women are better lovers. Second, women have prettier bodies, soft curves and smooth skin instead of bones and balls and hair in scratchy inappropriate places. Women are more cuddly and nicer to love. Third, women can't knock each other up. You don't have to spoil the beauty of the act messing around with birth control. You don't get frantic when your period is late. Fourth and most important, in a healthy lesbian relationship, you are equals as man and woman in our society cannot yet be. Back in the 1950's the lesbian scene was mostly butches and femmes. You were aggressor or receiver, and even if you were ki-ki like me, it just meant that you played one role or another depending on who you were with. Now we've freed ourselves from all that. You hardly ever see a dildo any more. We're not imitating men or cutesy-pie silly little girls. It is my sincere belief that the modern intelligent well-adjusted lesbian is the only person enjoying truly democratic sex.

Today women are discovering that they have not been allowed to design themselves. Sexually, and in every other way, we were forced to become what men wanted us to be. Now, as we start to search for our own sexuality, some women deem it best to withdraw entirely from men. Recently a prominent feminist confided:

I think it's wonderful that women have discovered masturbation, because it will enable us to keep apart from men as long as necessary. When you have work to do, you can't allow yourself to be diverted by sexual relationships. Masturbation is what male revolutionaries have always used to relieve themselves. Some of the women I know are so pathetic. They run around looking for a man, any man at all, just because they don't know how to masturbate.

But masturbation is lonely,[9] and a taste for homosexuality is not so easily acquired. (Indeed, certain new research suggests that homosexuality may be chemical, after all.[10]) Most of the women in my study were feminists, but

[9]The Ballad of the Lonely Masturbator (excerpts) by Ann Sexton:

> . . . Finger to finger, now she's mine.
> She's not too far. She's my encounter.
> I beat her like a bell. I recline
> in the bower where you used to mount her.
> You borrowed me on the flowered spread.
> At night, alone, I marry the bed.
>
> . . . I break out of my body this way,
> An annoying miracle. Could I
> put the dream market on display?
> I am spread out. I crucify.
> *My little plum* is what you said.
> At night, alone, I marry the bed.

From *Love Poems* (Boston, Houghton Mifflin Co., 1967)

[10]This evidence is still highly tentative, but there are many distinguished scientists behind it.

First, let's take a look at the older theories, which always seem to blame the homosexual's family. Unfortunately, most of these studies were based on homesexuals in trouble, prison populations, for example, or persons in intensive psychiatric treatment. Yes, they came from unhappy families, as people in trouble so often do, but as we recognize now, very little was known about homosexuals who were getting along well.

Recently the climate has changed, and homosexuals who are not in special trouble have been volunteering for studies. Also, our tests of certain types of hormone function are becoming more refined. In Los Angeles, Dr. M. Sydney Margolese found that the urine of homosexuals has a ratio of certain chemical breakdown products which resembles that found in the opposite sex.

In St. Louis, Dr. William Masters and his associates report that men who are exclusively homosexual have less testosterone in the blood and also lower sperm counts. Dr. Masters' homosexual volunteers were healthy college students in good academic standing. None had ever been hospitalized for a psychiatric illness.

These boys, as it turned out, came from normal families. Two-thirds of them recalled happy childhoods and strong dependable fathers.

But if homosexuality does have a chemical basis (at least sometimes) a very puzzling question remains, and it is this: Why

most of them like and need men. They want to educate men, not eliminate them. And sexually, these women are through faking it. They are learning that their own bodies are lovely. They are learning to think about their own sexuality and to talk about it.

"Perhaps all the dragons of our lives are princesses who are only waiting to see us once beautiful and brave."— RILKE

---

would hormone levels influence one's choice of a sex partner? (It is easy to grasp why a different hormone pattern might make individuals less sexy altogether, but gay people are not less sexy.)

The answer, when it emerges, may have to do with pheromones, a new scientific puzzle which is only starting to be explored. Apparently animals, and people too, may send sex signals by means of olfactory and other messages which have not yet been fully explained and charted.

Theoretically, subtle differences in hormones could produce equally subtle differences in the sex signals an individual sends or responds to.

The new homosexual findings may get parents off the hook, but many gay liberation spokesmen are not too pleased. They don't wish to be considered abnormal, chemically or in any other way.

Astronomer Franklin E. Kameny, president of the Mattachine Society of Washington, D.C., told *Medical World News* that he remains skeptical. In fact, Kameny suggests that these newfound differences might be due to the inferior sex lives of heterosexual males! "I'm wondering if a nagging, low-level, subliminal frustration in the heterosexual might not contribute to the difference in plasma testosterone levels," he commented.

CHAPTER THREE

100 SENSUOUS WOMEN—PART ONE

What does woman want? One thing is certain. She doesn't want a lover who follows sex manuals—anybody's sex manual—too rigidly.

One drawback to sex manuals is their tone and language. (Does the woman exist—anywhere—who yearns to be "manipulated"?)

A second drawback is their sexism. I was saddened to see that even "J," the Sensuous Woman, advises her sisters:

> Pin up on your bed, your mirror, your wall, a sign, lady, until you *know* it in every part of your being: *We were designed to delight, excite and satisfy the male of the species.*
> *Real* women know this.[1]

"J" also proposes that we wear wigs and costumes to jive up a flagging sex life, and she tells us it's "no threat" if

[1] "J" *The Sensuous Woman* (New York, Dell, 1971), p. 97.

our lovers and husbands dream of other women when they are with us.

> . . . a wig is fun now and then, especially if it's a different color from your own hair, for it allows him to live out (with no threat to you) one of man's common fantasies—that he's making love to someone new and mysterious.[2]

> . . . Sue greets her husband when he comes home at night in exotic costumes and creates a mood to match. One evening she may be a harem girl, the next a Lolita, a Ziegfeld Follies show girl, an eighteenth-century French courtesan, a gypsy fortune-teller, a prim schoolteacher who has to be coaxed into unwinding, a Roman slave girl, an Indian maiden. . . . If you learn to keep him off guard and curious about what you will be like next, he'll be too focused on you to stray.[3]

In his excellent review of sex manuals of the past 100 years, Dr. Michael Gordon, a University of Connecticut sociologist, points out that in the nineteenth century sex was almost strictly for men and in the twentieth century, while sex has been for women, too, the sexuality of women has been *denied autonomy*.

A typical nineteenth-century manual says, "As a general rule, a modest woman seldom desires any sexual gratification for herself. She submits to her husband, but only to please him; and but for the desire of maternity, would far rather be relieved from his attentions."

More recent sex manuals are still perpetuating a double standard, albeit on a more subtle level. In the still-influential *Love Without Fear*, Eustace Chesser writes: "The retention by each sex of its sex characteristics is of the first importance. Sexual freedom, which in blunt terms, means promiscuous intercourse, emphatically is not in the best

[2]*Ibid.*, p. 79.
[3]*Ibid.*, pp. 91–92.

interests of women in general. . . . Sexual promiscuity is entirely foreign to the true feminine nature."

Even "J," Gordon points out, holds to a "fairly conventional picture of what the relations between men and women should be like." Sex can be an extremely efficient way of landing a man. What mother did by revealing her domestic skills, you can do by revealing your erotic skills. *The Sensuous Woman,* Gordon concludes, might as well have been subtitled *The Way to a Man's Heart Is Through His Genitals.*

Sex and Marriage, a Planned Parenthood publication of 1965, makes this flat statement: "Men can enjoy sex in an animal sort of way, without love. Women can't." (The author of this statement, Dr. Robert Hall, has been a pioneer in the abortion movement.)

Another common fallacy of modern marriage manuals, Gordon points out, is the insistence that women mature sexually at a slower rate than men. "Woman is an early-leafing but late-flowering plant" is the way one writer put it.

The Kinsey studies may be responsible for this notion, for Kinsey pointed out that many American women do not attain their first orgasm until they are well beyond their teens. However, Kinsey blamed this on our cultural constraints, *not* on biology. Many writers have twisted their findings in a biological direction, making it appear that a "normal" unmarried woman is little troubled by sexual urges.

In short, the findings of modern sex researchers have been distorted by many popularizers, in the interests of justifying female chastity. It may be true (and I think it is) that a young woman can be turned off if her early lovers are fast and brutal, but that is a far cry from saying that she needs a marriage license in her bureau drawer before she can start to experience the joys of sex.

When, asks Dr. Gordon, will sex writers start to face and convey the really significant findings of modern sex researchers? The Masters and Johnson finding, for example, that woman probably has a superior orgasmic capacity to that of the male or the Sherfey conclusions about female insatiability?

All in all, your average sex manual is replete with misinformation, even today.

Take Dr. David Reuben, who had modestly assured us, in *Look,* that he is worth every penny of the $125 per hour he charges patients because he gets such "fantastic results." In *Everything You Always Wanted to Know About Sex,* he poses this question: "Is there any way a man can tell if a woman has really had an orgasm?"

Here is his answer:

> Since most women know what men want to hear, especially in the department of sex, they are *always willing* [italics mine] to acknowledge an orgasm, even if they haven't had one . . . if a man really wants to know, there are two accurate indicators.[*]

> Immediately after orgasm, a certain number of women experience what is called the sexual flush. . . . Not every woman experiences this, but they all exhibit the outer sign.

> Erection of the nipples always follows orgasm in the female. In spite of heaving hips, lunging pelvis, passion-

---

[*]How common *is* faking it? The best available estimate comes from Dr. Leah Schaefer, who submitted a thesis on the sexual experiences of thirty women to Columbia University in 1964. Of the thirty, seventeen pretended to have orgasms when they didn't, while one pretended not to have them when she did because her husband thought it was "disgusting and horrifying." Whereas Dr. Reuben indicates that any woman would fake the physical responses of orgasm, many simply lie to their lovers verbally.

With the rising feminine consciousness, it seems likely that the percentage of women who would fake an orgasm is diminishing. Nonetheless, it seems not unfair to estimate that perhaps half still do, usually to "avoid a hassle" with their husbands or lovers. This is a far cry from Reuben's insulting statement that it is in the female nature to dissimulate. The women who feel they must practice deception certainly don't enjoy it.

ate groans—no nipple erection, no orgasm. It is an accurate mammary lie detector—for those who want the truth.[5]

Have Mrs. Reuben and all those $125-an-hour patients been putting Dr. Reuben on? A sex flush, in those women who get it (see Chapter Two), develops *prior* to orgasm. Here is what Masters and Johnson say they have observed: "The sex flush reaches a peak of color concentration and its widest distribution late in the plateau phase, and *terminates abruptly* [italics mine] with orgasmic experience."[6] So, quite contrary to what Reuben says, the woman who still has a sex flush after intercourse is apt to be one who was aroused but *not* satisfied.

The same is true of nipple erections. Masters and Johnson have specifically noted that "postorgasmic nipple erection may be an indication of continuing sexual interest following insufficient orgasmic release."[7]

So Dr. Reuben's "mammary lie detector" is a big bust, if that is the term. All those men who are presumably checking out their ladies' orgasms deserve the confusion they must be reaping.

On the subject of menopause, Dr. Reuben is so insulting—and so inaccurate—that it's a wonder all the women past forty who bought his book did not tar and feather it, their booksellers, and him.

"Without estrogen," he writes, "the quality of being female gradually disappears. The vagina begins to shrivel, the uterus gets smaller, the breasts atrophy, sexual desire

---

[5]David Reuben, MD, *Everything You Always Wanted to Know About Sex but Were Afraid to Ask* (New York, McKay, 1969), p. 41.

[6]William Masters and Virginia Johnson, *Human Sexual Inadequacy* (Boston, Little, Brown & Co., 1970), p. 32.

[7]Masters and Johnson explain that women over fifty may retain "obvious nipple erection" for hours after orgasm. In general, then, the younger women who retain erect nipples after intercourse were probably not satisfied; the older women may or may not have been.

often disappears, and the woman becomes completely de-sexualized. Actually, it is a little worse than that.

"What could be worse?" he asks himself. "As the estrogen is shut off, a woman comes as close as she can to being a man. Increased facial hair, deepened voice, obesity, and the decline of breasts and female genitalia all contribute to a masculine appearance. Coarsened features, enlargement of the clitoris, and gradual baldness complete the tragic picture. Not really a man but no longer a functional woman, these individuals live in the world of intersex."[8]

Now it is quite true that most aging persons, male or female, slow down a bit sexually. The aroused woman takes longer to lubricate (minutes instead of seconds), and the aroused man takes comparably longer to raise an erection. The volume of seminal fluid which the male delivers is gradually reduced, as is the expulsive force with which he delivers it. After orgasm, his penis returns to its flaccid size more rapidly than before. The chances of his being able to rouse himself for an immediate encore diminish substantially.

The clitoris may become slightly smaller (not larger as Dr. Reuben says—that man is bad on nipples and clitorises)[9]—and it may also become more sensitive to touch. The vagina becomes less elastic, and why not? It need no longer expand to accommodate a baby's head. The time span of orgasm itself may be shortened in both men and women, and the number of contractions are reduced. However, enjoyment of orgasm need not be dimin-

[8]Reuben, *op. cit.*, p. 292.

[9]In his second book, *Any Woman Can*, Reuben reverses himself on the post-menopausal clitoris. Here he has it decreasing instead of enlarging (p. 57), but he does not even bother to correct himself in the paperback version of *Everything* . . . which came out while he was writing the second book. All told, his description of menopausal women sounds more like a rare medical disorder called adrenogenital syndrome. Dr. Reuben apparently doesn't know the difference, or didn't when he wrote *Everything*. . . .

ished. For some couples, it improves, in part because the aging male is much better able to prolong foreplay. Many aging males say that they enjoy foreplay far more than previously, for they do not feel as compulsively driven toward the big O, or moment of ejaculation.

After her early fifties, the woman is free from the fear of pregnancy and the bother of contraceptives. The man, very often, has better control and is more free to develop a pervasive sensuality like that which women enjoy from the beginning. Both are apt to change somewhat (sometimes for the better), and it is no more accurate to say that a fifty-year-old woman is no longer a woman than it would be to make the same statement about a fifty-year-old man.

It is not at all unusual to meet a woman who looks and feels better at fifty than she did at thirty-five. This is particularly true of mothers who have had large families. Their children grown and housework diminished, they now have more time and energy to lavish on their husbands and themselves. Quite a few married couples "rediscover" a waning love and sexuality when they get into their forties and fifties. This "second honeymoon" phenomenon is fairly common.[10]

[10]For some years now, Drs. Eric Pfeiffer, Adriaan Verwoerdt and their associates in the Psychiatry Department at Duke University have been gathering information about the sex lives of a large population of aging persons. Their findings confirm *some* popular beliefs about sex and aging—and dispel others.

Sex continues to play an important role in the lives of the vast majority. By age fifty, about half the men and women studied note some decline in sexual interest and activity, but some report an increase.

By age seventy, most of the men and women note a sexual decline. Even here, however, there is a minority who, for varying reasons, report an *increase* in sexual activity and interest.

Drs. Pfeiffer and Verwoerdt also note that "the oldest age group indicated higher levels of sexual involvement than did the next-to-oldest age group. This suggested that this oldest group actually constituted a group of elite survivors from whose midst less highly advantaged individuals have already been removed." In other words, there may be a connection between sexual vigor

It is true that some aging women start to find intercourse painful, but this is far less likely to happen when the woman continues to enjoy a regular sex life. One of the nicest things Masters and Johnson have found is that frequent intercourse helps keep the vagina youthful! With "regular usage," they say, it does not constrict significantly in size, and continues to lubricate well—and orgasms continue to be good.[11]

Painful intercourse is much more apt to occur in the older woman who has sex and orgasms only rarely. Naturally, if a woman were to believe one-quarter of the repulsive things Dr. Reuben has told her about herself, she would not feel very lovable and would hesitate to expose her coarse and hairy face and hairless head in public, much less reveal her atrophied breasts and shriveled vagina to a man.

Dr. Reuben advocates hormone replacement therapy for all women with quite as much exuberance as that other women's "friend," Dr. Robert Wilson, author of *Feminine Forever*. Dr. Wilson's book is still around, but his grants-in-aid from drug companies have shrunken even more than he and Dr. Reuben claim women's vaginas do, because the FDA has deemed Wilson's research unacceptable.

As if the likes of Reuben and Wilson were not enough, drug manufacturers are now themselves promoting estrogen replacement therapy directly to the female public. (This is contrary to the Pharmaceutical Manufacturers' Association's own code of ethics.) For example, Ayerst Laboratories, which manufactures Premarin and related products, maintains a public relations "service" called the

---

and longevity, though it is by no means necessarily a cause-and-effect connection.

Having an "interested partner" appears to be a major factor in the persistence of regular sex relations into old age. Husbands and wives agree that when sex relations cease in a marriage, it is generally the husband who is responsible for ending the relations.

[11]Masters and Johnson, *Human Sexual Inadequacy*, p. 342.

Information Center on the Mature Woman, at 3 West Fifty-seventh Street in New York City.

The information center mails free filler items, which subtly sell estrogen, to magazines, newspapers, and other mass media. In tiny print, these mailings acknowledge that "The Information Center on the Mature Woman is a service of Multidiscipline Research, Inc. through the support of Ayerst Laboratories." However, the average women's page editor appears to have no idea what Ayerst Laboratories *is,* for these features usually run without any indication that they were supplied by a drug manufacturer. The following column appeared in the Paterson (New Jersey) *News* on January 18, 1972 (note that only the second item deals with estrogen replacement therapy and that, *in toto,* the feature appears like a legitimate advice column of the Dear Abby sort. The basic formula of the information center is to sell estrogen in only one-third of its output, devoting the other two-thirds to nonphysical concerns of older women. Note also that readers are encouraged to make direct contact with the Information Center, without being told that "Miss Brookfield" is a drug company employee):

THE MATURE WOMAN
By Margaret Brookfield
Fellow Employes

Dear Miss Brookfield:

Can you tell me if women past the age of 40 or 50 automatically become self-appointed authorities on everything and anything?

I recently returned to business, working in an office with many women. They are always telling me where and when to buy clothes, where to go on vacation, what to serve for dinner, etc. These women aren't making helpful suggestions but giving orders. How do you stop them?

D.O.

Dear D.O.:

First, we have a question for you: how do they ever get any work done? You seem to be a buck private surrounded by generals. Our first bit of advice is to talk less.

Don't tell your co-workers about your shopping or vacation plans, and to avoid culinary chatter tell them you eat out every night.

There are some other alternatives: 1) start conversations along less personal lines, such as a new film you've seen or the latest news; or 2) (as a last resort) find a job in an all-male office.

* * *

Over-40 and Overweight

Dear Miss Brookfield:

I am 48 and overweight. I have tried strict dieting without success. I seem to have retained an additional five pounds with the birth of each child. Can my weight be due to the menopause? I am also irritable and depressed.

M.R.

Dear M.R.:

Many women have a tendency in their middle years to add a layer of fat around the hips and abdomen. But the extra weight, according to medical authorities, is not due to the menopause. Your depression and irritability may, however, be menopausal.

There are a number of symptoms associated with the menopause. Among the most familiar are hot flashes, night sweats, headaches, insomnia, fatigue, nervous tension, irritability and depression. Many women may not be bothered by any of these symptoms but it helps to know what they are, in case any one of them should develop.

Some of these effects are due to endocrine imbalance caused by the declining activities of the ovaries, according to the Public Affairs booklet entitled "Your Menopause." If so, in most cases these symptoms will vanish when the hormonal equilibrium is restored with estrogen replacement medication.

We would suggest you discuss your symptoms with your doctor.

* * *

Dear Miss Brookfield:

I seem to lose things constantly. One day I lose my wallet, the next day, my house keys. Today (would you believe it?) I misplaced a pair of shoes.

Sometimes I think I'm losing my mind. Does this happen to other women?

E.H.

Dear E.H.:

Yes (and don't lose this newspaper before you finish reading the rest of this answer). Try to make a conscious effort to have "a place for everything and everything in its place." It may be slow going for a while but keep trying.

P.S. How do you lose a pair of shoes?

* * *

Have you a problem as a mature woman, or with one? For advice and help, write to Margaret Brookfield, Information Center on the Mature Woman, 3 West 57th Street, New York, N.Y. 10019

Which is not to say that there aren't many reputable doctors who use hormone replacement therapy. But generally, they use it selectively and often only for short periods (to help a woman past her hot flushes, for example). Some women sail through menopause, and even for those who don't, there is a school of scientific thought which maintains that a good diet, with a special emphasis on calcium and Vitamin E, can alleviate many symptoms just as effectively as, but more safely than, hormones. Locally applied remedies come in handy, too—a simple lubricating cream, for example, if intercourse should grow painful.

The hormones most frequently prescribed for menopausal women are conjugated estrogens. These are different from the estrogens used in birth control pills in that they are usually manufactured from natural materials. Conjugated estrogens do not seem to cause blood clots or some of the other difficulties associated with the contraceptive pill.

However, there is always the nagging specter of cancer. It is not yet known whether estrogens can cause cancer in humans (although a team of Harvard researchers believe that they have recently proved it can; see Chapter Five, "How to Liberate Yourself from Your Gynecologist"), but is it quite well established that estrogen can speed up the course of an already-started malignancy. Since women of post-menopausal age face a not-insubstantial cancer risk, I know that I, for one, would hesitate to ingest any substance which might make matters worse. But this whole area is so "iffy" that one cannot take a blanket stand against estrogen replacement therapy. Certainly, if menopause is hell and nothing else helps, the estrogen cure may be worth the risks. First, though, it seems more sensible to try the three-pronged remedy of good diet, good sex and a busy and active life. Middle-aged women who feel as ugly and unwanted as Dr. Reuben would have them feel are understandably far more prone to change-of-life depression.

Here is how my own mother-in-law, who, besides being a busy wife, mother and grandmother, is a novelist and a woman who hitchhiked (braless!) to register at Cornell in 1918, describes her menopause: "I was fifty-two. At my annual checkup, my doctor asked, 'When was your last period?' It suddenly dawned on me that I hadn't had one for a while. 'Not for months,' I said.

"When I got home I checked the medicine cabinet. The box of Kotex I had bought just prior to my African trip the summer before was still almost full. 'What do you know!' I said. 'I haven't menstruated in a year. This must be menopause.' I was pleased, sort of. I called the doctor back and asked him if it was all right to throw away my diaphragm."

This is not to minimize the problems of those women who do have distressing symptoms at menopause. But many women don't, and it seems cruel, even bizarre, to frighten them needlessly, unless one owns stock in a company using mares' urine or some other similar source to make conjugated estrogen. You may have no evidence that your gynecologist has any connection with the hormone industry. (But as I learned from my misadventures with the pill and other pharmaceuticals, it is wise to retain a high index of suspicion toward any doctor who waxes too enthusiastic about any drug.)

At any rate, my mother-in-law never had one hot flush. Her periods just stopped, gradually, and she didn't even notice.

In the spring of 1971 my research assistant, Carol Milano, and I completed an informal but (we think) rather enlightening sex survey of 103 unusual women. They were, for the most part, highly educated, high-achieving career women or students. Several were famous, many more were "prominent," and at least two were wealthy—through their own efforts.

In the main my subjects or victims (or, in many cases, my friends) were women who are articulate, intelligent, educated, sexy, assertive and independent. They are the models of the new woman who enjoys more-than-average sexual awareness and freedom. Presumably, many segments of our female society are moving toward these same models. Certainly, our society is growing more liberal about sex, and women in general are growing more, well, demanding.[12]

Our survey was heavily weighted with physicians and writers—women who are exceptionally familiar with medical and psychiatric terminology. Most can loosely be counted as feminists or feminist sympathizers, whether or not they are active in the women's liberation movement.[13]

[12]Here is another finding that has been strangely neglected by psychologists, psychiatrists and the writers of sex manuals.

During the 1930's the late Dr. Abraham Maslow decided to test Freud's hypothesis that masochistic, self-effacing "traditionally feminine" women enjoy the best orgasms. Maslow studied 130 young college graduates and found that the opposite is true! The women who were assertive and self-confident felt freer to be themselves and experienced far greater sexual fulfillment than their more conventional and passive sisters.

Dr. Maslow, who served as president of the American Psychological Association, was one of the most revered and influential psychologists of his time. Yet his finding that, contrary to Freud's hypotheses, *unconventional women are sexiest* made little impact on his colleagues.

His research was published in *The Journal of Social Psychology* in 1939 and 1942.

[13]The questionnaires were given only to women who expressed their willingness to complete them. One out of three was actually returned. The key distribution points were:

— A meeting of the feminist caucus of the American Psychiatric Association.

— A meeting of feminist writers.

— A meeting of the women's liberation chapter at a New York City college.

— A consciousness-raising meeting of women in their fifties, sixties, and seventies.

— A New England rural commune of artists and crafts persons.

In addition, questionnaires were distributed to individual friends, relatives and colleagues who expressed interest.

The questionnaires, which were anonymous, were returned in self-addressed envelopes. However, some women made a point of identifying themselves. The youngest woman who specifically mentioned her age was nineteen, and the oldest was seventy. Most of the women were white and were either Protestant or Jewish, but some Catholics and a few nonwhites also responded.

Our respondents seemed to include approximately equal numbers of single women, married women and divorcées, as well as a few widows. Half or more were mothers, and at least 2 were unmarried

Certainly they all seem to believe that women are just as intelligent and capable as men—and just as entitled to sexual satisfaction. There was only one virgin. A majority of the women, even the young ones, had had extensive sexual experience. Many had also been in analysis, consciousness-raising groups or encounter groups.

In counterpoint to our investigation of comparatively "liberated" women, we also had the opportunity to review several hundred questionnaires that were filled out (*required* to be filled out) at a New York City abortion clinic during the same period in 1971. The clinic women, while sexually experienced (obviously), represented a much greater range of attitudes and social backgrounds. Generally, they are more conventional than the feminists, and much more naïve about sexuality and reproduction. And —this may come as a surprise to many readers—the conventional women in the abortion sample sounded much more hostile toward men. One of them said, for example, that her only hope for the future was to "cut off the penis" of the man who made her pregnant.

The women in my sample have a gentler ambition: They want men to become human.

As noted in the last chapter, the terms "vaginal" and "clitoral" orgasm have been widely used but ill defined. Men, failing to recognize the complexity of sensations in the female pelvis, assume that a "clitoral orgasm" means one that is clitorally induced, one that requires direct stimulation of the clitoris, either by the finger or the tongue.

Nearly half the women in our survey *do* require direct clitoral stimulation to achieve an orgasm at all. This is not to say that they downgrade the penis. While a small number expressed a clear preference for oral or manual sex, most of the women who need some direct clitoral

---

mothers who are raising their children without any male assistance.

In addition to the questionnaires, 14 women, representative of the groups already mentioned, were personally interviewed.

stimulation also stated that they obtain their best orgasm during intercourse, plus clitoral stimulation. This raises a disturbing question. How and why did the standard male-superior position become so popular in our culture? Admittedly, some women like it, but for the very large minority who require direct clitoral stimulation, it is one of the worst positions possible. Furthermore, it pins a woman down so that she cannot very conveniently rotate her hips.[14] For many women (and men, too, in other, sexier cultures) the pelvic movements of the female are a major source of sexual pleasure.

There were only 6 women in our survey who reported serious difficulty in reaching orgasm. This is not surprising, for as Dr. Maslow (again) demonstrated in the 1950's, people who are willing to participate in sex research without financial remuneration and without pressure from an authority figure (such as a professor or personal physician) are not, as a rule, ordinary or typical. *Voluntary* subjects are freer in their sex lives than most people, and less inhibited.[15]

[14]I understand that there is a variant on the male-superior position which may provide greater mobility and stimulation, for the woman. She thrusts her buttocks way up and places her feet or legs on her lover's shoulders.

[15]Dr. Maslow once asked a large number of college students to respond to a questionnaire on sexual practices. He then compared the personalities of those who consented to reply with those who declined. He found that there are consistent personality differences that separate those who are willing to answer personal sex questions from those who are unwilling. In other words, what sex research often uncovers is not a general range of attitudes at all but rather the attitudes of specific personality types—those who have fewer inhibitions than the norm and are more "self-actualizing."

Self-actualizing persons as described by Maslow have a healthy acceptance of themselves and others. They are relatively free of rigid defenses and role playing, relatively spontaneous, natural, and honest. They can accept their physical needs and discuss methods of gratification without guilt. They are able to accept qualities in themselves and others which would create anxiety and defensiveness in more conventional persons. They enjoy sex intensely, and often

Just over half the women in my study can obtain orgasm without direct clitoral stimulation. All these can reach orgasm from the thrusting of the penis inside the vagina, and a rather surprising number—about 1 in 6—have had orgasms from breast stimulation alone (including nursing a baby), kissing, books, paintings, mental fantasies and, in one case each, natural childbirth and watching animals copulate.

Yet even the women who do *not* require clitoral stimulation usually like it. Some said that they, too, have their *best* orgasms in positions where the clitoris, as well as the vagina, receives direct stimulation. Others noted that they like to have a great deal of clitoral stimulation before the man enters. There was, however, a large subgroup of

---

describe it as a mystical experience, but they are equally capable of lighthearted and playful sex. For them, Maslow has written, "Sex very frequently becomes a game in which laughter is quite as common as panting . . . their talk about sex is considerably more free and casual and unconventional than the average . . . what this sums up is an acceptance of the facts of life." (pp. 251, 244)

Self-actualizing persons also tend to reject rigid ideas of the sex roles people should play. "These people were all so certain of their maleness or femaleness that they didn't mind taking on some of the cultural aspects of the opposite sex role. It was especially noteworthy that they could be both active and passive lovers and this was the clearest in the sexual act and in physical lovemaking. Kissing and being kissed, being above or below in the sexual act, taking the initiative, being quiet and receiving love, teasing and being teased—these were all found in both sexes. It was considered a shortcoming to be limited to just active love-making or passive love-making. Both have their particular pleasures for self-actualizing people. . . . Self-actualizing people are not threatened by differences or strangeness. Indeed, they are rather intrigued than otherwise." From A. H. Maslow, *Motivation and Personality* (New York, Harper & Row, 1954), pp. 244, 245, 251, 259. Also from interviews with Professor Maslow shortly before his death.

It is interesting to note that the only un-self-actualizing persons willing to fill out Maslow's sex questionnaire were certain docile graduate students in psychology, who out of a sense of duty (to science and to their teachers) overcame their repulsion and forced themselves to cooperate.

In my survey, there were no such subtle pressures to comply working on anyone. There were no obvious pressures to comply, as

about 20 women who do not usually care to have their clitorises fussed over. They find it painful or irritating, or it brings on an immediate and (for them) less satisfying orgasm. However, a few women routinely have two orgasms at least, one during foreplay from oral or manual stimulation and one during intercourse. (These are not precisely the same thing as multiple orgasms, which occur in more rapid succession.)

Some of the women who can have vaginally induced orgasms prefer them to any other kind. They say that other kinds seem "less restful," "less complete" or "mere titillation." On the other hand, many women expressed no such preference. Some actually prefer clitorally induced orgasms, and others say that what they enjoy most depends on their mood, the circumstances, the partner's particular lovemaking skills and anatomy. (Sorry, fellas, but some

---

happens with *some* special samples, such as the abortion applicants who really had no choice. Nor was there any profit motive for the volunteers, who were not paid for their time.

And the time they gave was extensive. Some of the interviews continued over several days. Most of the questionnaires were far more extensively and thoughtfully filled out than we had anticipated. Comments such as "this was fun" or "I learned a lot from putting my thoughts and experiences into words" were frequently appended.

All told, 14 women were interviewed in depth, and 89 questionnaires out of 300 which had been distributed were completed and returned.

Dr. Kinsey was acutely sensitive to the possibility that his respondents might not have been typical (after all they all were "volunteers"), and he wanted very much to include all kinds of people. His books were called *Sexual Behavior in the Human Male* [Philadelphia and London: W. B. Saunders Co., 1948] and *Sexual Behavior in the Human Female* [Philadelphia and London: W. B. Saunders Co., 1953])—not "Sexual Behavior in Certain Selected Open-minded Types." Therefore, he used an interesting stratagem to secure the cooperation of persons who would not otherwise have responded. He would approach a group or club, contacting the leaders first, and announce that his goal was to secure 100 percent cooperation. Great tact and effort were used to round up the stragglers, and of course, as holdouts they felt social pressure to comply. (It was like being the only one in your office not to give to the community chest.)

highly experienced women maintain that—to them, and perhaps because of idiosyncrasies of their own anatomy— male anatomy does make a difference. Several women noted that penile *width* concerns them more than length. Others are affected by the *hardness* of the erection, and some do just like a big one.)[16]

Two women noted that a large penis seems to stimulate the cervix more. Others observed that a man with a large phallus can engage in a more exotic range of positions without slipping out.[17]

However, all but one of the women who commented so frankly on anatomical differences also noted that any handicap can surely be overcome by skilled and sensitive lovemaking, and that they much prefer a good lover to a man who is merely well endowed.

Still others pointed out that penis size seems to influence the type of orgasm they obtain and that they are more apt to have vaginal orgasms with either a large-phallused lover or a man who can hold an erection for an exceptionally long time. With men who are less generously proportioned or less self-controlled, they require additional stimulation of the clitoris. It has always struck me as strange that sex researchers seem to assume that a woman's capacity to have vaginal orgasm is entirely dependent on her—on her body, her mind or some combination of the two. It is quite likely that a man's mind and body bring a third and fourth

[16]One woman pointed out that she felt that one of the disappointing features of men who are very large is that their erections tend to be more spongy. (This corroborates the finding that there is less difference in size among erect penises than among flaccid ones.)

[17]One woman who said, "I am white on the outside but feel black on the inside and prefer, whenever possible, to socialize with blacks," mentioned that, generally, she believes black men *do* have larger phalluses. "What's so strange about that?" she added a bit defensively. "People from different parts of the world have certain unique physical characteristics. Any fool can see that many black women have especially voluptuous behinds. I'm not saying that this difference in phallus size holds 100 percent but I do think there's a *trend*. My cousin, who was a doctor in the Army, says that he agrees with me; there are more black men who are extra-large."

variable into the equation. For example, a woman may be so anatomically constituted that only certain types of penises—in shape, circumference, length or degree of hardness, provide sufficient traction on her labia minora to bring her to orgasm vaginally (see Chapter Two, "The Liberated Orgasm).

My survey did include a few extremist women who held to one of the following positions: (1) Any woman who claims that she experiences vaginal orgasms is either frigid or a liar. *There is no such thing.* The general tone of these returns was very angry, and several were illustrated with a raised fist. (2) The women who must have her clitoris touched in order to reach orgasm (ugh) is as good as frigid, and perhaps worse. The general tone of these returns was condescending, pitying. Although I have always sexually enjoyed my vagina and, as long as I am getting personal, even my cervix, which is somewhat more unusual (incredible to some people), I respect and feel for the angry returns, more than the supercilious ones. The many women who require direct clitoral stimulation (almost, you will recall, *half* the 103 in my survey) have often been treated quite condescendingly by their husbands or the psychiatrists to whom they turned for help.

One woman in my survey had her greatest orgasms during childbirth. Three others noted that their periods of greatest continual sexual arousal had occurred while they were breast-feeding their infants. (In addition to these, one other woman noted one orgasm during breast-feeding, but added that it embarrassed her a little and was a fleeting, if pleasurable, moment in her life, comparable to the orgasm she once experienced while watching Sonny Liston KO someone.)

Now, one could argue—and perhaps certain researchers such as Niles Newton would—that it is precisely this group of women, the small minority who are able to derive great sexual joy and release from their maternal functions, who are actually the most primordially "feminine." It is

Dr. Newton who has pointed out that the trouble with most research and writing about sex is that it is conducted by adult men, who think only in terms of intercourse since, being much more biologically limited than adult women, they cannot begin to appreciate, and, indeed, resent the limitless sexual components of pregnancy, childbirth and lactation.

So, if we are going to deal in snobbery and one-upmanship, if we are going to talk about "ultimate femininity," an excellent case can be made on behalf of the rare woman who has orgasms from breast-feeding and the even rarer woman who has orgasms from childbirth. Dr. Newton might say that these are the women who are truly natural, basic and eternal, who have best overcome all the inhibitions of our culture and who must have predominated at the beginning of our species when passionately devoted mothers mattered a great deal, while fathers and sexual connections with men counted less in survival terms.

Dr. Sherfey, if I may take the liberty (see Chapter One, "Is Woman Insatiable?"), has a somewhat different view of history and a different way of weighing evidence, although she and Dr. Newton would probably agree that at the beginning the sexual needs of women (whatever they were) were far more significant and central for species survival than the sexual needs of men. To Dr. Sherfey, the multi-orgasmic woman, the nymphomaniac, the woman who is totally responsive to and in tune with her biologic cycles, is most basic.

Finally, there was Sappho, among many others of lesser literary genius, who has (or should have) opened our eyes to the possibility that perhaps the most refined and delicate erotic delights available to woman can be garnered in homophile sex. And perhaps the most nearly perfect companionship and understanding exist here as well.

So, with basic issues like these to consider, the controversy over vaginal and clitoral orgasms seems very secondary indeed. Not that I think it isn't important. It concerns and inhibits some women and perhaps, today, an even larger number of men. But a time always comes to grow and move on, and I believe that most women who have been fortunate enough to retain and develop their own sexuality have come to view this raging controversy (vaginal or clitoral) as a less than serious matter. Or rather, they seem to feel that it is a matter which only becomes important when people, chiefly men, choose to make it so and choose to use it as a justification for their own personal phallic hang-ups or manual laziness.

It is sad that, indeed, the men in our culture are so much less flexible than the women. Despite brainwashing and all the cultural obstacles (nice girls *don't* until they marry. . . . It's all right for teen-age boys to masturbate, but not girls. . . . Vaginal orgasms are good, clitoral bad), the women in my survey have struggled, often valiantly, to establish their own sexual identities, to discover what it is they really like and want.

And then they learned that most of the men don't want to hear. For as various as these women were in their tastes and proclivities, their complaints about men were depressingly repetitive. Men make love as if they are following a program. . . . They are humorless. . . . They are too fast. . . . They are cruel to women who require finger stimulation, making them feel that this is a loathsome aberration. . . . They are interested in the "target" organs only, and they fail to appreciate the total body sensuality of women. . . . And, above all, they ignore the woman's statements about what she likes:

Not only do they fail to ask me what my preferences are, they seem reluctant to verbalize their preferences.

I guess I have trouble understanding men's bodies too, but at least I try. They have this inability to *believe* what I say about my own body.

Why don't [men] want to find out which parts of the body most stimulate a woman when paid attention to?

Nobody makes any mistakes with me because I've gotten very tough. A woman has to be very tough (unless she is very lucky) or else she'll wind up feeling used. I tell him right from the beginning that we're equal partners in this, and we do what I want, as well as what he wants, or it's no show. They can accept this if you make it clear from the beginning. If you wait to tell them, they are hurt. They take it as a personal rebuff. Lots of women complain that men are rotten lovers, but I think it's the woman's fault, too. She has to get over her inhibitions, and she has to stop worrying, "What will he think of me?"

I wish I were better at asking clearly for what pleases me. I've only known one man who encouraged me to do that.

After childbirth, my internal organs got a little less tight, or "sloppier." The old positions didn't work so well anymore. There was a distinct difference in what I felt. It was harder to have a really good orgasm. I tried vaginal exercise, but it didn't help much. . . . My husband wouldn't believe how serious the problem was (to me) and would only experiment half-heartedly with new positions.[18]

[18] Dr. Arnold Kegel of Los Angeles is probably the best known of the doctors who claim that if a woman has good control of her pelvic muscles, particularly the pubococcygeus muscle—her ability to achieve orgasm will be enhanced. Dr. Kegel believes that the same muscle which shuts off the urinary stream is the one which facilitates orgasm. To achieve control, a woman can practice shutting off the urinary stream. When she has thus identified the muscle, she is advised to contract and release it as a daily exercise. For further information, see *The Key to Feminine Response in Marriage*, by Ronald Deutsch (New York, Random House, Ballantine, 1968).

Dr. Kegel's exercise program may be particularly helpful to those women who find that their orgasmic capacity has been unfavorably affected by childbirth.

[Men] fail to discern their partner's preferences. They act as if they find the preferences unappetizing.

And an ultimate example of a husband who wouldn't listen to his wife's requests:

My ex-husband is a doctor. In medical school, he was scarred by a supposedly sexy gynecology professor, who gave the class a sex lecture and advised them, "Ride her high, boys, ride her high." What this professor meant is that if the man enters at a certain angle, he will supposedly provide more clitoral stimulation. But it didn't work, at least not for us. Or maybe I didn't need the clitoral stimulation. Every time my husband rode me high, it took away all the nice stimulation I was getting at the entrance to my vagina. Well, you won't believe this, but for ten years, every time I was about to come, the idiot would shift positions so that he could "ride me high"— and then I wouldn't come after all. I kept telling him not to shift positions, and he kept telling me I must be mistaken. . . . There's been an awfully high divorce rate in my ex's med school class. I wonder if a lot of it can't be traced back to that damn fool professor.

Many men don't spend enough time on foreplay and "romancing" to keep their women happy, according to my respondents:

Men shouldn't assume that a woman is aroused only by direct physical stimulation. They shouldn't assume that it takes a woman as little time as a man to become aroused.

Sometimes men don't spend enough time with preplay before intercourse. Also, sometimes they begin too forcefully. I think it is better to begin gently and then become forceful later. I think the man should see what the

---

Several women also mentioned that they had good results from following the Sexercise chapter in Bonnie Prudden's *How to Keep Slender and Fit After Thirty* (New York, Bernard Geis, 1969).

woman likes to do in this respect. (Gentle or forceful, many men don't know the possibilities of all kinds of touching and feeling.)

Lots of men just demand sex without any psychological love play beforehand.

All [men] are usually interested in is getting their rocks off. They aren't into a really long foreplay period, but rather are very goal-oriented toward "the great penetration and the big come."

They don't care whether a woman is satisfied, and usually the sex doesn't last long enough. If a man wants a quickie, he should masturbate—that's all. What makes [men] think we enjoy being treated like a receptacle for sperm?

Some men feel that foreplay is a grim necessity, a chore to prime the pump. I resent this attitude. Men seem to become stimulated so easily, and they get so impatient. Premature ejaculation is a problem.

Other women made the same points a little differently:

After the initial period they are too abrupt. They forget to tell a woman that she is still exciting. . . . Men want to call the shots. They don't encourage women to be expressive. Their foreplay is usually too brief and unimaginative. . . . They get right down to business. This turns me off. They don't understand erogenous zones and skilled provocative lovemaking. . . .

Sometimes, women complain specifically that their lovers don't pay sufficient attention to their clitorises:

Some (many?) men don't realize the clitoris is the source of my orgasm . . . and that they should provide a woman with orgasm any way they can do it, over and above intercourse. (Oral or manual.) Many men just don't care—they're selfish. Others try but are incompetent. To me a man is sexy if he satisfies me sexually . . . sees that I have an orgasm every time we make love.

Men do not realize the importance of stimulating the clitoris. In ordinary sex positions, I get *no* stimulation unless the man uses his finger. Many men think there is something wrong with a woman who needs finger stimulation.

Often, the women in my survey cited the common male hangup about being able to produce a female orgasm:

I don't know which is worse, selfishness and not caring if I reach orgasm, or caring too much—overkill!

[Men] achieve orgasm too quickly. They get very upset when you don't achieve orgasm. They make *you* feel guilty and inadequate. Their belief that women should have vaginal orgasms has obstructed more sexual lives than I care to think about.

The men I've known need desperately to feel that they can produce a vaginal orgasm. They insist on it, to the point where I still fake it sometimes to avoid a hassle.

Thank God my first lover was just a dumb teen-aged boy who didn't know I was supposed to have vaginal orgasms. He did whatever I liked, and we were very happy together. Men from twenty-five to forty are the worst. They usually think that they're the big expert. Older men often get more mellow.

Women are frequently disturbed because their lovers don't talk to them in bed or are too humorless about sex in general. Frequently, men lack imagination and sensitivity in their repertoire of techniques and positions:

. . . Few men are totally sensuous in their approach. They don't like to vary the positions and settings for lovemaking. They don't experiment with the stimulation of erogenous zones other than the genital areas and breasts. They won't even talk during sex.

[Men] are too rushed, and they want to stick to one position and the same old routine. They have little awareness of the total female body.

Despite their overtly liberated attitude, many men are still Victorians at heart. They don't really believe that women should enjoy sex, and they don't want to bother to be good lovers.

Men anguish too much over an event that fails. A man's capacity to satisfy is not negated by an episode or two of situational impotence. They're too performance-oriented and lack humor about sex.

I get annoyed by men who think you should only make love in bed (and usually late at night) and not in more spontaneous situations. The worst is men who fail to make me feel loved after lovemaking, the "roll-over-and-go-to-sleep type."

Men don't talk enough in bed or tell you what they feel. If they are turned on, they should show it, as this always turns me on all the more. Sometimes, men don't like to talk about the lovemaking afterward. That's stupid, because it could make it even better next time. Mostly, it appears that the sex center in the male brain is connected to the penis, and from conditioning, they can't enjoy all the other subtle things women enjoy.

It seems that the younger, less experienced women were more apt to make statements damning all men ("Men fall into two categories: those who don't *know* enough about sex, and those who don't care enough about sex"), while the women of greater years and experience were more bittersweet and compassionate (". . . I was unable to discuss my physical responses with my husband, partly from shyness and partly from ignorance of my anatomy as it really is. Take it from a couple who finally made it. The woman has to educate herself and then be honest with her husband. The husband has to care").

Are all these women "unfeeling bitches" who are overemphasizing the importance of technique? I don't think so. By and large they have happier sex lives than most women in America probably do. But they have learned to be discriminating, and they are clearly growing impatient with certain male attitudes.

The first orgasm came easily to some of these women (two mentioned that they had been masturbating to orgasm from the ages of five or six), but for some of the others, it followed a long struggle. Many women mentioned that their greatest obstacle to orgasm had been the fear of "letting go." It is not by coincidence that the French refer to orgasm as *la petite morte* (the little death) or *la morte douce* (the sweet death). When sexual tension is very high, a mild state of anoxia (lack of oxygen in the brain tissue) starts to develop. As a result, consciousness is sometimes clouded at the moment of orgasm.

I do not have comparative data for men, but I know that for many women this is a frightening experience at first. (I will hazard a guess that it may be *more* frightening for a woman since it is she who must bear the possible consequences.) Most women can only let themselves go in an atmosphere of caring and trust and warm communication. Certainly this is true of a woman who is young and inexperienced. Hence, the complaints we have heard about insensitivity go well beyond technique for technique's sake. A man may know every sex trick that has ever been printed in *Playboy* magazine, but if he only goes through the motions without regard for the individuality of the woman in his arms, how can she trust him and why *should* she let go?

There is a small percentage of women who will not recognize themselves in this discussion. They are the ones who can let go best with a stranger or even a callous or sadistic man. I believe that this is linked to low self-esteem. Such a woman suspects the man who treats her tenderly, for she does not deem herself worthy of love. Should she convince herself that he is sincere, she may be all the more reluctant to let go in his presence, for she fears that she may say or do something that will repel him. "If I like myself," one woman told me, "I'm very choosy about men. When I don't like myself, I'm not so choosy."

Only twenty years ago a distinguished Freudian analyst and expert on feminine sexuality gave a learned paper in which she suggested that all women are sexual masochists. Probably, most of her patients were. For the past several hundred years, and until recently, most Western women must have been masochists, or they would not have endured the thoughtless and even brutal treatment in bed that was generally their lot. Women believed that, being unequal creatures, they had no choice but to accept the sexual limbo man had designed for them.

As recently as August, 1971, the following statement appeared in the *Ladies' Home Journal:* "A woman can adjust herself to have an orgasm in a very short time. . . ."

Now that is just a male fantasy, cherished, in particular, by premature ejaculators. Some women *can* climax very quickly, but many women can't. A rather larger percentage of women can climax quickly on certain days of the month—particularly just before the menstrual period when progestin levels are high—but cannot, as a rule, climax so quickly at other points in the menstrual cycle. In societies where "frigid" women are unheard of, the men tend to spend much more time on both foreplay and intercourse itself than we do in the West.

Yet the source of the *Journal's* statement was an authority figure, a male psychoanalyst and psychiatry professor with impressive credentials. It is sad to think that among the *Journal*'s many millions of readers there were almost certainly a few who were just working up their courage to demand that their husbands slow down and who, upon reading Dr. Otto Sperling's blanket and arbitrary statement, probably slipped back into their old habit of self-blame. *Mea culpa* has been the cry of post-Freudian women in bed. Unlike her Victorian grandmothers who may in some respects have been more fortunate, or at least less unfortunate, because they expected not to enjoy sex at all, the educated post-Freudian woman has been *required* to enjoy sex, while the responsibility for making it enjoyable has rested almost wholly on her. "So he's a premature ejaculator," the message goes. "If you're a real woman, you'll learn to love it."

But let us not dwell too long. That Dr. Sperling's statement should appear in the *Journal* at this time is a curiosity, almost a throwback or a bit of nostalgia.[19] For women are changing very rapidly, and as Jean Genet, the French playwright who, like many homosexuals, understands the power struggle between men and women all too well, has discerned, "The emancipation of the modern woman obliges the man to give up old attitudes and find a new one, more in keeping with the less submissive woman."

But where are boys and men to learn these new attitudes? From Hugh Hefner? From Mary Calderone and her corps of blushing priests and physical education teachers who have suddenly been designated "sex educators"?

Margaret Mead pointed out long ago that in some of the primitive cultures she studied, female orgasm is never a problem. She wrote, "Societies like Samoa, that emphasize a highly varied and diffuse type of foreplay, will include in

[19]Most women reach orgasm more quickly during masturbation than during intercourse. Kinsey had data on the length of time it took 2,114 women to masturbate to orgasm:

45 percent	1 to 3 minutes
24 percent	4 to 5 minutes
19 percent	6 to 10 minutes
12 percent	longer than 10 minutes

the repertoire of the male, acts that will effectively awaken all women, however differently constituted they may be."

In modern America, it seems, the "repertoire of the male" is limited. By chance, he may be able to "effectively awaken" *some* women, but the ones who are "differently constituted" still freeze him or throw him into a panic. We recognize now that societies we once scorned as backward have been doing a far better job than we civilized folk of preparing their members for what remains a central concern of most lives: good sex.

On the Samoan Islands, the boys and the girls are instructed in sex—not how to curb it, but how to enjoy it—from the cradle. They get to watch a lot of it. At puberty, they get to learn by doing. Various older instructors and initiators are appointed to guide them. They don't just flounder around in the back seats of cars and have all sorts of horrible first experiences. (The women in my survey are not very high on Freudian psychology, but on one tenet they agree perfectly with the analyst: First experiences often leave a lasting impression.)

Perhaps the time will come when we will institutionalize real sex education (I for one wish I knew how to swivel my hips so I could teach my daughters; they're being encouraged to dance a lot, and maybe that will help), but here in Nixon's America the day does not seem imminent.

Whether they like it or not, Western men who wish to have a good and effective "repertoire" will, for now, just have to be taught by the women they bed down with. It isn't entirely natural for young women to perform as sex instructors, but there's no better solution at hand. The men who don't adapt are going to be stuck with leftovers, for in America and England, at least, female sexuality was so long repressed that it is bursting forth like Niagara, and only women of low IQ or vitality are still willing to accept the old-fashioned sex-is-for-men philosophies. Most men, having high regard for the seed of their loins, don't like to deposit it in women who are, incontrovertibly, less than the best available. Therefore, I optimistically predict that intelligent men are going to come around quite quickly and might even become eager learners.

But first, the women will have to know themselves. A man, after all, has plenty of opportunity to know his sex and reproductive organs as they are highly visible outside his body. A woman's are not.

Recognizing this problem, a kindly woman doctor once proposed an elaborate system of mirrors which, she thought, all women should set up in the privacy of their dressing rooms, for the purpose of self-examination. The idea never seems to have caught on.[20]

[20]Dr. Helena Wright, *More About the Sex Factor in Marriage* (London: Ernest Benn, Ltd., 1947).

"Arrange a good light and take a mirror and identify all the parts described. To find the clitoris, the thighs must be separated widely enough for comfortable vision. Then if two fingers hold apart the larger lips, the mucous membrane-covered hood will be seen immediately inside the front end of the space between the larger lips. The hood can be gently drawn backward by the finger-tips and inside will be seen a small, smooth rounded body (some-times it is very small and only just visible) which glistens in a good light. This is the clitoris. Its root runs upward under the hood, and the junction of the outer lips, and extends for about an inch. The two inner lips begin in the midline close together just under the clitoris, and extend downward and backward on each side of the smooth space in the middle, and come to an end by fading away at about the middle of the ring-shaped opening which is the entrance to the vagina."

Dr. Wright further instructed her readers in the art of establishing clitoral sensitivity. She recommends exploration with a small object, such as an uncut pencil or a toothbrush handle because "the fingertip is naturally itself sensitive to touch, and if it is used there may be confusion of effect between the feeling finger and the part felt."

One hand should separate the outer labia, Dr. Wright explains, and the other holding the "chosen object" should touch first one inner lip, then the other, and finally the clitoris. "The effect observed is that the instant the clitoris is touched, a peculiar and characteristic sensation is experienced, which is different in essence from touches on the labia or elsewhere."

"This difference has to be experienced; it cannot be described in words."

Dr. Wright further proposes that: "the rhythmic, caressing movements of the clitoris region can be designed to include adja-

In Washington, the D.C. Health Group, a feminist organization of women who are mostly in the health professions, have taught themselves to do pelvics on themselves and one another. A pair of valiant California women are traveling the country, teaching standing-room audiences at colleges and women's centers to explore their own pelvises. It's not a bad idea, but I doubt that many of us are yet ready to do pelvics on ourselves and our friends. However, two Washington women named Liz and Janet have hit on what sounds like an excellent compromise. They went to their gynecologist together and told the doctor they wished to watch each other be examined.

"The doctor recovered fairly rapidly from the shock of that suggestion," Liz reports, "and I saw a cervix for the first time. Several thoughts flashed through my head. I was freaked. That was my friend Janet. A cervix, which had always been just a word or concept, really exists!"

Liz adds that there is a second benefit in pairing off to visit gynecologists. One doesn't feel as lonely or as frightened.

Several recent sex books have included detailed instructions on how to masturbate. The question came up in my consciousness-raising group: "Does the knowledge gained here help a woman in interpersonal situations, or doesn't it?"

---

cent areas of the vagina and so express the idea that the two regions can function as a unit. . . . The effect is as if the vividly sensitive nerve-endings in the clitoris were saying to the sleeping capacities of the vagina, 'Come, do as we do, wake up and feel.' "

She informs us that there are an indefinite number of ways this can be done, and she suggests three, for starters:

1. "a downward stroke beginning just above and beyond the root of the clitoris, passing over the clitoris and on down the midline, into the vaginal entrance following the front wall of the passage and ending a little way inside."

2. "the reverse of the first, and a rhythm of these two alternating movements."

3. "gentle stretching movements of the front part of the ring of the vaginal entrance. . . . Two fingertips can easily be slid into place and gently and rhythmically moved."

There are two schools of thought. Some women felt that masturbation had improved their interpersonal sex lives, but others feared that it might have made them too exclusively clitoral. One of the women in the group, a journalist, had recently interviewed "J" and asked her, "You gave good instructions on masturbation—how do you transfer them to sex with a man?" "J" smiled, and snapped her fingers. "I knew I left something out of my book," she replied.

While some women masturbate vaginally, or vaginally *and* clitorally, the majority rely largely on clitoral stimulation most of the time. This has led many psychiatrists, and some women, to speculate that perhaps too much reliance on direct clitoral stimulation makes vaginally induced orgasm harder to attain.

On these grounds, psychiatrists have cautioned not only against masturbation, but also against petting to climax. However, Dr. Alfred Kinsey's findings seem to refute this. He found that wives who had experienced orgasm prior to marriage had a far better rate of orgasm during marital intercourse. "There was no factor which showed a higher correlation with the frequency of orgasm in marital coitus than the presence or absence of premarital experience in orgasm."

Under what circumstances did the first premarital orgasm occur? *For only 10 percent did it happen during intercourse.* Forty percent had their first orgasm during masturbation, 24 percent during petting with boys or men, 5 percent during an erotic dream, 3 percent during homosexual play and 1 percent during a fantasy or other head experience in which there was no bodily stimulation of any kind.

This is not to deny that some women who got used to clitorally induced orgasms (from masturbation and petting) in their teens *believe* that this early reliance on direct clitoral techniques has made it more difficult for them to transfer feelings to their vagina. But perhaps they believe it only because their analysts have suggested it. The analysts have no hard data, whereas Kinsey's thousands of case histories seem to go in the opposite direction. Kinsey felt that the significant hurdle for a girl or young woman is learning how to abandon oneself to one's sexual feelings—by whatever method. Women who have had no orgasms prior to marriage are the ones most apt to have problems later. Not that it is ever, necessarily, too late. Kinsey found a few women who did not experience their first orgasms until after they had been married a quarter of a century.

By stark contrast (how sexually variable is woman), the Kinsey group also established that some babies and small girls masturbate to climax. Slightly under one-half of 1 percent of the women in his study remembered having reached orgasm before the age of three. By eleven years of age, 9 percent had reached orgasm, and all told, 14 percent experienced it before adolescence. Even babies were observed masturbating to climax. (This was not new. In the nineteenth century a report appeared in a medical journal of a baby girl who, sitting in her high chair, would rub her thighs together, stiffen, stare, and then apparently recover, perspiring. Her parents thought she was having epileptic seizures.)

Kinsey found, also, not only that preadolescent boys masturbate to orgasm, but that they frequently have the ability to attain multiple orgasms which, as a rule (but not always), they lose at the age when the male climax starts to be accompanied by the ejaculation of semen. The Kinsey researchers actually observed twelve young boys who could achieve orgasm more than ten times in succession. One boy, eleven months old, had fourteen orgasms in 38 minutes. The youngest boy whom Kinsey researchers observed reaching orgasm was five months old. The youngest girl was four months. (We mature faster.)

A recent report in the *Journal of the Society for the Sci-*

entific Study of Sex also raised the question of masturbation. The doctor who wrote the report concluded that with some women masturbation helps, and with some it doesn't. (He wasn't just speculating. He had instructed his patients to try it.)

There was some indication that among the women in my survey, those who had masturbated freely as children grew up to be sexier adults. But it is impossible here to separate cause and effect. Perhaps these women masturbated *because* they were endowed with a higher-than-average sexuality.

There is no question that the consciousness-raising groups, in which so many women are currently participating, are helping most of them to think and talk about sex more freely. One realizes that one's body is not loathsome and that one's sexual desires and frustrations are anything but abnormal.

A consciousness-raising group is simply a leaderless group of women who meet weekly to discuss their *feelings and problems as women.* Consciousness-raising groups come in various sizes, but somewhere between five and twelve seems to work best. Naturally, sex is not the only topic discussed, but it does tend to come up often, especially after the group has developed trust. In some groups, the women take turns speaking, but in others they speak or not as they wish. Most successful consciousness-raising groups adhere to only one firm rule. When a member complains about a situation in her life, the group *does not* allow her to assume that she must not be pretty enough, or smart enough, or woman enough to cope as well as mythical others do. Instead, the group helps her explore how societal conditions might be responsible and tries to help give her the courage to think of practical ways of changing her situation.

In the next chapter, we shall discuss the kinds of lovemaking that women who have had their consciousness raised (in a group or outside of one) like, and we shall learn some surprising things about their most gratifying sexual experiences.

CHAPTER FOUR

100 SENSUOUS WOMEN—PART TWO

The late gynecologist and sex researcher Robert Latou Dickinson often remarked, "It takes two people to make one frigid wife." He was referring, of course, to the woman herself and her husband.

Contemporary psychotherapists have been wont to look at the situation a little differently. They blame three people—the woman, her mother and perhaps her father. It is really remarkable to see how deft they are at getting husbands and lovers off the hook. (Husbands, of course, are often the ones who pay the therapy bills, and I suspect that this very practical factor may have some influence on the collective psychiatric unconscious.)

How weird it has all been. The frigid wife consults a male expert, and he spends months and years helping her find the root of *her* problem. Only recently, a relatively small group of psychiatrists—the family therapists—have pushed to include husbands in the treatment of sex problems. Most, even today, would agree with the *Ladies' Home Journal* "wisdom" of the Dr. Otto Sperling quote in the previous chapter. A woman, if she's a good one, should be able to overcome *her* blocks—with a little help from her psychiatric friends. If she doesn't overcome these blocks despite trying, well, her parents (especially her mother) must have been really awful.

The evidence from our survey and from anthropological studies seems to contradict this position. It appears that the first sexual experience *with a man* may be the most crucial factor and that women who encounter a sensitive lover the first time out are often spared the years of agony over establishing "heterosexual responsiveness" that seem to be the lot of so many American women.

Obviously, this isn't always true. Some women have had such a repressive upbringing that Casanova himself might have failed to stir their juices. But these cases are extreme. The fact is that most girls in America still have a fairly repressive upbringing (depressingly similar in the vast majority of middle-class families, actually), and yet a few turn on to men very happily and easily, while most have to struggle. Could it not be that most of our boys and men—in depressing contrast with, say, the Mangaians—are simply unfit to initiate virgins, being too fast, too fumbling and too unmindful of the sexual feelings of women?

A happily married psychologist, now in her thirties, gave us the following history:

> My parents wouldn't threaten me with anything if I touched myself, but they would swoop down and "distract" me. By the age of four, I had given up masturbating. I don't recall that I had ever reached orgasm from it anyway, so it didn't seem a great loss.
>
> They were bugs on cleanliness, though. When I went to the bathroom, they made quite a fuss about seeing that I wiped myself in the right direction. They didn't do this to my brother. I got the impression that my bottom could be dirtied more easily than his—from the transmission of wastes into the wrong parts. (I still find it difficult to let myself go if I haven't had a bath between the last time I moved my bowels or even urinated and hav-

ing sex. Maybe I can reach orgasm in intercourse, but I feel dirty about oral sex or letting my anus be touched. I just want to get it over because my body doesn't feel clean.)

At the age of nine I had a traumatic experience. I came rushing into the bedroom one evening when my father was dressing to go out. He had an erection. My, I thought it was ugly and strange. I almost wanted to throw up and I often recalled it with disgust afterward. Until then I had only seen my younger brother's genitals, never with an erection, and to me, they were just like a silly little lump. One thing helped reassure me about my father. Maybe it was just a fortunate accident. Our teacher took us to the Brooklyn Museum, and among the primitive art statues there was a fertility god with a huge erection. It got me to thinking that maybe my father didn't have some loathsome disease or shameful condition after all. Maybe penises that stuck out were just one of the mysteries of adult life. Incidentally, neither my father nor mother ever "discussed" the incident with me or tried to reassure me in any way. Daddy, who was a rather rigid lawyer-accountant, was clearly humiliated, and it was just left to me to puzzle it out or make my peace with it.

They never prepared me for menstruation either, and in talking to my friends, I've concluded that most of them were at least a little bit better prepared than I was. I mean at least they got a book called *The Stork Didn't Bring You*. I didn't even have that. Luckily, I had two slightly older girlfriends who started before I did and clued me in a little. I mean I didn't think I was suddenly bleeding to death or anything.

Then, when I was thirteen, I got very lucky. We were playing spin the bottle at a school party. There was this very shy artistic boy who was about a year and a half older. I'd noticed him and thought he seemed a little interesting and "different," but I'd never had any daydreams about him or anything. I'd never been consciously attracted to him. For one thing he wasn't a sports hero or an especially popular boy. He did have lovely soft eyes, but his skin wasn't too good.

Well, he really kissed me. It was totally different from the other fooling around I'd been doing at parties. He opened his mouth and explored mine with his tongue, and it was completely sensuous. I just loved it. He walked me home, and after that we started going together. We were just right for getting each other all juiced up. When my hygiene teacher warned us that "boys were after one thing only," I couldn't believe it. I didn't know what she was talking about. Tommy and I were obviously after the same thing. We just liked to go off together and cuddle.

He moved away. I was heartbroken. I dated other boys, and I had fun, but they weren't too great to pet with. Everything they did seemed contrived and amateurish. Well, what the hell. They were only fifteen or sixteen. Tommy was exceptionally sensitive—or gifted. He never rushed anything or seemed stiff or jerky or embarrassed. He was a natural.

Just after my fifteenth birthday I met Martin. He was smooth, a college senior, and much more "studied" than Tommy but also very good. He courted me extravagantly, taking me to the theater, coming down from his college to meet me after school so he could ride me home on the subway before he went to work. One night in Central Park we were lying on the grass petting, and it just happened. It was such a beautiful night. I lost my head. First I had this great orgasm, and then I said, "Wow—this must be sexual intercourse." I wasn't even sure, and I had to *ask* Martin who confirmed that it was. I never had that feeling, "Is this all there is?" To the contrary, what I didn't understand was, "Why *didn't* anyone tell me?"

On the basis of my experience I don't think that what your parents or teachers do is that essential. If you're a fairly young healthy female animal and you chance across the right boys, you're going to be crazy about sex. I didn't get pregnant from Martin, which was good, but on the other hand, he did leave me after a few months to marry an old girlfriend. I missed him, and I cried some, but young as I was, I didn't feel suicidal or anything like that. I was and always will be rather grateful to him, and rather smug about that night in Central Park. On thinking back there is one thing I can say for the "sex education" meted out by my parents. At least they didn't give me this horseshit about saving myself for the one and only. I mean I didn't feel one bit ruined after Martin. I felt smug and, in a kindly way, a step ahead of the other girls in the class. I know I was just lucky. After long experience, I've realized that Tommy and Martin were both, in their own way, superior to most male lovers. And both were right for me at the stage I was at—Tommy to warm me up, and then Martin to "put it all together," as they say on Mad. Ave.

The psychologist from whom we just heard adds that she has totally rejected the popular theory that contemporary woman's childhood is usually to blame for her inability to adjust to the sexual demands, however crude, of men. She views this generalization as a "male copout" except in extreme and unusual cases.

"Most of the women in our society don't have an ideal sexual upbringing," she continues. "But most of the boys and men don't either. In extreme cases this can paralyze a person, but male psychotherapists seem to be conveniently overlooking the fact that *in the normal range* few men are paralyzed and many women are."

Some readers will object that the preceding history has little to do with *technique,* as they understand the term. The narrator, they will say, was merely fortunate in being awakened by two young men (or a man and a boy, actually) who were gentle and tender. These, they will say, are traits of character and have to do with caring or "digging" each other.

Quite so. And there is no question that there are a few

men—such as the artistic young boy described in the preceding paragraphs—who seem to know instinctively how to stimulate and satisfy a woman, without pushing her too far.

But the fact remains that most boys and men in our culture apparently do not have this instinct. Our adolescent males bear little resemblance to Margaret Mead's Samoan boys of broad repertoire, who can "effectively awaken almost all women."

Nor do a majority of our grown men bear much resemblance to the "erotically civilized adults" described by Van de Velde,[1] who, according to the Dutch sexologist, would never be so indelicate as to roll over and go to sleep without afterplay. Rather to the contrary, four of the women in our survey complained that their mates or lovers sometimes stopped short in the middle of lovemaking to smoke a cigarette!

The play *Oh! Calcutta!* opens with an amusing bedroom scene, in which a woman is giving her lover so many frenzied instructions that she reminds the viewer of a traffic policeman. Some of the men I know adore that scene, and when their wives or girlfriends are so forward as to suggest, for example, a new position, such men are apt to recall the scene with glee and say, "Aha, you're acting just like *her*."

Psychotherapists, too, love to cite *Oh! Calcutta!* triumphantly. See what happens, they say, when women become assertive. It scares the men off. They can't perform. That's why (ominously) impotence is on the rise.[2]

[1] Th. H. Van de Velde, *Ideal Marriage* (New York, Random House, 1930, 1957).

[2] But psychiatrists also make a somewhat opposite complaint. A couple of years ago, at the annual meeting of the American Psychiatric Association, I heard a distinguished Chicago psychoanalyst wax wroth because—get this—"the adolescent girls are getting so aggressive that it is no longer possible for me to make a differential diagnosis, in boys, between schizophrenia and adolescent turmoil."

Such psychotherapists reveal an appalling ignorance of epidemiology. As any student of public health *should know,* when one disease is cured, others which had been confused for it, or absorbed into it, start to become manifest. Psychiatrists are hearing more about male sexual inadequacies because modern woman, no longer a sexual masochist, is refusing to lie still for them.

Consider premature ejaculation, which is extremely common, although there is no standard definition of it. If a man regularly climaxes the moment he enters a woman, or, as in many cases, before he can even make entry, then clearly his ejaculations are premature.

But what if it's not quite that bad? Some doctors say that a man is a premature ejaculator if he cannot sustain intercourse for at least thirty seconds to a minute. Others say two minutes. And here's a gorgeous example of psychiatric wit and wisdom, apt to be overheard at least twice at any party where therapists gather: "If the guy comes faster than his doctor does, he's a premature ejaculator." Masters and Johnson hold a two-way view of premature ejaculation; if a man can't control himself for long enough to satisfy his partner, then, as far as that "unit" goes, he is premature.

Despite Dr. Sperling's good words about any woman's being able to train herself, etc., etc., women are starting to rebel, and when they encounter a premature ejaculator, they are apt to protest. Yes, even if they love him. If they

---

Here, approximately, is what the gentleman said: We all know that some adolescents act so crazy that it can be difficult to distinguish what we call "adolescent turmoil" which usually passes with maturity, from schizophrenia, which requires more vigorous treatment. In the past, the most reliable clue was to ask a boy, "Have you ever made it with a girl?" If he said yes, you could be pretty sure that it was just "adolescent turmoil." If he said no, you would conclude schizophrenia, because schizophrenic boys rarely make it in their teens.

But now (he was furious) you cannot count on this anymore because the girls are so forward that they are taking these passive, disorganized boys to bed with them.

It almost sounded to me as if the doctor were jealous.

expect to go on loving him for long, there is all the more reason to insist he seek help.

Perhaps some of the Victorian women who were "lying back and thinking of England," totally unaroused, were able to love their husbands for a lifetime despite the lack of sexual satisfaction. (As best we know, these women were not consciously frustrated.) It is also true that even today a mature and experienced woman does not view one or two mishaps or failures with any alarm. (Indeed, a number of our most sensuous women said that it was too bad men cannot take "occasional" failures in better grace.)

But it is *not* true that an aroused woman can go on indefinitely "just enjoying the nice feelings and closeness of sex" and not minding if she fails to reach orgasm. Why, it's even bad for her physically (see Chapter Two). As one of the women in my survey pointed out, "Sneaking into the bathroom to relieve oneself with one's own finger is not conducive to the course of true love." The idea that women don't need orgasms to be healthy and happy is just another male supremacist fantasy. At least it doesn't apply to women who have been aroused and who believe that they too have sexual rights.

So that is why the therapists are hearing more complaints of prematurity and impotence. Instead of tolerating a bad situation, as before, women are sending their lovers and husbands for help.

What women are expected to tolerate is sometimes rather grim. I have learned from the women in my survey that New York abounds with men who favor anal intercourse. I have also learned that the woman who truly likes it must be rare, although some do enjoy having their anuses gently touched or stroked. Of the 103 women we queried, only *one* expressed even mild enthusiasm. In her words, "I am slightly on the positive side of neutral."

Here is the harrowing tale of a social worker in her late twenties:

My husband and I lived together for almost two years before we married. The sex was quite good. He used to fool around with my anus a lot and sort of rub his penis against it, but I didn't mind that. Then we got married and flew to Europe on our honeymoon. He begged me to try anal intercourse. I complied, and it was very painful. After that it was all he wanted to do, except once in a while as a big favor. I developed all kinds of rectal problems, but he still wouldn't stop. I adored him, but after six months I couldn't take it anymore. I was in constant pain, so I moved out. He went into therapy, and one day his analyst asked me to come for a joint session. All he did was give me a lecture about how everyone has some quirky tastes and if I loved my husband, I should accommodate. But there was nothing in it for me, so I'm glad I'm out of it. I'm still seeing a doctor about my rectal problems. The last I heard, Gordon had turned gay. I'll bet that's what he really wanted all the time. Good luck to him.

Did the analyst blame Gordon's "rejecting wife" for his crossing over into homosexuality? We don't know. But we do know that some of the men who have been using women in bizarre ways, to mask or to act out their own forbidden fantasies, are suddenly finding fewer women who are willing to submit. If this is leading to more diagnosed sexual problems in men, so be it. I'm not even sure that homosexuality *is* a problem. Certainly, as psychiatrist Robert Seidenberg has pointed out, the important question is not what makes a homosexual, but what makes society persecute him. If Gordon is making a boyfriend happy, that seems better, for all, than making a wife miserable.

Well, then, were any of the *wives* in our survey happy? Yes, indeed, many of them said they were. For example, "My husband and I have been happy all our lives. Not every sexual experience was perfect, but more satisfying, fun, fulfilling than the first. Who could ask for anything more?" and "If you're any sort of woman, and he's any sort of man, you can work things out. We did."

There was also a group of loving wives, however, who complained that in their thirties and after, their sex drives had outstripped that of their husbands:

> I think it is true what Kinsey once said about women wanting more as they get older and men wanting less. . . . Over the years I've learned that the only way I could be comfortable and accomplish anything is to deliberately turn myself off. I'm no great beauty, but when I start letting myself "go" with my sex urges, I send off so many signals that ugly little strangers are always trying to pick me up. I want to be faithful to my husband because I love him, but I know that if I allow my full sex drive to emerge, I won't be, so I keep the lid on it, which isn't too bad, but isn't too good either. . . . I was analyzed, and my analyst, a woman, said she had no answers. She finally admitted that she had the same problem.

> One gets "imprinted" with one or two men. No one else seems desirable. . . . As an adolescent, I thought of myself as a freak because I had strong sexual needs and masturbated. Now I frequently masturbate because my desire outpaces my husband's, and I have strong doubts, and no desire, about finding extramarital satisfaction. The difference is that now I think of myself as well within "normal range."

Without question, the women in our survey who seemed to be the most *pan-sexual,* who had explored and developed their eroticism to its outer limits, were the single and divorced women in their thirties, forties and fifties.

A single or divorced woman, living alone, may sometimes get lonely and wish that she had a permanent connection. If she has no children and she is a maternal sort, she may become a baby-carriage peeper or develop "twitching ovaries" from time to time. Nonetheless, many of the single women, including some who were far from young, were enjoying the happiest sex lives of any women in the survey. Many of these women expressed no desire to marry, and others said that they might marry if they were absolutely sure, but they definitely preferred the single life to the generally bad or "mediocre" marriages they see around them. Some commented gratefully that in big cities at least, the last social pressures against single women are lifting. They no longer feel embarrassed or inadequate if, for example, they wish to attend a concert or movie with a woman friend.

I'm thirty-three, a senior editor in book publishing in New York, but have lived most of my life in the Middle West. I have been a part of so-called group sex before it was a common term, but the participants have always been extremely close friends. The groups consisted of one man and two women, two men and two women, two men and three women (not two men and myself, which I would like sometime). I do not find myself physically drawn to women except in a group, where I have made love to and been made love to by women and enjoyed it. I have masturbated since the age of six, using my hand, but sometimes with a vibrator, a candle, a dildo. I've had intercourse with about twenty men, and about half have been extremely good sexual partners. . . . They have mostly been artists or teachers. . . . Frequently I have wished I could make love to several men during the same time span, and I have, but I am truly a woman who is the most comfortable with an emotional, physical, involvement with one man at a time . . . [I have had] orgasms by the stimulation of other erogenous zones alone, *e.g.*, anus, breasts, earlobes, toes. And orgasms without any physical touch, *i.e.*, reading books, seeing paintings, movies, watching animals have intercourse.

It is time for a realistic look at the position of unattached women in America. Marriage is traditionally viewed as a triumph for women and a defeat for men.

Even today young girls are still being pushed into marriage—by their mothers, fathers and friends—before they have any chance to discover themselves or to look around and decide whether the married life is what they want.

And yet consider the rather startling mental health statistics.[3] As confirmed and reconfirmed in many studies, the facts are: Despite the serious economic discrimination that still persists,[4] women alone fare much better than do bachelors. Single men are the most unhappy and neurotic group in our population. Married women are next worse off, followed by single women and married men.

Dr. Genevieve Knupfer of the California State Department of Mental Health is one of the half dozen or so researchers who have so reported but who have, apparently, gone unheeded and unheard.[5]

[3]These have been clearly established for a decade or more, but I am one of the very few mass media writers who have even bothered to bring them to the attention of the public. One or two articles are never enough to change national clichés, although once in a great while, perhaps a book can—*Uncle Tom's Cabin, The Feminine Mystique* for example.

[4]Just consider how difficult it is for a single woman to get a mortgage or a charge account. Consider what sociologists have recently reported. Of all the "occupations" recognized by the Census Bureau, there are only four or five where women have the same chances for advancement as men. Even in traditionally feminine occupations, such as elementary school teaching and nursing, less capable men, simply because they are male, are often promoted over better-qualified women.

There are some occupations where men and women do exactly the same work, but the salary scale for men is higher. In book publishing, for example, a male senior editor averages a one-third higher salary than his precise female counterpart.

[5]Similar conclusions were reached by the following investigators:

a. N. M. Bradburn, *In Pursuit of Happiness* (Chicago, National Opinion Research Center, 1963).

b. D. Caplovitz and N. M. Bradburn, "Social Class and Psychological Adjustment: A Portrait of the Communities in the 'Happiness' Study: A Preliminary Report" (Chicago, National Opinion Research Center, 1964).

c. W. Clark, "Notes on Anomie: 1897–1959, Drinking Practices Study," working paper no. 3, 1965.

Several years ago, when she presented her findings to the American Psychiatric Association, Dr. Knupfer speculated on the reasons.

She has found that in the college and post-college age marriage scramble, it is often the best and strongest women who get left out. These women are occupied not with finding a husband but with the more logical first task of finding and developing themselves. By the time they feel themselves formed and look around for a husband—if they should—most of the men are taken.

The bachelor leftovers are apt to be undesirable, for women, as a rule, select men they can look up to. Thus, some of the worst men (in the sense of being desirable "husband material") remain unmarried at thirty, along with some of the best women. (In the sense of being strong, intelligent, independent, self-actualizing.)

Dr. Knupfer has also remarked that woman alone seems far more successful at making and keeping close personal attachments than is man alone. A woman maintains close contact with and frequently entertains her friends. If she is an aunt, she is probably an important part of her nephews' and nieces' lives. (Yes, the old saw about the maiden aunt who is like a "second mother" to her sisters' or brothers' children is perfectly true, whereas few bachelor uncles are so actively involved.)

With a bachelor, on the other hand, as his friends marry

d. E. Durkheim, *Suicide,* trans. by J. A. Spaulding and G. Simpson (Glencoe, Ill., The Free Press, 1951).

e. G. Gurin *et al., Americans View Their Mental Health* (New York, Basic Books, 1960).

f. G. Gurin *et al.,* "Tabular Supplement to Americans View Their Mental Health" (Ann Arbor, Mich., Survey Research Center, 1960).

g. G. Knupfer and R. Room, "Age, Sex and Social Class as Factors in Amount of Drinking in a Metropolitan Community," *Social Problems,* 12:224–40 (1964).

h. C. Leplae, "Celibacy in Belgium," *Acta Sociol.* 8:15–26 (1964).

i. L. Srole, *et al., Mental Health in the Metropolis: The Midtown Manhattan Study* (New York, McGraw-Hill Book Co., 1962).

off, he seems to get more and more lonely and isolated. He does not ordinarily retain too much involvement in the lives of others.

Dr. Knupfer suggests also that the responsibilities of marriage seem to have a maturing and strengthening effect on men, whereas marriage (at least as it has been constituted in the United States) often has an infantilizing effect on women.

So there we are. The tired jokes about lonely and frustrated spinsters seem to be quite inapplicable to many of those living today in our larger American cities. And as noted, the spinsters in my survey had active and sometimes remarkable sex lives.

We have dwelled rather long on the sexual inadequacies of the American male. Let us look now at the bright side. Almost all the women we surveyed had enjoyed some wonderful experiences with men, which, of course, made the bad ones seem all the worse.

Here is a list of male characteristics that women said turned them on. (The list varied tremendously, of course, from woman to woman, and qualities that some found appealing were inconsequential or even negative to others.) Physical traits mentioned were:

Rhythm in dancing.

An air of virility.

Dress plays an important part because it conveys something of his personality.

Cleanliness. I could never be attracted to a man with dirty fingernails.

Dark, black hair, eyes, thin. Must have a penis (and balls). Never like blonds or men who are at all brutal or sexist.

A man is sexy [to me] as a result of individual preferences that I am now in the process of revamping and trying to rid myself of since they are based on all sorts of
fucked-up social roles and stereotypes.

It's not a question of short or tall or blond or brunette
(or even bald) but rather what shape his body is in.

I can't turn on to a man who isn't close to six feet tall.

A short and compact male body is best in bed.

Beautiful hands are the sexiest physical trait to me,
masculine but poetic hands. It might sound ridiculous,
but in my experience men with such hands are usually
superb lovers. Soulful eyes are the second most important trait.

A mustache.

Lots of hair on face, body or both.

I can't turn on to hairy men.

A good body with a nice smell and nice feeling skin.

Tall, stands straight, not fat, smiles.

At my age, any man who can maintain a nice firm
erection starts to look pretty good.

For me there is no single combination of sexy qualities. They vary so much from man to man.

Some men just have a sensitive way of looking at a
woman.

For me, looks are inseparable from total personality,
though I would be curious to see how it would be if you

just picked a sexy-looking new guy and he never opened his mouth.

The way he dresses. His smell while having sex. His smile. His voice. His eyes. The shape of his body.

Eye contact.

I like conventional-looking men with athletic good looks.

Ugh. I can't stand all-American muscle boys.

Dammit, I have to say it. This question of size of penis which looms so large in current mythology *is* a factor, although not the most important one.

I like a nice fertile man who can get me pregnant (namely, my husband), as my most glorious sex experiences by far have been the two indescribable orgasms that accompanied the natural childbirth of my daughters.

His voice sends tingles down my spine. Not an artificially low and cultivated voice, but one that is naturally sexy.

Men who don't wear deodorants. The natural aromas of a healthy male body are great. Also, I hate the smell of certain soaps men use. I'm just terribly nasal. Always have been. My sex antennae all seem to be in my nose.[6]

A masculine physique is more important than a handsome face.

[6] The 1960's have seen a great upsurge of research into olfactory physiology. It is now believed that in the animal world, sexual life may revolve around smell even more than vision or hearing. In the male golden hamster, mating behavior is completely eliminated by removal of the olfactory bulb. Data on humans is more conjectural.

I hardly notice bodies unless they are truly grotesque. It doesn't matter to me whether he is built like Gable or he's just a middle-aged desk-man with a spare tire. What I do like are piercing eyes and a large, aristocratic nose.

An attractive or even interesting face. A good or even fairly good body.

But almost two-thirds of the women surveyed didn't mention physical traits at all! When asked what makes a man seem sexy or desirable, many cited personality factors exclusively:

A considerate and tender man is sexy.
I agree completely with Rollo May, who points out that intimacy is what you remember, not how many orgasmic contractions. My peak sexual experiences were with lovers who made me feel truly close and truly needed. My most memorable time with my husband was when he suffered a truly crushing defeat at work, and he came to me to be restored. A less than sexy man turns away from women during crises in his life. He retreats into himself, nursing his wounds or tensions alone, or he seeks the company of male companions and advisers. A truly sexy man brings all his pain and grief to his woman, and she restores him, and they are infinitely close.

Yet there was another group of women who, while also downgrading looks and other sheerly physical qualities, emphasized lovemaking technique much more than personality or emotionality:

Physically, men differ—a point which is often overlooked in *Ladies' Home Journal*-type discussions. Some are better in bed than others in every way. I give emotions their full due—but I still think there's a physical competence no amount of pressure can change.

I like a man who is physical in ways that are not at all sexual, like back rubs, holding hands, affectionate embraces that are not just preludes to intercourse.

The majority of women emphasized personality, technique *and* the quality of the relationship:

Tenderness!

I desire most the men who make me feel most womanly—the men with self-respect and confidence, a sincere interest in me as an individual and as a woman, and with whom I feel a genuine rapport and closeness and trust.

When a man makes me feel I am sexy and desirable, and at the same time he makes me feel that he is his own man.

A man is sexy if he satisfied me sexually . . . sees that I have an orgasm every time we make love. But if a man is not desirable in other ways, sex is not enough. . . . It's like being hooked up to a machine.

A desire for me plus tenderness plus self-confidence in bed. Desire for me is really uppermost. I want to feel that he is turned on to me especially, not just any female with the right-type equipment.

I think a man is desirable if he has high self-esteem, is intelligent, and is independent. The way he treats a woman is also very important. If he is appreciative of what she is and is affectionate.

Gentleness, cleanliness, lack of condescension, warmth.

Warmth, gentleness and self-confidence without excessive ego-tripping.

Humor and independence.

Largely, the attention he pays to you makes a man sexy.

I would now say that any man or woman could be attractive to me if I felt good about them and cared for them.

Being aware of your physical self and complimenting you. Teasing.

Sensuousness and sensitivity, a sense of style, appreciation of the woman, adventurousness and experimentation but not too soon in the relationship, ability to abandon himself to sincere passion, rather than having a studied technique.

Warmth, affection, strength (emotional) and humor.

A man is sexy if he is sensitive to my sexual needs, and responsive to my overtures.

Consideration of a woman as an individual, relaxation and honesty.

Aloofness—a qualify that connotes he knows me better than I know myself. He also must appear to be interested in me, although hard to get.

Complete openness and warmth.

Gentle, persistent staying power. Indicating to me that I am attractive and I turn him on.

The thing that is primary is a good feeling between the two people. Some of the best lovemaking I have ever had has been with lovers who were only fair but who I cared for very much and who felt the same toward me. It is not hard to find a "good lay." What is hard to find is "good men" and there lies the problem!

His ability to be tender. His capability of at least putting into words what he is feeling for you. An understanding of what makes you respond and what things are important to you.

De gustibus non disputandum est.

Awareness of the female body. Being able to relate.

Tact and discretion.

If I love him. The best experience is a unified one for two people, completely in touch and loving. Yet love is not always the key. There are no absolutes. I take sex very seriously and am upset if I feel unsatisfied. Yet, if I don't have a regular sexual outlet (men, masturbation, friendship), I don't want one. The best conditions are often the most fulfilling, but not always.

Intense concentration. The ability to convey, at least for the moment, that you are the one and only woman in the world.

While I greatly enjoy intercourse, I am simply mad about oral sex, or genital kissing as it is sometimes called. I myself have become very skilled at performing the genital kiss, simply because I am so interested. I have been told by a number of men that they had no idea how exquisite it could be until they met me. My own happiest memories are of men who, like me, are extremely interested in and skilled at the voluptuous techniques of oral sex. I realize that this is a highly individualized and specialized taste and would definitely not apply to all women. I much prefer having ordinary intercourse with a man who is only fair at oral sex. I am talking about the real specialists. They must know how to suck very hard and use their teeth a little (at the right moments) without giving you that awful slobbish feeling that they are going to devour you and without dribbling saliva all over the place. I do not really think that this is a technique that can be studied because one or two men who have loved me very much have read everything they could lay their hands on about oral sex, plus listening to my instructions, yet they never became really first-rate. I believe that greatness at oral sex is related to your sincere dedication to it. The greatest sexual moments of my life occurred, I am somewhat ashamed to say, with the husband of one of my closest friends. She was away for the summer, he was lonely, and together we explored the most consummate physical heights. And yet her friendship—we have been close since kindergarten—means so much to me that I wouldn't think of trying to break up her marriage. Actually, I don't even consider her husband good enough for her, although she loves him. But in a strictly isolated way that might be difficult for other women to understand, he provided my moments of greatest ecstasy.

In life I abhor men who are sadistic, but in bed I adore a touch of pain. I am most fortunate in having worked out a delicious compromise with my wonderful husband. On weekends he doesn't shave and by Sunday evening he has just the right growth of scratchy beard and mustache. Thus, without committing any sadistic acts he is able to cause irritation by kissing me vigorously all over my body.

I prefer men who are imaginative and willing to try *anything*. I am totally bisexual, extremely stimulated by the male and female body together, so my greatest sexual experiences have been threesomes with one virile man plus another woman. I have made love in completely mirrored rooms, but just watching myself with a man is not the same thing at all.

I like any man who is freewheeling enough to be completely uninhibited by orgies. The sight of all those writhing bodies in one big room excites me more than anything. I am free and independent, and I don't want to be anyone's one and only.

If he doesn't convey that I am the one and only, forget him. I am forty-two and have thus far had fourteen arrangements or relationships or affairs, most of them lovely and happy, but they were always totally monogamous while they lasted. Sex is so intense for me, and such a total commitment, that I couldn't think of sharing it with more than one man at a time.

A sense that he finds me as intelligent and interesting as he finds me sexy, and vice versa. Plus the inexplicable chemistry between us.

Clicking right along with you is the sexiest quality. Being very close and understanding, and yet your complement or opposite.

I am most fulfilled with the man who is more my opposite than any other I have ever known—my husband. I am like Chatty Kathy in bed, while he is silent or just grunts. I like to wriggle around a lot, whereas he quickly finds his sex rhythm, and stays with it. Yet he thrills me far more than any other man I have ever known.

I believe the Greek myth is correct. How male and female once were one, but mischievous gods separated them. Now they wander the earth, looking for their opposite half. I haven't found mine yet, but the men I prefer sexually are very different from me in character. I have some dear male friends and I have tried very hard to turn on to them, but just can't. (It would be nice if I could.)

A man has to be a good friend first. I respect and value my own body, and my mind, and my own corny brand of humor. Therefore, I couldn't give my body, much less my mind, to a man who hadn't been a sweet, humorous companion for quite a long time. I don't fathom instant sex at all. It's just not for me. There was another lawyer in my office I was quite fond of. We worked so well together and saw practical problems the same way. We were on the verge. Then he took me to see *Brewster McCloud*. I thought it was one of the funniest movies I had ever seen. He just sat there stony-faced. I knew we would never make it together. I am only twenty-seven, but I have had a rich and varied and gratifying sex life, and I now see no point in going to bed with a man who isn't just right for me. It's too easy to masturbate. I can have splendid orgasms alone or with a man I really like, but never with a man I only half like.

I am only nineteen, but I have learned that sex is completely a head experience. You dig each other or you don't, and that's all. The rest is mere rationalization.

Any man who doesn't think sex is a dirty word, who values it and loves it the way I do is OK in my book.

I've concluded that how I respond to a man or (on a few occasions) a woman, has far more to do with my own readiness than with him. At times I am terribly absorbed in my work, and I have rejected overtures from terribly nice and likable people. At other times I have been looking or cruising and have accepted overtures from some people who did not meet my usual standards. After opening night of a play, for example, I am ready for people, for love. My intense concentration and absorption shift from myself and my work to others.

I am very much a creature of my menstrual cycle. My husband can be acting like a six-year-old bully, but if it's just before my period, I fly to bed with him, and I love it. Other times he can be so tender and seductive, but I hardly notice. I hope he forgives me.

I like a man who is gutsy and physical and doesn't

have taste or manners in the drawing-room sense. I really appreciate a man who is not ashamed to fart, if he needs to, or swig down a bottle of wine, making thirsty, swallowing noises. A totally physical creature. It's a myth, incidentally, that such men are always truck drivers or manual laborers—or game-keepers. Painters and especially sculptors are just terrific.

The love of my life (twenty years on and off but mostly on) is to the world a cold, calculating and tough-minded captain of industry. The contrast, between his exterior person and the intimate self he reveals to me, positively blows my mind. When I see him on the television news, totally in command, and I recall the things he has cried out to me in moments of passion, I instantly have an orgasm, sitting right there in front of the TV set.

A sweet, gentle man who is reliable, dependable and consistent, an oasis and tower of strength in a too rapidly changing and frightening world.

A man who is childlike and innovative, full of wonder and full of surprises, who has lots of highs and lows and isn't always predictable. I like younger men, but definitely not for their bodies, of which they have less control and mastery than older men do. I like them for their whimsy.

These are the only qualities that matter in a man: sweetness, intelligence, gentleness, sense of humor, considerateness, taste; a real human being.

All these women are talking about sex, not love, although for many of them the two are clearly inseparable. (For many others they are not.) The old clichés telling men how to act with a woman (gallant, civilized, very, very delicate) have been replaced by new ones (it's all mechanics, just memorize the program and you're *in,* and by the way, let your hair grow if you want a young one) which are equally inapplicable to all, or even most, affectionate and sexually responsive women. It is quite obvious that women have an infinite variety of tastes and even moods within the same general framework of taste. They have needs and proclivities waiting to be awakened, however inexperienced they might be. One of the women who expressed a strong general preference for men who are warm and egalitarian added this: "The only man with whom I have ever had multiple orgasms got great psychic delight out of his cool during my excitement. (Though not in a mean way at all. He was a demanding lover but a tender companion.)" While not a brute, he was clearly a little bit different in temperament from the men with whom she usually prefers to consort. Yet he awakened one particular feature of her sexual response which had remained dormant until then and continued to be unexpressed afterward.

The man who yearns for success with "real" women, women who are comfortable with themselves and their own sexuality, must simply learn to be *himself*. He could grow a mustache or not, depending on what suits him, and the same even applies to baths. He should study up on oral sex if he likes it, but plenty of women will never miss it if he never learns to do a butterfly flip. If he is cool and controlled, let him be that way—some women dig it—and if he is passionate or even childlike, let him be that way, too. Clearly, the right men and women would have much less difficulty finding each other and having good sex, even great sex, if they would all stop playacting and striving to do things which seem unnatural, emotionally or technically.

The only man who is in real sexual trouble with women is the man who cannot listen to or see them, the man who has such rigid ideas about sex roles and appropriate feminine behavior that he cannot shift focus enough to satisfy any normal woman except once in a while, through accident or luck.

The man who cherishes fantasies of being loved by all

or most women is in some trouble too, for women are just too variable. I hope that my husband and I will succeed in teaching our son that life is far too short for playacting and that if one engages in too much of it, he is apt to miss or bypass precisely those persons with whom he could have engaged in genuine sexual passion or love. (I believe that our daughters already know this. Somehow, through an accident of genes or conditioning or both, males have more difficulty grasping this.)

There is an informally constituted group in New York City which calls itself The Sons of Shrinks. (Pretty soon, now, I suspect, they'll be calling themselves the kids—or offspring—of shrinks, if they haven't already.) I just hope that they will be wiser than their fathers (or their mothers, in cases where the qualifying parent was female) in avoiding the obsession with vaginal orgasm which has hung up so many otherwise gentle and intelligent psychiatrists and, through them, a rather large segment of the educated lay and laying public.

Even in our group of possibly overeducated women, including so many doctors and doctors' wives, psychologists, writers, actresses, professors, there was a substantial minority of sexually joyous women to whom the whole controversy over the vaginal-clitoral orgasm was wholly without meaning. These women had literally never experienced any distinction between types of orgasms:

I don't know the difference. They're all alike to me.

I don't know what kind of orgasm I have. I just have them. I usually have an orgasm more than once. It depends on how long one makes love. In order to get an orgasm, I usually need both vaginal and clitorial stimulation.

My only preference is for an event that's timed right between the parties. I know it's not essential, but it makes it so much nicer.

I have never been able to understand the distinction. What is it? Is there one?

The controversy is invalid except in politicopsychological terms.

I have had what I considered to be a vaginal orgasm, but the recent publicity over orgasm has confused me.

I'm not sure of the difference. The greater the degree of arousal, the higher the pleasure. All orgasms feel good.

Another group of women, well read in modern anatomy and physiology, described their experience of orgasm in terms of the Masters and Johnson findings or variations of them.

I experience orgasm through vaginal stimulation alone, but because of female anatomy, I am unsure that it is possible to stimulate only the vagina. The clitoris inevitably is stimulated through motion and friction during intercourse. Therefore, I feel that "vaginal" orgasms are most often really mixed orgasms. I prefer orgasms during intercourse. I like the combination of vaginal and clitoral sensations. I like having a penis inside of me.

Vaginal orgasm is both fact and myth, fact in that it occurs, myth in that it is thought different from orgasm resulting from manipulation.

I believe that orgasm occurs only in the vagina, triggered by clitoral stimulation.

I think that any other orgasm involves some sort of clitoral stimulation, no matter how unconscious. I'm not certain that an orgasm isn't simply an orgasm. I occasionally have an orgasm from breast stimulation alone, but I *feel it* in the clitoris as well as in the vagina.

In my case the orgasm seems to start in the clitoris and go to the vagina from there.

From masturbation and oral sex I have orgasms that seem mostly clitoral. From intercourse, when it's good, I have orgasms that seem mostly vaginal. But the best orgasms are (a) under circumstances that are highly emotional and (b) involve the stimulation of all parts. I have no trouble reaching orgasm, but in twenty years of sex I've had maybe twelve that were really extraordinary. Your inner and outer layers flow, the earth does move, and all that. You feel it everywhere. You are not aware whether these extra-special orgasms are vaginal or clitoral. You even feel them in your scalp and the soles of your feet. It's much more than pleasant relief from tension. In fact, contrary to my experience with routine orgasms, I find it hard to sleep afterward.

A third group of women preferred what they called vaginal orgasms. By this they appeared to mean an orgasm from intercourse, experienced deep in the vagina and generally induced by penile thrusting alone, without additional, direct stimulation of the clitoris.

A few, as I noted earlier, sounded a bit snobby about it:

Clitoral orgasm is mere titillation; only vaginal orgasms are real.

I doubt that I've ever had a clitoral orgasm. I wouldn't want one.

Clitoral is less desirable because it merely creates the desire for vaginal orgasm.

But most were more flexible:

Vaginal is more emotional. On the whole, clitoral is slightly less desirable, but it will do.

Clitoral orgasms which occur in masturbation and oral sex are very nice. But my preference is for intercourse and for vaginal orgasm.

I have many kinds of orgasms and I like them all. Perhaps vaginal is a bit more emotional and restful, so, yes, I'd have to say that is my preference. But its importance has been detrimentally overrated and has made many women feel inadequate because they only have clitoral orgasms.

Vaginal is a little bit nicer because it implies sharing and seems more complete. But it is also harder to attain. Lots of times I settle very happily for clitoral. The only bad orgasm is no orgasm as far as I'm concerned.

Clitoral orgasms are not *necessarily* less desirable, but they can be and often they are.

Vaginal orgasm is real, but the psychologic palaver about it is ridiculous.

A few of the clitoral women were quite emphatic about their position:

I have never had a vaginal orgasm because it doesn't exist. The myth is kept alive because it aids in maintaining male supremacy in sex. To say that a clitoral orgasm is less desirable is like saying *an* orgasm is less desirable than none.

But most simply believed that different women have different experiences:

I know that lots of women don't need as much clitoral stimulation as I, but I also know that lots of other women do.

Most of the women who need direct clitoral stimulation

had found men who were willing to provide it and had grown relaxed and even philosophical about their proclivity. Many attributed it to anatomy. Yet about 1 in 3 expressed some confusion and bitterness. As noted in the last chapter, many had been treated rather scornfully and cruelly by men. Others merely expressed a vague feeling that perhaps, after all, they were missing something:

> I can see no reason why I have never achieved a vaginal orgasm, unless I have some physical abnormality. I have never had any psychological hang-ups about sex and am better sexually adjusted than most due to a very liberal upbringing. No guilt attached, no religious feelings. So I'm still waiting, feeling that perhaps I've been deceived about the vaginal orgasm although I have felt something like it approaching on occasion; it has never been accomplished.

Perhaps the greatest surprise in our survey was the frequency of multiple orgasms. Almost two-thirds of the women had experienced them, some regularly or frequently, and some only occasionally or only with one particular man. (Sex researchers generally estimate that between 12 and 15 percent of American women have experienced multiple orgasms, so the frequency in our sample was dramatically higher. On the other hand, as noted in Chapter Two, there are primitive societies where it is assumed that the women will have several orgasms for each *one* achieved by the male. Obviously, the capacity exists and is "normal," but it is only now starting to manifest itself widely in certain subgroups in America.)

The circumstances were extremely variable. In some women multiple orgasm was linked to physiological events, such as menstruation or pregnancy, while in others the duration of intercourse seemed to be the key. Several women noted that they always or almost always had at least two or three orgasms, which they were uncertain how to define as the first usually occurred in foreplay and the subsequent ones during intercourse. Some women experienced multiple orgasms during masturbation or oral sex only, while others could only have them during intercourse. One woman said:

Sometimes I masturbate with a vibrator, applied to my clitoris, but the orgasm doesn't seem nearly as complete as intercourse with a man's penis inside me. With a vibrator, the first orgasm relieves me but doesn't really satisfy me, so if I have the time and privacy, I go on and on until I get sleepy. Usually three or four climaxes suffice, but I believe I've gotten up to fifteen or sixteen. The first, or maybe the second or third are usually the best, but not always. Sometimes the best one occurs later on.

By contrast, another woman said:

If I must masturbate, it is just to relieve myself, like scratching an itch. I don't even have any fantasies, which is too bad because I know that some women can have a delightful time. After I finish, I couldn't bear to go on. My clitoris feels too sensitive. However, in a prolonged event with a man (intercourse) I often have several orgasms. The longer he holds out (up?) the more I have. Once I had a boyfriend who had some psychiatric problem where he couldn't ejaculate. (He had discovered his wife making love to their dentist, and it started after that.) He would go on for an hour or longer, and in one sense it was delightful. But since he never climaxed, it got to be too unbalanced, and I stopped seeing him. He was very popular.

Many women explained that their multiple orgasms did not fall into any distinctive pattern.

If I like someone a lot, or sometimes when I'm just horny, or I don't know when.

If I'm unusually frustrated, if my sex partner is good or if I'm totally uninhibited, in which case it is very much a "head" experience.

With a few exceptions, these women did not seem to place any special value on their multiple orgasms. (Perhaps the male—sex researcher or lover—is more interested or titillated by the thought of such orgasms than the thrill to the woman herself actually warrants.) In describing their favorite events and experiences, few of the women spoke of multiple orgasms. They spoke of letting go, the oral sex, and group sex and clitorises and vaginas, erections, pregnancy, nursing, childbirth, tastes and smells and timing, but they mentioned multiple orgasms only in passing and rarely attributed any central importance to them. One of the women who seemed most deeply concerned and worried because she could not experience "vaginal" orgasms was also highly multi-orgasmic, having frequently experienced "twenty or more" in one session of lovemaking.

Some of the women who have not had multiple orgasms are puzzled by the concept:

Before I have what I consider to be my main orgasm, I have many small very pleasant contractions. The sensations can go on for a very long time. However, once I have a big orgasm, I can't bear to have my clitoris touched. Perhaps I haven't waited long enough to start up again, but I can't imagine having another orgasm in the same night. Because I am usually sated.

Our data on the fantasy life of these 103 women is limited, as I did not ask about fantasies on the questionnaires. However, some volunteered information, and the smaller group who were personally interviewed were questioned about their fantasies.

We have information on 21 women, and their answers

were extremely varied. Eight have no fantasy life, except for occasional erotic dreams.

> If I'm attracted to a man and I don't admit it consciously, sometimes I just dream that we're having sex. Nothing fancy, no surprises except for some of the people who turn up in the dreams. Once it was a building inspector. (I suppose there was some profound meaning there.) Once, to my horror, it was my own three-year-old daughter. Well, she is luscious, but I was so disgusted with myself that I woke up shaking.

> Well, naturally, if my husband is away, I sometimes think about him and pretend I'm in his arms. But it never gets too specific. I must lack imagination.

One lesbian, one bisexual, and four women who had never had a homosexual experience admitted that they frequently have fantasies about women. Perhaps latent lesbianism is more common than is generally supposed.

A heterosexual woman who has homosexual fantasies said:

> I'm never attracted to real women whom I know, but occasionally I may see one on the street whom I think about later. They are always slim young girls with tiny breasts and pointy nipples. The way some of the girls in New York City are revealing their cute little tits now, I don't know how the man can stand it. I'm surprised there isn't more rape.

Another heterosexual woman (white) said she always fantasized large-breasted black women when she masturbated:

> I suck on her breasts. I am both intrigued and repelled. I never had a black nanny if that's what you're thinking, not even a cleaning woman.

All but two of the women denied that they use fantasy when they are actually making love. In one case:

> I sometimes pretend there is a third person in bed with us, male or female. Sometimes I like to think about my husband with another woman, but I never pretend that he's a different man.

In the other case:

> I sometimes pretend that he is whipping my titties or vulva, but only for a minute. It gets too painful.

Most of the women commented that when they were children or teen-agers, they fantasized frequently, sometimes picturing themselves as movie stars or the heroines of novels but that, as adults, they had more or less ceased. The most common fantasies were "rehearsals" for sex, with a known partner who was away or with whom the relationship had not yet been consummated. Only two women said that they mentally undressed attractive strangers, one "constantly" and one "very rarely, usually on the beach."

It appears that the fantasy life of women, even women who are highly sexual, is less intense and varied than the fantasy life of many men. Some observers believe that this will change as women emancipate themselves from sexual Victorianism, but others maintain that this is a real and enduring difference between the sexes.[7] For the present,

[7] Two German investigators (Gunter Schmidt and Volkmar Sigusch of the Institute of Sexual Research at the University of Hamburg) have predicted that as women became "resexualized," such differences will disappear.

The process is already under way, at least in terms of reactions to pornography. A generation ago Kinsey found that men, but rarely women, become sexually aroused on viewing pornography. In a recent Schmidt-Sigusch study of "six hundred sexually emancipated" young men and women, the women reacted to pornography almost as much as the men.

men might be disappointed if they knew how pale the fantasies of most of their women actually are.

In general, these 103 women seem to be vastly different from their mothers and grandmothers and quite possibly many of their own contemporaries, in the ease and frequency with which they reach orgasm. They also display much wisdom about their own bodies, a great deal more than is usually found in sex manuals. Many pointed out that menstrual cycles influenced their sex drive, and others had observed that pregnancy and childbirth seemed to have altered it. Some women felt sexier during pregnancy, perhaps because the distention of veins and arteries created physical pressures. (See Sherfey section in Chapter One, "Is Woman Insatiable?") With each subsequent delivery some women continued to feel sexier, again perhaps because of varicosities, but others found themselves confronting new sex problems, apparently connected to childbirth damage.

As new situations arose, these women generally adapted to them. One group who experienced sexual problems, however, were married women whose sexual needs had outstripped those of their husbands. (The male's sex drive according to Kinsey usually peaks at around the age of nineteen. The female's doesn't peak until the late twenties or thirties and, in some of the women in my survey, later. For some it peaked *after* menopause.) Several of these women said that while they loved their husbands, they wished they had the courage not to be monogamous. In only one case had the wife and husband agreed, openly with each other, to have extramarital affairs. The wife claimed that it was working for them but added that she could not have done it without her husband's consent, for "that would betray the trust of our marriage. We are very close." Whether or not this will become a more common pattern is something that cannot be predicted now. Many of the wives felt that they would not want to risk their good marriages with such an arrangement. "It's too dangerous. I get too attached to a sex partner. It's not in my nature to have sex without getting emotionally involved, and my husband, I believe, is the same way."

These women often had problems finding men who shared their generally healthy and joyous sexual attitudes. They claimed that many men lacked humor, imagination or self-control, that some of them still feel that it's wrong for a woman to enjoy sex and, above all, that they seem to be offended when a woman attempts to tell them what she likes.

The older single women were surprisingly happy, often as happy as or happier than the married ones. The married ones often mentioned the joys of family life and children, but some of the single women seemed to be living sexually at a "higher" or more interesting plane. They did not complain as frequently as the married women that they were not getting enough sex.

A very small number of women who still have orgasm problems did participate in the survey. I regret that we did not have a greater range of returns from such women, but as explained in the previous chapter, this was predictable. The women with remaining problems who did participate were working hard at overcoming their difficulties and had at least grown comfortable with sexual concepts and terminology. (This may be an important first step for such women, since guilt or shame or even anatomical misunderstanding sometimes underlie sexual difficulties.)

It is very difficult for me to have an orgasm. I get very close, but then nothing happens. I have never had orgasms during intercourse. It has happened either before or after with the man massaging me around the clitoris. I have had some different kinds of feeling during intercourse, that I used to think was a vaginal orgasm. It was an almost unbearable sensation, sort of "pleasure-pain" that was so intense that I couldn't continue. There was no physical relief after we stopped, as there is in what I feel to be a clitorial orgasm, or an orgasm, period. One time after this happened, the man massaged me, and I had an orgasm, but it was the most intense orgasm that I ever had. I don't consider that I had two orgasms that time, only one.

I see a psychiatrist, and we have discussed my problem with having orgasms. He thinks the reasons I can't have one are that I always have to be in control of myself and that I prevent the orgasm because of that. Orgasm is the total lack of control—it isn't something we can control. That is where the inhibition lies. The only other inhibition I have about sex is that I don't like the man to ejaculate in my mouth. It happened to me once, and I don't like the taste.

As mentioned earlier, a number of the women who now reach orgasm freely noted that they had once had similar "letting go" problems. Perhaps when this young woman meets a man who is completely loving and uncritical, as well as being a skilled lover with a large "repertoire" of techniques to awaken her, she will become trusting enough to let go.

A noteworthy thing about all these women is their shared belief that woman has the right to enjoy sex fully as much as the man. Furthermore, they believed that orgasms, perhaps not every time but certainly most of the time, are their due and their *need* fully as much as it is a man's due and need.

Men would think it was ridiculous if psychiatrists went around saying that many of them don't really need orgasms. They should be content just to be affectionate and share love, etc., etc. Yet unfortunately, many men still hope or believe that this male supremacist myth about women is true. Let us hope that they will soon recognize the error of their ways and the unkindness of their attitudes.

CHAPTER FIVE

HOW TO LIBERATE YOURSELF FROM YOUR GYNECOLOGIST

You rape 'em—We scrape 'em.
—Sign in a Silver Spring, Maryland,
gynecologist's office

Obstetrics and gynecology constitute one broad specialty, although gynecology has to do with the physiology and pathology of the female reproductive organs in the non-pregnant state, while obstetrics deals with the pregnant state and its sequels.[1]

There are about 18,000 obstetrician-gynecologists in the United States.[2] (From here on, we shall call them gynecologists for short.) They are not stupid, although other doctors tend to think that they are and often remark that "catching babies is an easy specialty."[3]

[1] Eastman, Nicholson Joseph, *Williams Obstetrics,* 10th ed. (New York, Appleton-Century-Crofts, 1950).

[2] About 11,500 are board-certified, which means that they have had several years of hospital training in gynecology and have also passed an exacting test. Another 2,500 have completed specialty training but have not yet taken or passed the certifying exams. In addition, there are about 4,000 general or "family" practitioners who do gynecology and obstetrics.

Only about 3 percent of the gynecologists in the United States are women.

[3] In their recently completed "profile" of young gynecologists Drs. Michael Newton and Frederick P. Zuspan reported that 19 percent had earned Phi Beta Kappa keys, 46 percent were in the upper third of their medical school classes and only 7 percent were in the bottom third.

The main functions of a gynecologist are *preventive*. Only rarely does he encounter an exotic or challenging disease. Most of his practice is quite routine and quite repetitive. And yet it isn't easy to be a *good* gynecologist, for, ideally, he combines the skills of a surgeon, an internist (the pregnant woman is like a "different species" biochemically, and should she have diabetes, heart disease or any one of a number of other special conditions, she requires the most expert handling) and even a pediatrician. (It falls to gynecologists to look after newborns when no pediatrician is available.) Furthermore, the alert gynecologist informs himself on nutrition (two human beings are mightily affected by what his one patient eats, and many disturbances of pregnancy are believed to be dietary in origin), anesthesia and endocrinology, to name only three additional areas.

The perfect gynecologist, if he exists, is a very patient man. He plays a waiting game, reading and informing himself, keeping up in all the areas we have mentioned and more, but using his hard-gained knowledge and skills only occasionally, for—and this is the crux of the problem —most of the patients who come to his office are *not ill*.

Nor are they children. Yet quite unintentionally, I am sure, gynecologists have been a significant force in keeping modern women infantile and immature, for their authoritarian attitudes deprive women of autonomy over their own natural functions. (It is one thing to act like an authority figure with a sick patient who is frightened and lacks judgment, and quite another to frighten a healthy woman into believing that her destiny is not and cannot possibly be in her own hands.)[4] Consider the fact that

[4]Recent studies of dying patients indicate that *even they* often need and desire more autonomy than our modern medical care system usually grants them. Needless authoritarianism is certainly a charge that can be aimed at many physicians in many different specialties. Yet it seems especially pervasive in gynecology, and especially indefensible. Women use birth control more effectively if they understand how it works and if they have been allowed to

gynecologists usually call patients by their first names, while expecting the patient to address them formally as *doctor*.

Consider a letter which I received recently from Dr. Michael Newton, director of the American College of Obstetricians and Gynecologists.[5] I had asked Dr. Newton to provide me with the names and addresses of the organizations to which gynecologists who are interested in natural childbirth belong.[6] Dr. Newton replied:

"Each physician makes his own decision on whether or not he agrees with the tenants [*sic*] of natural childbirth, based upon his examination of the patient and his personal preferences. Therefore we have no list of obstetrician-gynecologists who exclusively practice this method of delivery."

Instead of a list of natural childbirth organizations, Dr. Newton enclosed a directory of *all* Manhattan gynecologists who belong to his organization!

What are we to make of such a reply? Evidently, it all sounds reasonable to Dr. Newton, perhaps because, in this

---

select a method that pleases them, just as they have healthier and happier pregnancies and deliveries when they are allowed to be full decision-making participants.

Long ago Plato made a sharp distinction between physicians treating slaves and free men. He urged that in treating a slave, a doctor should prescribe like an authority figure, as if he were absolutely sure of himself and his potions. In treating a free man, the physician was expected to "enter into discourse with the patient *and* his family" and not entitled to proceed with any medication or surgery until the patient was "convinced."

[5]September 9, 1971.

[6]A list of doctors in your region who practice natural childbirth can be obtained from the following organizations:

The American Society of Psychoprophylaxis in Obstetrics, Inc.
7 West 96th Street
New York, New York 10025

International Childbirth Education Association, Inc.
251 Nottingham Way
Hillside, New Jersey 07205

country, certainly, gynecologists are trained to "treat us as patients, not people," serving us with "reassurance instead of the information we need."[7]

Perhaps Dr. Newton thinks that women rarely talk among themselves and that we do not know that many, if not most, American gynecologists are reluctant to go along with natural childbirth under any circumstances.[8] He seriously expects us to believe that doctors have such "magic" that they can *tell* at the time of the first prenatal examination whether or not natural childbirth will be suitable for a given patient.[9]

Why are American women shaved, humiliated,

[7]From *Our Bodies and Ourselves,* by the Boston Women's Health Course Collective (Boston, New England Free Press, 1971).

[8]I know that many people prefer the phrase "prepared childbirth" but I shall use "natural" instead, since it is still in commoner usage.

[9]No doubt there are certain rare physical conditions, such as a deformed pelvis, which make natural childbirth inadvisable and which a gynecologist can spot very early in pregnancy. But most of the conditions which require strenuous medical intervention develop late in pregnancy or at the time of delivery.

Perhaps Dr. Newton means that gynecologists can detect women who have the "wrong personality" for natural childbirth. But that is almost like suggesting that they, the gynecologists, are mind readers. My first gynecologist thought I had the "wrong personality" for breast-feeding and did everything he could to discourage me. (He even prescribed a postpartum laxative that went straight to the milk and gave my baby severe diarrhea. Ironically, it was a book by Dr. Newton's own wife, Dr. Niles Newton, that taught me how to overcome my gynecologist and breast-feed anyway—for nine months.)

For my second and third babies I had a different gynecologist. He didn't think much of breast-feeding either, but as I was firm—having a successful experience behind me—he didn't lay any obstacles in my path.

(It's not just the gynecologists. If you want to breast-feed, you have to hold out against many of the nurses and other hospital personnel. For example, they try to get you to put nupercainal or other goo on your nipples or, at the very least, to wash them with alcohol or phisohex. Common sense should tell you that any such chemicals are injurious to the nipples and repulsive, if not poisonous, to your baby.)

drugged, painted and stuck up in stirrups to deliver their babies? Why are they pinned into a position which is totally unnatural and inconvenient for the mother?[10]

Why are delivery rooms managed and run for the convenience of the doctors, not the patients?

The gynecologists think they are marvelous at psyching *us* out. I have spent much time interviewing many gynecologists and can think of only seven who didn't start generalizing about this type of woman and that type of woman within the first fifteen minutes.[11] So let us psych *them* out for a change. Let us ask:

[10]There are five basic positions women assume during delivery in various cultures: lying down, standing, sitting, squatting and kneeling. The lying-down position preferred in the United States is among the least popular in primitive societies. There are various natural advantages to some of the other positions, particularly, many observers believe, squatting. But American doctors are generally unwilling to experiment with other positions, perhaps because a woman in labor seems most helpless, and her attendants most "superior," when she is lying strapped on her back.

The "American" position may not even be a desirable one for Caesarean sections. In 1956 Dr. Virginia Apgar, who is probably the world's leading authority on the health of newborns, suggested that there might be advantages for both babies and mothers if Caesarean sections were performed with the woman lying on her side. (Among other benefits, the drainage of amniotic fluid and blood is improved.) Australians have gone ahead and followed her advice and are very favorably impressed with the results. But, to Dr. Apgar's knowledge, no one in the United States even has tried it. (*Medical World News*, July 16, 1971.)

At the April, 1970, meeting of the Society of Gynecologic Investigation, Drs. Gordon G. Power and Lawrence D. Longo reported the following: Childbirth on one's back was introduced as a civilized innovation in sixteenth-century France, apparently for the convenience of obstetricians. This position has the tendency to raise the mother's blood pressure in the critical area of the placenta. As she lies on her back, the weight of her womb presses on the inferior vena cava which is the venous trunk for legs and torso. As blood backs up, it can cut off umbilical circulation by creating distention in the placenta. This is called the sluice flow mechanism. In many cases the baby's heart rate (a sign of fetal distress) slows down when the mother is on her back.

The treatment is simple, Drs. Power and Longo state: Turn the mother on her side, or let her use a birth stool.

[11]And if they wonder about gynecologists' attitudes toward them,

1. Why would a man consecrate his life to the female organs?

2. What leads a physician to specialize in reproduction and female disorders?

3. Isn't it hard to believe that voyeurism or some special love-hate relationship with women doesn't play a part?

In a provocative paper entitled "Art Versus Violence," Dr. Lawrence J. Friedman, a psychoanalyst, discusses

---

women would be dismayed and hurt if they could see how the prescription drugs they use—especially birth control pills, hormone replacement therapy and tranquilizers—are advertised in medical journals. (It is true that the pharmaceutical companies, not the doctors, write these ads, but no doubt, the companies would drop them if they were not a big hit with readers.)

Discussing such pharmaceutical advertising in her testimony before the U.S. Senate Small Business Committee on July 23, 1971, Dr. Natalie Shainess said:

It presents "reprehensible imagery, emphasizing the worst, distorting reality and furthering contempt for women.

"Basically, the images presented are of two types:

"1. The young, attractive, sex-object type—usually employed for ads for contraceptives, and furthering the *physician's fantasies,* and notions of woman as temptress. Oracon, a product of Mead Johnson, is advertised showing a checkerboard of girlish beauties. Apparently the woman over thirty—or perhaps twenty-five—no longer has need of contraceptives. Further, women are depicted nude in a distressingly unnecessary number of times.

"2. The 'old uglies,' are the images presented for everything else, and especially for replacement hormonal therapy of later years. Here, Searle's ad for Ovulen is a good example. One would think that even a woman's bony facial structure alters after thirty to become ugly, and of course—that warts appear also.

"A particularly low blow is struck at women by Searle, in showing a picture of a battered child for the same product with the heading: The Unwanted Child and Birth Control. I do not doubt that maternal hatred results from forced motherhood—it is an important issue. But showing this picture is most unfair to women, most of whom have done pretty well, choice or not. But the *visual impact* of a picture of this kind is great. But further, it is inaccurate—something more is required for child-battering—it takes an extremely disturbed or dangerously antisocial person. It is not necessary to twang the heart-strings of doctors, furthering dislike or contempt for women—a majority of their patients—in order to sell contraceptives, and using a rare, unfortunate behavioral expression."

man's historical envy toward woman's reproductive organs, and motherhood:[12]

> The history of civilization, primitive, ancient, and modern, is full of man's expressions of his hostility and envy of women, and his severe ambivalence toward them. They have been mistrusted, persecuted, treated as second-rate humans in practically every culture. They have been discriminated against in every religion. Idealization of the Virgin Mother on the one hand and centuries of denunciation by the Church as the source of all evil on the other. The witch-hunting, taboos and ceremonies of primitive societies expressing ambivalence toward women fill volumes. What about its expression in the artificial mother-culture of our own times? The highly-idealized "sainted mother" who is reviled and ridiculed the moment she stops being a mother and becomes a mother-in-law.
>
> We talk a great deal about penis envy, and there is no question that it exists. We also know how universal is masculine bias, demonstrated in man's deprecation of women and over-valuation of his own sex. Expressions like, "Congratulations, it's a boy!"—or, "Too bad, it's a girl. Better luck the next time!"—are as old as history. What is only beginning to be recognized is that behind man's ambivalence toward women is his envy of her ability to create life.
>
> ... Our daily language dealing with creativity is revealing. A man is "pregnant with" or "gives birth to an idea" —has an "abortive thought" or "brain-child." Very common, too, are such expressions as "This is my baby, my creation. I thought of it first!"—and the fight over priority can be fierce. I know a writer who published his first book the week his first child was born and, subsequently, another book every time his wife gave birth. And the feelings of emptiness, even depression, after completing a

[12]Lawrence J. Friedman, "Art Versus Violence," *Arts in Society*, Vol. 8, No. 1 (1971), Madison: University Extension, The University of Wisconsin, pp. 325–31.

major work are very familiar to creative men and are similar to the feelings of women after childbirth.

The pity of it is that women accept and identify with this masculine bias, and even outdo men in their own deprecation. They themselves denigrate their roles as mothers, label outstanding women in business or the professions as masculine, and equate lesser intelligence and passivity as femininity.

Man's knowledge that he cannot create but can only destroy life—life created by women—has undoubtedly affected the entire course of civilization. It is reasonable to speculate whether it may not be the driving force behind his incessant urge to make wars throughout history. Today, as the "father of the hydrogen bomb," he is in a position to threaten with destruction all life created by women.

"This is my baby, my creation!" Are gynecologists (secretly and unconsciously) trying to usurp the childbearing functions they, and presumably all men, envy?[13] It would

[13]Dr. George Vaillant, a Tufts University psychiatrist, has shed further light on the motivations of gynecologists. (And his own psychiatric colleagues as well.) Thirty years ago, 268 male college sophomores, all good students, were chosen for intensive study by a university health service. Their lives have been followed ever since. Of these 268 men, 46 went on to attend and graduate from medical school. Generally, the doctors have more problems than the other men, including more bad marriages (47 percent as compared to 32 percent) and more hospitalizations for psychiatric illness (17 percent as compared to 5 percent). However, it was found that the difference was even more striking when the physicians who had chosen specialties with "primary responsibility for patient care" were separated from the other physicians. Most of the physicians who had gone into "primary" specialties—namely the gynecologists, psychiatrists, internists, and pediatricians—seemed *more unlike* the controls than did the other doctors. It was the physicians in the primary specialties who had the largest share of emotional difficulties in adult life and who had also experienced the most unstable childhoods. Vaillant concludes: "Some physicians may elect to assume direct care of patients to give others the care that they did not receive in their own childhoods."

In other words, our gynecologists (not to mention some of our other doctors) may be unhappy men who want to mother us, in

sometimes appear so. Consider the anger so many feel toward natural childbirth (where the woman has much more control and participates more fully), even though they know that unmedicated babies are apt to be born in better condition.

Consider the remarks one often hears from gynecologists as they make their rounds at hospitals. "*We're* in labor," a common expression goes. "*We're* four-fingers dilated," and so on. (Fancy a surgeon saying, "*We're* having an appendectomy," or a psychiatrist, "*We're* hallucinating.")

Many traditional gynecologists are kindly, good-natured chaps. They practice what we might call a "benevolent paternalism." But despite their good intentions, the outcome, for their patients, is not so good. Consider the findings of Dr. Deborah Tanzer, who compared the pregnancy and birth experience of forty-one women, twenty-two of whom had their babies by natural childbirth methods.[14]

The natural childbirth mothers had a more positive

---

order to prove themselves better "mothers" than their own mothers were. On one level, their careers can be seen as an admirable and altruistic resolution of their conflicts. But the problem remains; we, not they, are the mothers and are entitled to a measure of self-determination.

It may also not be accidental that in quite bizarre fashion, large numbers of gynecologists have found a way to become super *fathers* and, at the same time, draw pay for doing the same thing as Mrs. Portnoy's son.

Sperm donors today earn an average fee of $25 to $40. Gynecologists performing artificial inseminations tend to send such business to their younger colleagues, the gynecologists still in training who are perpetually short of funds.

At one distinguished New York City hospital, at least half the gynecology residents regularly serve as sperm donors. Some earn as much (for their sperm) as $10,000 a year. A senior gynecologist who is one of the chief purchasers of all this sperm tells me that in most cases the residents' wives do not know.

Question: If Dr. Smith earns $10,000 a year for selling his sperm at the rate of $40 per ejaculation, how many times a year must Dr. Smith masturbate into a jar? Answer: 250 times, or an average of once per working day.

[14]Dr. Deborah Tanzer, Brandeis University doctoral thesis.

labor. They had been taught exactly what to expect when labor started, and they approached it more confidently. They experienced less pain and less fear. Their attitudes toward their new babies *and* toward their husbands (who had remained with them during labor) were more positive. Natural childbirth proved more beneficial to the mother-child relationship, the father-child relationship *and* the marriage. Most important, says Tanzer, "the natural childbirth women experienced a significantly greater growth in their self-concepts and emerged from the experience *closer to the ideal image they held for themselves.* Use of the natural childbirth method produces greater lasting improvement in a woman's view of herself and of her capabilities as a person, and as a woman."[15]

What Tanzer found to be objectively true, was given a more subjective airing in a recent issue of *Off Our Backs,* a woman's liberation newspaper.[16] Two young mothers compared their childbirth experiences:

First:

. . . Each week [of natural childbirth classes] was a

[15]Some women who are trained in natural childbirth techniques develop unexpected complications and must be anesthetized and delivered traditionally after all. In a situation like this, the gynecologist's skill and equipment become crucially important. Tanzer believes it would be a great psychological benefit if *all women* were trained for natural childbirth, with the understanding that should medical conditions necessitate it, their doctor would intervene and employ traditional methods. The training alone is beneficial, for it gives the mother-to-be a clear understanding of what is going on within her body.

One hears occasional reports of physicians who are so devoted to the precepts of natural childbirth that they may fail to intervene as promptly as they should, when circumstances warrant. One friend of mine who is a slim, small woman was in heavy labor for sixteen hours with her eleven-pound son, her first baby, before her doctor decided to perform a Caesarean section. She is pleased that she had natural childbirth training, but bitter that her doctor allowed her to suffer—fruitlessly—for so long.

It would be nice if more gynecologists were devoted to their patients, not their theories.

[16]*Off Our Backs.* October 25, 1970, pp. 12, 13.

different subject, including female anatomy and conception, the growth of the fetus, and the physiological and emotional aspects of birth and labor. I also learned about breastfeeding and about how with the aid of my coach (husband), Mac, I would be able to work with my body to deliver our baby.

I went into labor four weeks before the baby was due. It was a precipitous four hour labor, but with my knowledge of labor combined with Mac's . . . support, it went well. Because labor was so short, I arrived at the hospital only twenty minutes before Nathan was born and a half hour before the doctor arrived. Nathan slipped out in good condition for a baby so early. If I, and in consequence, he, had been drugged, he might have been in sluggish condition, too full of mucus to breathe.

Because he was only five pounds, the OB said he should stay in bed with me day and night. . . . His staying with me was much preferable to an incubator for both of us. I could provide a loving atmosphere at exactly the right temperature and I was really disbelieving and tremendously excited to see him. . . . Over all, I had a remarkably good experience. How good I didn't realize until later when I talked with other women who hadn't had a chance to learn about the different methods of childbirth.

. . . Natural childbirth is almost unknown especially among poor women and for obvious reasons: it takes more time to teach a woman about her body and how she can help herself and, it takes away from the doctor's status as babybringer, if it is obviously the woman herself who brings forth the child. Trained childbirth is one alternative to childbirth with anesthesia. Each woman should be able to choose her way unpressured by doctors or peers. If a woman is knowledgeable of her anatomy, the emotional and physical aspects of birth, and the techniques by which she can work with her own body, she can choose the method that allows her to give birth with dignity.

The second mother, whose doctor acquiesced to her demand for natural childbirth only if she would agree to "take his advice on anesthetics if *he felt the situation called for it*," found herself being injected with drugs almost as soon as she arrived at the hospital, in labor. She describes the events which took place after she had been intravenously given the hormone pitocin to stimulate a quicker labor:

Three hours after my arrival my doctor decided my pain was too much for me and despite my admittedly feeble but persistent objections, he administered a cervical block (an injection of a pain killer around the cervix through the vagina). The drug made me nauseous, dizzy, and panicky. That will pass, I was told, and don't I feel better now?

I heard a woman screaming in the next room. She was swearing in Spanish and I passed several minutes translating her profanity. I asked the doctor if there wasn't something they could do for her. "Oh," he said, "she doesn't know what's going on. She's anesthetized. She won't remember a thing." Then he and the nurses exchanged cracks about how funny some women sound when they are "under." With the drug and the pain (which returned double when the pain killer wore off) I was becomingly increasingly panicked. I didn't trust anyone, but here I was, drugged, fat, and helpless. I started to cry and that was all they needed. My doctor decided I was too exhausted to stay awake. Reminding me with a fatherly smile of our agreement, he approached me with a hypodermic and asked if I could be anesthetized. I nodded and there was nothing more.

He had told me it would be hours before the birth, but less than an hour later, my daughter was delivered with forceps. "You were so stubborn under the drug," my doctor scolded me later, "we had to use forceps because you wouldn't push." I guess I was supposed to feel guilty, but instead I felt angry. I had learned that Nembutal relaxes the muscles as it allows you to escape the present.

Since delivering a child requires intense muscular effort, such a drug can only be detrimental to the final pushing. It was not a decision I could make. I was *unable* to push.

After delivery, the uterus contracts to expel the placenta, and complete the birth process. If this last muscular activity doesn't happen, the mother can hemorrhage, and I did. Again my doctor attributed this to some quirk of fate rather than to the drug he had administered.

. . . When I awoke in intensive care having transfusions, I felt sick, alone and totally confused. . . . I had to work hard to remember that, ah yes, I'd had a baby. . . . When they finally brought her to me I was beyond even feigning joy. Who was this baby? The total incompleteness of the last nine months was a shattering reality. I had carried her for nine months dreaming of our first encounter and then was robbed of the logical connection that nature puts between pregnancy and raising the child —the birth experience.

I am convinced that the male dominated medical profession has so distorted the natural validity of the mother's role in childbirth that they see themselves as the hero of every delivery they attend. The whole attitude of "well, this labor would be a snap if I didn't have to contend with this *woman*," is sick and destructive to both mother and child. The perversion of a natural event until it becomes a fearful and elaborate production is one way women are kept in their dependent, subservient role.

In addition to the psychological benefits of natural childbirth, there are physical benefits. Many of the complications of childbirth—to mother and to baby—are due to excessively vigorous intervention, particularly the excessive use of drugs.[17]

[17]In rather roundabout ways, some hospitals acknowledge that this is so. Dr. Anne Seiden, a Chicago physician, tells a curious story about her experience as an intern in San Francisco: "We interns were assigned to work in pairs in the delivery room. One of us was the 'gynecologist,' and the other was the 'anesthesiologist.' The anesthesia seemed to work, and yet I became suspicious that the machine had been set up to deliver 'placebo' amounts when we

Most laymen are inclined to assume that medically at least, if not psychologically, pregnant women in America receive the best care available anyplace. Sadly, this is very far from true. Our mortality figures, for mothers and babies alike, are substantially higher than in most other fully industrialized countries.[18]

It is generally (although quietly) assumed that about half the maternal deaths in this country are "preventable."[19] We also lose some 20,000 babies each year and,

---

interns were using it. One day when the delivery room was not in use I went in and tried to anesthetize myself. For an hour I kept pushing the buttons and there was no effect. Virtually nothing was being delivered. As a result of this experience I realized that hospitals sometimes play rather extraordinary games with women in labor. The personnel *know* that it's better for them not to get much anesthesia, but they believe that the woman must think she is being anesthetized, to relieve her fears. They don't even let the interns in on this game, much less the mothers. After my internship I had two children without anesthesia and without too much discomfort because I had learned that childbirth need not always be painful."

[18]Sweden, Great Britain, Japan, Czechoslovakia and even Taiwan are among the dozen or more countries which outrank us, according to U.N. figures. In Sweden and the Netherlands, to name only two countries, infant mortality rates are some 50 percent lower than they are here!

When questioned about our poor showing, the president of the AMA recently commented that if it weren't for our black women (who, the theory goes, do not even know enough to seek adequate prenatal care), our comparative world standing would be very good indeed. However, in their October, 1970, report on "Higher Education and the Nation's Health," investigators at the Carnegie Commission noted that our mortality rates for white mothers and babies are also very poor: "The rate of 19.7 infants deaths per 1,000 live births for white people in the United States in 1967 was above the overall rate for ten other countries in that year."

The Carnegie report scolds, "Not only are our rankings low, but the gaps between the United States' rates and those in the highest ranking industrial countries are substantial."

[19]See Dr. C. K. Fraser, "Report on Confidential Inquiries into Maternal Deaths in the District of Columbia, 1950–64," *Medical Annals of the District of Columbia,* Vol. 37, No. 3 (March, 1968), pp. 149–159; and Eastman, Nicholson Joseph, *op. cit.*

among the survivors, an appallingly high number have cerebral palsy, mental retardation and other nervous system impairments which can often be traced back to methods used at delivery.

But methods used at delivery are not the whole ugly story, for an astonishing new battle has arisen between gynecologists and nutrition experts. As the reader knows if she has had a baby, American gynecologists tend to be quite hung up on limiting weight gain during pregnancy. Many advise their patients that fifteen pounds is "ideal" and anything more than twenty is "immoral." Not long ago I had lunch with a friend who was in her eighth month of pregnancy. Her "meal" consisted of a diet pill and a few forkfuls of salad. Susan explained that she had an appointment with her doctor the next morning and that she always "crash-dieted" before her monthly checkups because "if I've gained more than two pounds, he yells at me so loud it practically makes the building shake."

In contrast with the fifteen-pound weight limit which Susan's doctor held so sacred, the gynecologists in most of the countries which outrank us in infant and maternal health encourage their patients to gain an average of twenty-five to thirty pounds.

There is a growing body of evidence that excessive dieting during pregnancy may be extremely harmful to infants, for (as our grandmothers warned us) it leads to small babies. Small babies, it has now been ascertained, have a far higher incidence of serious birth defects. A recent report of the National Academy of Science–National Research Council states that low birth weight is the most important determinant of infant death, neurological abnormality, and impaired intellectual development. And Dr. Janet Hardy of Johns Hopkins, who has directed a massive study of infant health on behalf of the National Institutes of Health, makes the following observation: "In Europe, where pregnant women have not been restricted in their weight gain, the neonatal mortality has been substantially less than in the United States.[20] Stillborns and newborn deaths are some *thirty times* more frequent in babies weighing under five and a half pounds than in larger babies, and a firm relationship has even been established between low IQ at four years of age and low birth weight. An average maternal weight gain of up to thirty pounds is now estimated to be the most desirable for infant health and well-being.

American mothers-to-be who submit to their natural hunger pangs and allow themselves to gain the twenty to thirty pounds decreed optimum by both nature and modern science are often ridiculed, humiliated and bullied by their doctors.[21] They are encouraged to crash-diet and even to take dangerous diuretics and appetite suppressants, some of which are highly toxic and which pass through the placenta to the fetus. Why?

The theory behind rigid dieting during pregnancy is that it prevents something called toxemia, which may not even exist. Dr. Rudolf Vollman, chief of the Section on Obstetrics of the National Institute of Neurological Diseases and Stroke, has this to say: "The word is a misnomer, a term invented by obstetricians to describe the various effects of pregnancy—substantial fluid accumulation, increased blood pressure, metabolic and hormonal changes—which are normal characteristics of gestation. It was a convenient way of teaching medical students who, when they became doctors, went right on believing this bugaboo themselves."

[20]See National Academy of Science report, *Maternal Nutrition and the Course of Pregnancy*. Also see Dr. Hardy's book, *The Women and Their Pregnancies* (Philadelphia, Saunders & Co., 1972). Also see William Cole, "Are Mothers-to-Be Starving Their Unborn Children?" *Family Circle* (February, 1972), p. 32.

[21]When Maureen Kiss, assistant to the health editor at *Family Circle* magazine, became pregnant recently her doctor placed her on a rigid diet. Maureen was familiar with the recommendations of the National Academy of Science, and she cited them to her doctor. "Who are you going to believe," he roared, "*your* doctor or some silly nonsense that got printed in a woman's magazine?"

It is difficult to understand why gynecologists persist in torturing their patients about weight gain when there is so much evidence that they have been wrong on this score. (Perhaps unnaturally slim mothers and small babies make the doctor's life easier at the time of delivery.)

Perhaps gynecologists will change on this issue, for a growing number of their leaders have lately become quite outspoken. For example, Dr. Kenneth Niswander, chairman of the Department of Obstetrics and Gynecology of the University of California at Davis, has stated in a speech:

> The relationship between low-birth weight and early death and neurological damage in the infant is well established. There are, of course, many factors which may have an effect on birth weight—for example, genetic and environmental characteristics, maternal condition or events occurring during pregnancy. But our studies strongly indicate—as do those of other investigators— that the maternal weight gain of the mother during pregnancy is the most important factor in determining the birth weight of the infant. The larger the maternal weight gain, the less the risk of a low-birth-weight infant.
>
> In European countries where obstetricians do not restrict the weight gain of their lighter weight patients and where slimness generally is not so grimly and relentlessly pursued, pregnant women, on the average, gain more than they do here. With the result that there are far fewer premature babies. It seems certain that American women would also gain more weight during pregnancy, if it were not for the reign of terror instituted by our physicians.

Diet is one matter over which pregnant women can— and should—fight back. Unfortunately, there are other problem areas where it is far more difficult for the woman herself to intervene. But at least she can ask questions every step of the way—and demand honest convincing answers.

One study, in Rochester, New York, has revealed that a major cause of childbirth difficulty is the artificial stimulation of birth when there is no justification for it, except the gynecologist's own weekend schedule. Artificial means of induction such as oxytocin, the birth-stimulating hormone, have been established as something which should never be used frivolously. In a Cleveland study of 199 induced births among women with five or more previous children, four mothers suffered ruptures in spite of constant observation, and two of the babies died.

The Rochester study also revealed that impatient doctors sometimes use instruments when they should not, delivering children prematurely. Episiotomies are frequently not performed when they should be (the failure to perform this minor surgery, which prevents a mother's tissues from tearing, often leads to future sexual difficulties), and frequently predictable emergencies (Caesarean section, the need for blood transfusions) are not prepared for in advance.

Almost as a matter of course, some impatient doctors perform completely unnecessary Caesarean deliveries.[22]

In March, 1968, a grim little study appeared in the *Medical Annals of the District of Columbia*. Written by Dr. D. C. Fraser, it was entitled "Report on Confidential Inquiries into Maternal Deaths in the District of Columbia, 1950–64." Dr. Fraser found that "physician negligence" is a common factor in maternity cases that end badly. He cites three examples: ". . . Hemorrhage due to rupture of the uterus was noted in 8 patients. . . . It was associated with labor, intrauterine manipulation, and

[22]Most women who have Caesarean sections are inclined to believe that their lives were saved by the procedure. They have no way of judging whether it was actually necessary or even advisable. However, when Dr. Alan Guttmacher was asked to review the records of thirteen typical Caesarean sections performed on New York City women (see remarks about "Teamster" study farther on in this chapter), he concluded that in seven of the cases there was "serious question" about the necessity for surgery.

questionable use of oxytocic drugs. The obstetrician must be mindful of age, parity, previous uterine surgery. . . . The factors needed to avoid this complication are obstetric judgment and consultation. . . ."

Anesthesia was responsible for a number of other deaths. "Spinal anesthesia contributed to 3 deaths due to lack of prudent safeguards after the anesthetic agent was administered. There are numerous avoidable factors in the area, shared largely by the physician, due to errors of judgment and technique . . . the risk could have been reduced by the selection of another anesthetic agent and the adherence to established reasonable standards in its administration."

Hemorrhage owing to ectopic pregnancy was a common cause of maternal deaths.[23] "Delay in diagnosis and surgery contributes heavily to death. Factors in avoidability were largely errors in judgment in recognition of the condition, failure to adequately treat the initial shock. . . ."

Overenthusiastic use of anesthesia, labor induction and even Caesarean section . . . failure to diagnose or prepare for emergencies. . . . On the one hand, the doctors are doing too much, and on the other, they are doing too little, because that's the way obstetrics is practiced in the United States. With all their good intentions, obstetricians interfere with normal pregnancies more than they should, while failing to look to emergencies as sharply as they might.

A few are glaringly incompetent, but the medical fraternity is such that doctors rarely "tell" on one another, and few of the incompetents are ever censured. In their excellent book, *The Medical Offenders,* Howard and Martha Lewis cite these examples of malpractice, among many others:[24]

<hr>

[23]Ectopic pregnancy occurs when the fertilized ovum is implanted outside the uterine cavity, usually in the fallopian tube. The wall of the fallopian tube usually ruptures.

[24]Howard and Martha Lewis, *The Medical Offenders* (New York, Simon & Schuster, 1970), pp. 211–13.

A doctor attempted to bring on labor in a patient who was "due" shortly, despite the protestations of the four-time mother that she was not near labor. When a pill failed to change her condition, the doctor administered chloroform and endeavored to grasp the baby manually. Having no success, he tugged for several minutes with his forceps. As the patient began to bleed, the doctor removed his shoes, climbed onto the bed and, bracing his feet against the woman's thighs, pulled at the forceps for a half hour. Although warned that he was harming the baby, the doctor silently and determinedly continued tugging until finally the father intervened by insisting his wife be taken to a hospital. The doctor arose and renounced his involvement with the patient. At the hospital a few hours later, the woman expelled the totally bruised corpse of the baby. The mother's condition was described by the examining physician: "I've never seen anyone butchered up like that."

A mother delivered her child without anesthesia and witnessed the following tragic scene. The baby was pronounced perfectly healthy immediately after delivery, but after a few minutes in the ice-cold delivery room, she turned blue-black. The doctor placed the baby in a bassinet and applied a resuscitator, while the mother grew increasingly fearful. The doctor bypassed the nearby airlock incubator (complete with oxygen tent and measuring gauge) in favor of a primitive method—a funnel-like oxygen outlet which he held to the baby's face. Her squirming and head-tossing caused oxygen to escape from the funnel. The doctor informed the mother that the baby had a fatally malformed heart. (He was wrong, however, for the baby survived and her heart has no defects.) After forty-five minutes of oxygen administration, the doctor left, in order "to beat the traffic" going home. He left no instructions for the baby's care, and consequently she received no special attention. Her temperature was taken three days later, when she was placed on the critical list. The baby's exposure to the cold delivery room had led to shock, which produced the oxygen deficiency that caused her to turn blue. The brain might have survived the deprivation if oxygen had been carefully applied with the air-lock incubator. The child's brain damage was irreversible. Blind, deaf and dumb, she has no sense of touch, no muscle control, and is subject to convulsions and twitching.

The Lewises also point out that another area of "negligence in obstetrics is connected with substandard care in circumcisions." They describe one lawsuit involving a baby boy, who was routinely circumcised at two days of age. A black spot soon developed at the tip of his penis. It was gangrene. Although noticed, the spot did not motivate the doctors who observed it to call in a pediatrician or urologist to treat it. The baby was discharged from the hospital. When the black spot continued growing, the parents took their son to the hospital emergency room, where the doctor on duty that Saturday told them to return during clinic hours on Monday. The black spot spread so rapidly that the parents brought the baby to the hospital again on Sunday; that day's doctor likewise asked them to return on Monday. On Monday, the appropriate specialist, when finally seen, had no choice but to amputate the forepart of the baby's penis.

Fraternal loyalty is also, apparently, what keeps doctors from taking action against the admittedly small number of gynecologists who take sexual liberties with their patients. But even if the number *is* small, the effect on the young girl or woman is often so devastating that (I believe) these practitioners should be run out of their profession.

Two psychiatrists who were close friends and associates had been referring many of their patients to a gynecologist who seemed to take an exceptionally warm and understanding interest and who was also willing to perform low-cost abortions. After a time, the psychiatrists learned from their patients just *how* warm and how interested the gynecologist was. In the course of doing "pelvics" on attractive young women he frequently provided clitoral massage, at no extra fee.

As patient after patient told her psychiatrist about this unprofessional behavior, the two psychiatrists, naturally enough, stopped sending women to the gynecologist. But that was *all* they did. "We discussed it," said one, "and after all, we didn't really have any proof. If we'd tried to bring him up on ethics charges or something, we would have to drag our patients into it. Most of them have enough problems."

Much more common is the paternalistic but kindly practitioner who wishes to spare his young patients embarrassment. So delicate is he that he may fail to render the service he contracted for.

After college, Joan spent the summer in her home town in Ohio. At college she had had one affair, and her boyfriend had used condoms. In September, she would be starting a new job in New York, and she decided to arrive prepared with a diaphragm. Not wishing to take her chances at an impersonal birth control clinic, she visited her mother's gynecologist, the same doctor who had delivered her twenty-one years before.

"He seemed a little embarrassed," Joanie recalls, "although he was very nice. He didn't even send me a bill. The trouble was, his instructions weren't too clear, and when I tried to practice using the diaphragm I never could be sure that I was finding the cervix.

"When I got to New York, I made friends with a girl at my office who told me that the Margaret Sanger Research Bureau, in honor of its founder, takes great pride in its diaphragm success rate and gives the best instructions around. They have you practice putting it in, and then you have to come back and they give you a test. Well, that sounded fine to me. My college roommate almost died from an illegal abortion, so that was something I wanted to avoid. So I made an appointment at Sanger, and guess what. Not only was I using the diaphragm incorrectly, but the one my mother's doctor had given me was two sizes too small! Can you beat that? I guess he thought I was still a little girl."

Other doctors have brought their intrauterine device patients confusion and worse, by not preparing them for cramps, occasionally severe, which may occur at insertion or afterward. "If I'd had any idea," recalls a Los Angeles woman, "I would have asked my husband to come with me, or my sister. But all the doctor said was, 'Don't worry, it only takes a few minutes, and then you won't even know you have it.' Well, I made my appointment to get fitted on an ordinary weekday, and I even brought along my four-year-old daughter. What a mistake. Driving home, the cramps started coming, as bad as labor pains, and my labor pains were really something. My daughter got frightened, and I almost crashed the car. It was a bad scene all right."

Perhaps the most common and dangerous contraceptive negligence is the casualness with which many doctors hand out birth control pills. Despite the fact that there are hundreds of lawsuits pending against drug companies and doctors for deaths and permanent damage connected with the pill, and despite the fact that plaintiffs have won settlements of a half million dollars or more, some doctors continue to prescribe the pill as if it were sugar candy, without taking a careful patient and family history and without warning the patient of the serious danger signals to watch for.

A tragedy that could have been avoided occurred in Buffalo, New York, when Ann St. C., wife of a professor at the local university, mother of three and a user of the pill, called her gynecologist and asked, "Is the pill safe? Should I be taking it?"

Dr. K. snapped, "Of course it's all right for you to be taking the pill. If it weren't, I'd never have prescribed it."

Ann never had a chance to clarify the reason she was calling. In the preceding two weeks she had experienced several attacks of dizziness and double vision. She had also suffered from stiffness in the neck. If she had not been so readily cowed by the doctor's brusqueness, she might have detailed her symptoms. In that case, the doctor's reaction to her question might have been quite different.

Ann had a stroke exactly eight days later. She was sitting at her dinner table and suddenly began to cough and choke. Her husband thought something had stuck in her throat and pounded her vigorously on the back. She continued to cough and choke. Their six-year-old cried out, "Look, Mommy's mouth is all twisted!" Ann was partially paralyzed and totally unable to speak.

She spent two months in the hospital and then slowly recovered her speech and most of her physical functioning, except for weakness in the right arm or leg.

The neurologists who have been treating strokes occurring in young women on the pill have repeatedly noted that there is often a prodromal period, or time of warning. It may last for weeks or even months. The most common symptom is sudden, severe headache.

According to the doctrine of "informed consent," a patient is entitled to know the nature of any procedure performed on her or medication given her, the reasons for it and the possible dangers. This doctrine is blatantly ignored by most gynecologists and their associates. At birth control clinics for example, various methods are described to applicants, but the only information given about them (as a rule) is the efficacy rate.[25] The various methods are presented as if all are desirable, easy to use, and pretty much trouble-free. Thus, while women may *consent* to use one method or another, they are most certainly not informed. This generally chin-up policy does not advance

[25] And efficacy rates are not always what they seem, as we shall see in the chapter on birth control. There can be a substantial difference between "theoretical" effectiveness and "use" effectiveness.

the cause of effective birth control use, for different women have different needs and hopes and fears.

Women, especially young ones and poor ones, who are disillusioned with a birth control method often stop using it *without* reporting back for another. They feel as though they've been taken (they have), and they try to make do with withdrawal or a vaguely practiced kind of "rhythm." It would be far better for fertility control in general, and individual feminine health in particular, if the prescribing doctors and birth control clinics were honest to start with.

The issue of informed consent—or lack of it—in gynecology came to an ugly head last year in the Goldzieher matter. Dr. Joseph Goldzieher is a gynecologist at the Southwest Foundation for Research and Education in San Antonio. (A researcher Dr. Goldzieher may be, but an educator—well, you decide.)

In March, 1971, Dr. Goldzieher gave a paper at a meeting of the American Fertility Society in New Orleans. It was very well received. The paper described a double-blind[26] study he had performed, to determine whether the incidence of headache, nervousness, nausea, vomiting, depression and breast tenderness would be substantially higher in women taking the birth control pill than in women taking a placebo. The women in the study were mostly poor Mexican-Americans who went to the San Antonio center to get contraceptives and who were placed in the experiment without being told that some of them would get a dummy pill instead of a real contraceptive. Dr. Goldzieher—who concedes that all of the women had come to the clinic to prevent conception, not to assist in research—persists, nonetheless, in calling these women "volunteers."

The "volunteers" were also provided with a contraceptive cream and advised to use it as well as the pill. Of sev-

---

[26]A double-blind study is one in which two or more methods are given in such a fashion that neither the patient nor the doctor knows which patient was getting which until the study is over.

enty-six women who received the placebo, ten were pregnant at the end of four months.

When Barbara Yuncker of the New York *Post* questioned Dr. Goldzieher about his procedures, he replied, "If you think you can explain a placebo test to women like these, you never met Mrs. Gomez from the West Side."[27]

Now I submit that if a physician in any other specialty had dared to perform an experiment like this, we would have heard an outpouring of criticism from quite a few of his colleagues. In Dr. Goldzieher's case there was hardly a ripple from the gynecologists themselves. The last I heard, Dr. Goldzieher had not in any way been censured.[28]

One gynecologist has spoken out against Dr. Goldzieher —unequivocally but anonymously. He told *Medical World News* that he considered the experiment "totally unethical" but declined to let the publication use his name.[29] "My school," this "noted gynecologist" explained, "would never allow me to conduct an experiment in this manner."

The Planned Parenthood Affiliate in San Antonio had referred many of Dr. Goldzieher's study patients to him. I asked Dr. George Langmyhr, medical director of Planned Parenthood International, whether he regretted this participation. Dr. Langmyhr seemed most concerned that a fund to abort the pregnant women had not been included. "If I were the investigator," he declared, "there would have

[27] New York *Post*, April 22, 1971.

[28] In spite of the fact that, in 1968, Dr. Christopher Tietze of the Population Council had pointed out (in "Statistical Assessment of Adverse Experiences Associated with the Use of Oral Contraceptives," *Clinical Obstetrics and Gynecology*, Vol. 11, September 1968, pp. 698–715), "It is obvious that oral contraceptives cannot be studied by means of an ordinary double-blind trial involving a placebo. No responsible investigator would take it upon himself to expose women seeking protection to the risk of pregnancy by ostensibly giving them contraceptive tablets which, in a certain proportion of cases, would contain mere glucose, or at best some vitamins."

[29] April 16, 1971, p. 19.

been such a fund—even if we had to fly the women to
New York." (This sounds more responsible, but it still
doesn't take into consideration that perhaps some or many
of these women have religious scruples against abortion.)
Dr. Langmyhr was also concerned with the problem of
"whether the informed consent procedures were carried
out properly." However, he said that neither he as an individual nor Planned Parenthood as an organization had any
plans to repudiate or censure the study, or to stop working
with Goldzieher.[30]

Sad to say, the furor over Dr. Goldzieher's methods has
arisen *not* among his colleagues but in other quarters. A
woman's liberation group, The Third World Woman's
Caucus, is attempting to bring legal action against him.
And Robert M. Veatch, associate for medical ethics at the
Institute of Society Ethics and the Life Sciences, devoted a
long critical article to Dr. Goldzieher's experiment:[32]

> . . . Informed consent is a classical ethical norm of ex-
> perimentation on human subjects. Anyone who thinks he
> can get "fully" informed consent is naïve, but was there
> even any semblance of consent to this experiment? Why
> could patient/subjects not be told, as one critic suggests,
> that there is a placebo group in the experimental
> design? . . .

[30]This seems a bit shortsighted, in light of a recent paper on the
feelings of the black community toward family planning programs,
which was prepared by Dr. Charles V. Willie of the Syracuse University Sociology Department. (See footnote 31 on this page.) Dr.
Willie writes, "I must state categorically that many people in the
black community are suspicious of any family planning program
initiated by whites. A substantial minority . . . view family planning
programs as a plot to eliminate blacks in the United States." On this
basis alone—the desire to build trust—one would think that Planned
Parenthood, like other groups trying to bring family planning into
ghetto areas, would be dismayed at Dr. Goldzieher's manipulations
of Chicano women.

[31]Charles V. Willie, PhD, "A Position Paper" in Perspectives
from the Black Community, Washington, D.C. *Population Reference Bureau,* No. 37, (June, 1971).

[32]Robert M. Veatch, " 'Experimental' Pregnancy," The Hastings
Center *Report,* No. 1 (June, 1971).

In many research institutions and funding agencies, review procedures are now established. What are the procedures in effect at the Southwest Foundation for Research and Education? The study was funded by Syntex Labs, a manufacturer of oral contraceptives, and the federal government's Agency for International Development, an agency with primary interests in an area other than biomedical research. What was Syntex's interest in this project, and what review and control procedures do they use? Would the experiment have been approved for funding by the National Institutes of Health? If not, is the moral that if one wants to conduct questionable research, he should seek out research facilities and funding where fewer questions will be asked? And can a study funded in large part by the drug manufacturer be expected to be as impartial as one funded without a vested interest? . . . Are the researchers and the founders of the research now prepared to provide financial and other support for the products of their experiment?

Perhaps you have heard of the Goldzieher matter. There was just enough public attention (and women's liberation is keeping it alive) to make many better-informed women aware of the experiment. But in gynecology there are other scandals which hardly seem to surface publicly at all.[33]

[33]There is a very serious obstacle to good medical and health reporting. A general assignment writer cannot be trusted to cover medicine and health adequately because she (or he) usually lacks the background and technical knowledge. Recognizing this, newspapers and magazines assign articles to specialty reporters, who, as a rule, concentrate on one beat exclusively.

When you become a specialty reporter, in this or any other area, you soon find yourself uncomfortably dependent on your sources. A full-time police reporter rarely tells "all" he knows about the chief or the district attorney because if he broke certain "rules" of protocol, they would punish him by failing to inform him when a big story is breaking. The same tends to be true of medical and health reporting. You can criticize your sources but only within certain unspoken "limits," or else these sources will cut you out.

Consider what happened when a controversy erupted over the nutritional value of packaged breakfast cereals. A nutritionist and university professor, rose up to defend these food products, and his

For example, consider the results of medical audits. An audit is a procedure whereby specialists who are recognized experts in particular diseases are called in to review the work of other doctors. In audit after audit, in many parts of the United States it has been found that perfectly healthy uteri, ovaries and fallopian tubes are excised all too frequently. One doctor, Norman S. Miller of the University of Michigan School of Medicine, has dubbed these operations "hip-pocket hysterectomies," because the only benefactor is the surgeon's wallet.

---

remarks were widely publicized (and accepted). The general reporters who covered the story couldn't have been expected to know that the same professor was also a consultant to the industry he was defending. The specialty reporters knew it, but few mentioned it in their stories, perhaps because the professor (and the eminent university) is too valuable a source to embarrass.

This dilemma is not in any way unique to health reporting but afflicts the press generally. As our society becomes increasingly technical and specialized, it is necessary for reporters to become specialists too. But as they become immersed in their specialties, they tend to identify with the problems and the welfare of the public figures and organizations they cover, instead of the problems and the welfare of their own readers.

Medical practice in America today is wracked with disappointment and scandal. Nobody's life expectancy is improving much, and it has become increasingly clear that the delivery of medical services in this country is just appalling. Both research and clinical practice function at a poor level, and malpractice suits are multiplying. Most new drugs or procedures which are hailed as great advances fade into nothingness or, at the least, soon prove to have many drawbacks and limitations.

Many of the most significant advances in longevity have been due *not* to improvement in individual physician skills, but to public health measures, such as inoculations and improvements in sanitation. Few women realize, for example, that the most drastic reduction in maternal mortality this country has ever experienced occurred when obstetricians finally became convinced that it was necessary to wash their hands.

Today the percentage of patients who are hospitalized for iatrogenic (doctor-caused) illness is steadily increasing and is now estimated at about 20 percent. (Adverse reactions to prescription drugs are the prevailing reason, but patients are also frequently hospitalized for reactions to other medical procedures.)

According to testimony given by Drs. Leighton Cluff and Robert Moser before the U.S. Senate Small Business Committee, 1,000,000

A particularly distinguished—and disturbing—series of audits was performed in New York City in the late 1950's and early 1960's. These audits were supervised by Drs. Ray E. Trussell and Mildred A. Morehead of the Columbia University School of Public Health.[34] They had been requested by the Teamsters Union Joint Council 16 which represents almost half a million New Yorkers. The union was troubled by the high costs of medical care its members were receiving and wondered whether these costs were justified by good services.

A review of 406 hospital admissions was made by various outstanding specialists. It fell to Dr. Alan Guttmacher, now the director of Planned Parenthood, to review the gynecology cases.

The auditors reported that:

"Essentially there were two causes for care that was judged to be inferior. One related to surgery performed on essentially normal organs (removal of the uterus) where the grave suspicion of patient exploitation could be raised.

Americans are hospitalized each year owing to adverse reactions to drugs. Only 1 in 5 is suffering from an adverse reaction to an over-the-counter medication; 4 in 5 are reacting to drugs prescribed by their doctors. In addition, 10 percent of patients who are hospitalized for *other causes* must have their hospital stay extended owing to adverse reactions to drugs administered in the safe bosom of the hospital.

The academic leaders of the medical profession are well aware of these problems and are striving mightily to change and upgrade the quality of medical education. Review committees at our better hospitals are keeping tabs on staff practices and making ever sterner appraisals. But perhaps the future lies with "relicensing," which is being initiated in at least one state. If relicensing were required, doctors would have to take their exams over and over at periodic intervals, and this would force more of them to keep up.

If at least half the health articles in your favorite magazine or newspaper aren't fairly critical or skeptical, you can pretty much assume that you are *not* getting an accurate picture of what's going on.

[34]Morehead and Trussell, "The Quantity, Quality and Costs of Medical and Hospital Care Secured by a Sample of Teamster Families in the New York Area" (New York, Columbia University School of Public Health and Administrative Medicine, 1962).

The other factor . . . was inferior care resulting from poor clinical judgment. . . ."

In the mishandling of general disorders, incompetence was apparently to blame. But in the handling of gynecological disorders, and gynecological disorders almost exclusively, the auditors found evidence of *deliberate exploitation*. They even noted that most of the unnecessary hysterectomies were performed by highly qualified specialists.

The auditors raise the question of gynecological exploitation several times, in several different ways: "Essentially the gynecological cases that received poor rating stemmed from surgery that is suspected as 'unnecessary.' In general surgical cases, however, the majority of the poorer ratings were caused by poor judgment in operative techniques or inadequate clinical management. There were very few of the general surgical patients for whom an operation was felt to be unnecessary."

In its net effect, medical incompetence is just as harmful as deliberate exploitation. But the intentions are different. Earlier in this chapter I raised the question of whether gynecologists, as a group, are more prone to observe shoddy medical ethics than practitioners in other specialties. I believe that the findings of this Teamster audit lend support to my thesis. To many gynecologists, however well trained, their patients are less than the fully functioning responsible "free" adults described in the Platonic medical ethic. They occupy some nether region which falls close to the territory occupied by the livestock and pets whom veterinarians tend to. (But at least the pets and livestock have active and vociferous humane societies watching out for their welfare and even their rights. Who is protecting the rights of women against the gynecologists?) Men and women alike are so worshipful of physicians that they hardly dare raise any question about the care they receive. Those who do raise questions are usually regarded as eccentric or neurotic, and are sharply reminded of the long years of medical training, etc., etc. One of the most depressing statements in the Teamster report was this:

> The relationship between the patients' opinion of the medical care they received, and the surveyors' judgment of the level or quality of the care given, indicated considerable optimism on the part of the patients. Three quarters of those whose care was considered less than optimal, felt they had received the best of care. On the other hand the surveyors agreed with five of the six individuals who strongly felt they had received inferior care.

So we see that patients err not in criticizing their doctors too much, but quite in the opposite direction. All told, of the 406 hospital admissions studied, only 57 percent were judged by the auditors to have received "good" or "excellent" care. The remainder were equally distributed between "fair" and "poor" treatment. Thus, of 80 or so people who received "poor" treatment, only 5 recognized it. Only one patient erred in underrating the care received.

How common were unjustified hysterectomies? To quote the Teamster audit:

> There were 60 cases in the sample where a hysterectomy [removal of the uterus] had been performed. From a review of the records, including the operative report and the pathology findings, the surveyor felt that one-third were operated on unnecessarily, and that question could be raised about the advisability of the operation in another ten percent. At the very least, these women should have had a dilation and curettage (scraping of the uterus) followed by a period of observation prior to the hysterectomy. In many instances, the dilation and curettage alone would probably have alleviated symptoms.

Dr. Guttmacher's findings about Caesarean sections were equally distressing: 7 out of 13 may have been unnecessary.

All told, 126 obstetrics-gynecology admissions (routine deliveries excluded) were reviewed by Dr. Guttmacher. Close to half of these patients were handled in a less than satisfactory way. Here is an example of an unnecessary hysterectomy:

A 42-year-old woman was hospitalized for a three-month history of vaginal pruritis and occasional premenstrual staining. A consultant in Obstetrics and Gynecology recommended a Papanicolaou Smear and a dilation and curettage, and advised that further management should be determined after the results of these examinations were known. Neither of these procedures was done. The attending physician operated, with a preoperative diagnosis of ovarian cyst. No cyst was found. He then performed a hysterectomy; the pathology report showed only two small polyps. The surveyor noted, "There was no excuse to do a hysterectomy. A dilation and curettage would have removed the small polyps and almost certainly cured her post-menstrual staining. This was bad medicine." Six days following discharge, this patient was hospitalized with thrombophlebitis of the broad ligament. The surveyor noted that if an unnecessary hysterectomy had not been done in the first place, the second admission would also not have been required.

An example of a pregnant woman with heart disease, whose case was tragically mismanaged:

A Teamster's wife in her thirties, with living children, was hospitalized five times in 1959 and 1960 for complications of rheumatic heart disease and pregnancy. Both of the physicians she consulted were foreign-trained and had no hospital appointments. She was under their care in an accredited proprietary hospital for the first admission. Her Blue Cross coverage ran out and three subsequent admissions were in an unaffiliated municipal hospital. Finally, she was taken by her family doctor to a voluntary accredited hospital outside of New York City for her fifth admission. These hospital admissions ranged in length from four to 21 days. During three she was pregnant and finally was delivered of a stillborn baby. She was treated symptomatically for current symptoms (spitting of blood) on each admission with little attention or recognition given to the underlying heart disease. The obstetrical surveyor stated: "This was a very ill woman and the gravity of her illness was unknown to her and not sufficiently appreciated by her physician. It was dangerous to discharge her during her pregnancy. I certainly would have hospitalized her continually until delivery; for the five month period during which she was pregnant and ill. Furthermore, after the stillbirth, sterilization should have been considered. It is possible she would have refused on religious grounds. However, there is no evidence in the record that it was even thought of, much less suggested. During each hospital admission, she was allowed out of bed too often and too soon."

The surveyor of the heart disease cases noted, "There is little question that this seriously ill, pregnant, cardiac received inadequate medical care and management. There is no evidence that the basic cause of her numerous admissions, which were related to rheumatic heart disease, mitral stenosis, and embolic pneumonia, was ever appreciated. Her cardiac failure remained untreated for some time. It is appalling that a pregnant cardiac with repeated pulmonary emboli was so casually treated."

From the interview, it was learned that she was still under the care of the two family physicians, who told her that she had no cardiac disease. The amount of work-up that she received in the proprietary hospitals was practically negligible; even the voluntary hospital did little more than take one chest film. More work-up was done in the government hospital, at least on her medical admissions; however, when she was admitted to the obstetrical service, there was no attention paid to her cardiac condition.

Her husband also suffers from cardiac disease and during 1959 was able to work only part of the year. During the first six months of 1960 the family spent over $300 on drugs. The patient at the time of interview was again pregnant.

Regarding the questionable Caesarean sections, the report states that they "not only failed to have x-ray measurements taken but also other practices consistent with good obstetrical care were omitted. Included among these for one or more patients were failure to obtain a consultation, failure to rupture membranes, and failure to stimulate labor with pitocin."

The handling of minor procedures was frequently questioned also, and Dr. Guttmacher suggested that some of the patients need not have been hospitalized at all.

No. 146—26 years old, hospitalized for three days. Dilation and curettage for three month history of postmenstrual and occasional postcoital staining. Preoperative diagnosis of polyp, but no report of same in operative note or pathology report. "Therefore, I assume there was a very small polyp which could have been twisted off in the office, cauterized, and very likely have eliminated complaints without hospitalization. No preoperative Papanicolaou smear."

No. 161—35 years old, hospitalized two days. Incision and stretching of hymen for difficulty in coitus. This operation is largely abandoned; no indication that proper sexual counseling or conservative office procedure (stretching) had been undertaken.

But hasn't the situation improved since the Teamster audit was published a decade ago? Aren't the gynecologists "policing themselves" and, at the very least, eliminating the unnecessary surgery?

There is little reason to think so.

In the United States today, 516 hysterectomies are performed annually for every 100,000 women. In England and Wales, the figure is only 213—well under *half*.

Dr. John P. Bunker, a Stanford University anesthesiologist, reviewed this extraordinary situation in a recent article in *The New England Journal of Medicine*.[35]

Surgery, in general, is more prevalent in the United States than in England, but the difference in female surgery is especially dramatic. Dr. Bunker concedes that some of the difference is philosophical. In the case of breast operations, for example (278 per 100,000 in the United States; 171 per 100,000 in Britain), Dr. Bunker allows that there is a legitimate difference in "enthusiasm" for these procedures in the British and American medical literature. "In keeping with the national character," Dr. Bunker observes, "the American surgeon is more aggressive. He appears to hold higher expectation of what surgery can do in the treatment of disease, whereas the British surgeon is more modest in his expectation, possibly more realistic, but also possibly missing opportunities for surgical cure."[36]

[35] John P. Bunker, MD, "Surgical Manpower," *New England Journal of Medicine*, January 15, 1970, pp. 135–43.

[36] Radical mastectomy (removal of the breast) is, of course, a traumatic experience for many women. In some cases there is no question that it is necessary, to save the patient's life, but in other cases a "wide excision" of the tumor appears to serve just as well. Dr. John Hayward of Guy's Hospital, London, has been comparing the results of these two operations. After ninety months, there was no significant difference between the percentage of patients remaining alive who had received the smaller operation and those who had received the larger. With radical mastectomy 64 percent were alive; with wide excision 67 percent were alive.

In women with small breasts even the excision operation made a cosmetic change, but in women with larger breasts it was barely noticeable.

Psychological tests were used to determine the emotional effects of the two operations. Among those who had received the radical operation 14 percent were found to have a "poor attitude." Among those receiving the smaller operation only 4 percent had a poor attitude.

According to an article in the *Medical Tribune* of October 6, 1971, the English, who are approaching breast surgery in a more cautious way than the Americans, are getting just as good a result physically and a far better one emotionally.

On the subject of unnecessary hysterectomies, Dr. Bunker sounds altogether cynical:

> When a plan for reimbursement of surgical fees was offered to the United Mine Workers some years ago, there seemed to be an excessively large number of surgical procedures performed—that is, an excessive number of surgical bills were submitted. The Mine Workers Fund was concerned with the large amount of what appeared to be unnecessary surgery, particularly the number of gynecologic operations. . . . When a requirement was added that all operations be endorsed by pre-operative special consultation, the number of [hysterectomies] fell by as much as 75 percent. . . .

Well, isn't it better to be "safe than sorry," have the organ out if there is any question about it? Dr. Bunker explains that while we know the mortality rates associated with most operations, we do not know the comparable risks of *not* operating. It has been established, however, that for at least one illness where a great deal of excess surgery is performed, appendicitis, the overall mortality is lower when appendectomies are *not* performed.

Dr. Bunker suggests that there are several factors—beyond philosophy—which influence the great surgical disparity between the United States and Great Britain.

First of all, our surgeons are poorly distributed, with a shortage of them in many areas and an excess in many others. In our big cities many surgeons have time on their hands. And idle hands make mischief, as my grandmother used to say.

Second, "consultation is the way of life under the British National Health Service. . . . The British surgeon . . . sees patients only as they are referred to him by the general practitioner or internist, and he is entirely hospital-based. The American surgeon, by contrast . . . may accept patients without referral, or he may be the primary physician . . . referring the patient to himself for surgery and thus creating his own demand . . . when two differing points of view are brought to bear on the problems of a single patient, it is very much to the patient's advantage. . . ."

Third, it is possible, Dr. Bunker suggests, that under the British National Health Service, ordinary people may get better preventive care, leading to a decreased need for hospitalization and surgery.

"Finally," says Dr. Bunker, "the method of payment appears to play an important, if unmeasured, part. Surgical fees in the United States, although perhaps not as large as a generation ago, are still much greater than those in other areas in medicine, and the opportunity for large incomes may attract a disproportionate number of physicians. . . . In addition, the 'incentive' of a fee for service may tend to increase the number of operations in cases in which indications are borderline."

Certain misconceptions about hysterectomies ought to be cleared up at this point.

They make you safe from uterine cancer. Not entirely. Some hysterectomies are only "partial." The cervix or neck of the womb remains, and the patient is as likely (or unlikely) to get cancer of the cervix as she was before.

Women who get fibroid tumors ought to have their uterus out. Fibroids are not malignant. There is even some evidence that women who have them are *less* apt to get uterine cancer. It is believed that *over half* of all women past childbearing age develop fibroids.

Hysterectomies can cure backaches, headaches, nerves and other complaints of menopause. There is no evidence of this, and yet, according to one study, about 10 percent of hysterectomies are performed to "treat" complaints such as these.

To monitor needless surgery, many better hospitals have established "tissue committees." These committees review the laboratory findings concerning organs that have been removed surgically. If a doctor is removing too many healthy organs, his tissue committee gets after him. The problem is that some of the more avid hysterectomists spread their work around at a number of hospitals and thus manage to avoid discovery.

How are you, then, to get honest medical care? In the first place, do you really need a gynecologist at all? Certainly you need him as a consultant, from time to time, but are you sure you need him as your main doctor?

A surprising number of women do rely on gynecologists as their main doctors, sometimes out of ignorance (many do not know that an internist or GP is usually well equipped to do routine checkups which include the female parts) and sometimes out of devotion. For example, my friend Maria adores the gynecologist who delivered her two sons almost twenty years ago. Although she is now in her middle forties, she still considers him her "main doctor" and consults him first about any and all of her ailments. "If he gets your babies out wisely and well," she comments, "I guess you're his for life."

However, there is much to be said for using an internist or family practitioner, rather than a gynecologist, as a "main doctor." The internist or family practitioner is more apt to see a woman as a "total person" and to check her general health adequately. He is more apt to concern himself, for example, with whether she has a general condition which might make the pill inadvisable (say a family history of cancer or a tendency to get high blood pressure) or which requires special watching during pregnancy (heart disease). Traditionally, internists are guardians against surgery, and in light of the extraordinary figures for excess gynecological surgery on women, it seems only sensible to have a trusted internist in one's corner.[37]

[37] See "With a Life at Stake" by Edward M. Brecher, *McCall's* magazine (October, 1967). In this extraordinary article, Brecher, a medical writer, describes his wife's death from cancer. When symptoms developed, the Brechers went straight to a top gynecological surgeon, who operated at a leading university hospital: "Doctors came and went; no one of them was in command. One

This is not to suggest that gynecologists aren't the ones to deliver babies or perform surgery *when truly necessary*. But I believe that it is best to view the gynecologist as a consultant and to ask one's internist to help select him.[38]

---

of them told Ruth one thing, the same doctor or someone else gave me an altogether different report, and there was no one to whom we could turn to tell us which version was true." The gynecologist advised limited radiation; the radiologist advised extensive radiation. "We could only wait helplessly to see which department would win the tug-of-war in which Ruth's future was at stake." Ruth wrote to a cousin that she felt "like a character in a novel by Kafka or in a play written by Ionesco for the Theater of the Absurd."

Finally, Brecher took a step which he "fervently" urges on other families: He secured the services of an internist, who took charge of his wife's case, coordinating the other specialists and seeing that she was made comfortable, emotionally and physically. "His first step, quite simply, was to get to know Ruth. He asked her about her children, her work, her plans, her beliefs, her relationship with me. He treated her like an adult rather than like a child in need of professional smiles and empty reassurances. Moreover, he gave her an opportunity to get to know him. . . . Later, he reviewed her physical condition with her in detail, the nature of her illness, the various courses of treatment still available, the hazards ahead and the probable outcome. He let her talk. He listened. He answered questions. If he didn't know the answer, he said so—and looked it up or consulted another specialist. He was not afraid to call a cancer a cancer—a small point, but one which favorably impressed us both."

Brecher concludes that internists are exceptionally well prepared "to take responsibility for a patient's entire care," for the internist was and remains today a specialist in diagnostic medicine. If you go to him complaining of headaches, he does not hurriedly write you a prescription for aspirin or something stronger. Instead, he seeks to identify, and if possible remedy, the cause of the headaches. Like anyone else, of course, he may make a diagnostic mistake . . . but the internist's mistake won't result from his being too busy to get to the heart of the matter. [He] can also save you from unnecessary surgery or other procedures—not just by keeping you out of the hands of unscrupulous men who operate or overtreat at the drop of a hat but in subtler ways as well."

[38] A good argument against having a gynecologist as your main doctor is that he may be too busy to give you adequate attention. Gynecologists handle an average of seventy-five patients and twenty births a week and already spend more time seeing patients than any other medical specialists. Obviously, if he is doing his job well and personally presiding at middle-of-the-night deliveries, he will be

The pregnant or hoping-to-become pregnant woman should read widely and consult her friends.[39] She does not have to panic and find a gynecologist the moment she suspects she may be pregnant. Her internist, who presumably knows her, is perfectly capable of confirming the pregnancy and helping her to find a suitable gynecologist.

Many women have definite ideas of whether they want natural childbirth, rooming-in, husbands in the delivery room, even one type or another of anesthesia. Yet women are afraid to "shop" for gynecologists and they should not be. Look for a gynecologist whose approach to pregnancy is compatible with yours. Your internist, it is hoped, can supply you with a list of names. Your friends will also

---

more fatigued and less able to concentrate than other specialists who aren't up all night on a regular basis.

Many women complain that their gynecologists don't tell them enough and that their doctors give them brushoffs when they ask questions. Often new mothers encounter conflicts between their gynecologist and pediatrician, as, in my own case, when a laxative that goes straight to the milk was prescribed.

As a patient, you have the right to insist that your gynecologist answer your questions completely and in a way that you understand. It may be helpful if you prepare a list of questions before your examination. No woman needs to use a doctor who sees himself as a mind reader and believes he can correctly judge how much she should know about her condition.

The kind of low which communications between gynecologists and their patients can sometimes reach is illustrated by a story which Grace Naismith reported in *Family Health* magazine: "One woman didn't know what the thin scar on her abdomen signified until the gynecologist discovered it and asked if she had had a hysterectomy. 'What's that?' she said. Although her uterus had been removed because of a tumor, this woman was still taking birth control pills she had obtained from a different doctor, unaware that the removal of her uterus, or womb, had made pregnancy impossible."

[39]Three books I like very much are: *The Family Book of Child Care,* Niles Newton (New York, Harper & Row); *Maternal Emotions,* Niles Newton (New York, Harper & Row); *Women and Their Bodies,* Boston Women's Health Course Collective publications (Boston: New England Free Press, 1970 [if any reader is interested in purchasing this publication, write to Boston Women's Health Course Collective, c/o New England Free Press, 791 Tremont Street, Boston, Mass. 02118]).

have suggestions, but if all things are equal, it's desirable to find a gynecologist who has worked with your internist before. Sometimes this won't be possible, as, for example, in cases where there may be only one or two gynecologists in your community who are interested in natural child-birth.

You have every right to call gynecologists and ask their views on whatever questions concern you, before you select one and contract for his services. Before you buy a washing machine, you check into the price and the guarantee offered by different dealers, don't you? Your pregnancy is much more important. Remember that there is no reason to feel like a sick or frightened person. If you are a healthy young woman, your pregnancy, medically speaking, would probably come out fine if you just had your baby in the woods. Not that this is recommended; should complications arise, skilled intervention is crucial. None-theless, the overwhelming odds are that nothing will go wrong, and therefore, you should be shopping for a doctor, and a hospital, which will help enhance the experience emotionally. In the long run, *your view of yourself as a woman and mother* is what is most apt to be either enhanced or dampened by your pregnancy and birth experience.

The choice of hospital is far more crucial than the average laywoman realizes. In the Teamster study, it was found that whether care was good or bad was more influenced by the quality of the hospital than the quality of the doctor. Even an excellently trained doctor may turn in less than his best performance at a second-rate hospital, and the reverse is also true. The authors of the report suggest: "The differences in care is a result of different behavior patterns in these settings."

Apparently, there is a hospital mystique. In some, almost everyone is cautious and professional, while in others the standards are "looser."

The best hospitals are those affiliated with medical

schools, and if you can find a doctor you like who can book you into one, I would strongly recommend it.

Next best are those not affiliated with medical schools, but approved for internship or residency training.

The least desirable hospitals are those which have no training programs at all. Among these, those which are "accredited" are apt to be better than nonaccredited institutions.

Many women past thirty-five believe that they must see a gynecologist for an annual or semiannual checkup. This is not usually necessary. Your internist should be entirely capable of doing a routine pelvic examination and Pap smear. If for some special reason, further consultation with a gynecologist is advisable, he will arrange it.

Be on guard against fee splitting.[40] An unscrupulous doctor who does not perform surgery himself may nonetheless rush you into it for the sake of his own kickback. Again, your best guardian against fee splitting and other shoddy practices is to find and stay with one central family doctor whom you are sure you trust.

Don't be seduced by big names. Some of the biggest names in gynecology are actually highly paid salesmen for a product and, it is my belief, that product often comes before the welfare of their patients.[41]

It is foolhardy for the woman seeking youth and beauty, or a transformed sex life, or instantly delightful childbirth, or completely carefree birth control to telephone a gynecologist-promoter whose name she saw in the newspaper. Life itself—and health care in particular—is very scarce on miracles and even on compromises that are suitable for all.

Maturity, I think, is the ability to live with ambiguity. I would be equally wary of the gynecologist who practices

---

[40]See Lewises *The Medical Offenders* and John R. Lindsey, "The Whole Town's Splitting Fees," *Medical Economics* (November 9, 1959).

[41]See chapter on birth control for details.

natural childbirth exclusively and the gynecologist whose only philosophy is hit-'em-on-the-head-the-instant-labor-starts-and-don't-wake-'em-till-the-hairdresser-shows. Some labors and deliveries will follow a course where natural childbirth is desirable and feasible—if that is what the mother wants. Others will follow a course where safe natural childbirth is not possible.

You will come to face *your* birth control and pregnancy and menopause decisions out of your own personality and background.

Some of you will come fearing drugs and not wanting the pill, eager and willing to use a local method if your doctor will take the time and trouble to show you how it can work. Others will feel that almost any risk is worth the avoidance of having to stick a greasy finger into one's vagina. Even here, however, we all have our own priorities and fears, and this is certainly our privilege. . . . When Martha asked her doctor if she should take the pill, he gave her the full poop on blood clots. "The risk," he told her, "is up to you." Martha decided to take them, but when she stopped the pill, wanting to get pregnant, her periods never came. She consulted a fertility specialist who told her, "With your menstrual history, you should not have been given the pill. It seems to be women like you, whose periods were sparse to start with, who are apt to suffer from an 'oversuppression' effect." The fertility specialist gave her a drug which helped her conceive—a multiple pregnancy, which she miscarried. He has now advised against further therapy and says that *perhaps* her normal periods will come back if she just waits.

Martha and her husband are suing the original gynecologist, even though the fertility specialist who expressed such dismay has declined to testify on their behalf. ("I couldn't really say that it was normal medical practice to warn you about this side effect," he apologized. "The whole area is rather delicate, and plenty of competent gynecologists just don't have a good enough understanding of fertility. It's like neurosurgery. All surgeons and most doctors are technically licensed to perform it, but the average practitioner would cut into your head with no more safety than your local butcher. I'm afraid that most gynecologists are not fertility experts, actually.") "That's great," says Martha, sarcastically. "It's really a comfort to know that my gynecologist 'shouldn't be blamed' for his lack of subtle understanding. I'm 'all woman,' and I'm not obsessively interested in the details of pharmacology. I was willing to risk blood clots for the sake of a good sex adjustment in my marriage, but my future babies I would never have risked. If he had only told me that there was the slightest chance the pill could make me sterile, I would have used something else. That's just my hang-up, I realize, but I was entitled to know, and he should have been keeping up."

Medicine is very far from being a pure science. It is, as any sincere and intelligent doctor should be willing to admit, a craft or art, punctuated by many profound question marks and doubts.

In my opinion, a good gynecologist, like any good doctor, is a human being first, not an all-purpose authority figure.

He should be willing to listen to his patients and he should not pretend that he always has easy answers to their questions. When he doesn't know something, he should look it up. The doctor and patient are partners in the patient's health and welfare, not master and serf. The doctor who must act like a master may have psychiatric problems, in my opinion.

And let's face it. Doctors are not, by any measure, the healthiest group in our society. Psychological studies of students who enter medicine (the studies are always of men; I have not yet found one of men versus women, although I suspect that there might be a difference because the boy who enters medicine is doing something very conventionally approved, whereas the girl who enters medicine is doing something that is still daring and iconoclastic) show that a majority of doctors are somewhat rigid, authoritarian and socially inept. They are, apparently, happiest when in command.

There is a special type who puts on a good act. He has learned how to cavort like warm, backslapping "folks," but it's all a social patina—he still doesn't *listen*.

Men in our society are not too accustomed to listening to women. It isn't easy to find a hairdresser who listens, much less a husband, a lover or a personal physician.

But such doctors do exist and in growing numbers for medicine and even gynecology are slowly becoming less authoritarian. Concepts such as "informed consent" and "patient rights" which were barely mentioned in passing when my husband attended medical school twenty years ago, are major concerns at most of the better academic centers today.[42]

Gynecologists will change, if women insist on being treated as full partners in their own health. To put it another way, *we* can demand that they stop shooting us up—and shutting us up—with their clever combinations of hormones, tranquilizers, anesthesia, and fear.

---

[42]I wish to thank Dr. Ernest Drucker for pointing out how medical training in the United States almost forces doctors to think of patients as "objects." Drucker is a psychologist who runs a seminar for freshman medical students at the Albert Einstein College of Medicine. "On the first day of medical training," Drucker notes, "these students are introduced to 'their' cadaver and instructed on how to start chopping it up. No one prepares them for this shocking experience. To be able to cope with it—this traumatic introduction to their careers as doctors—they *have* to shut out any feeling that this object on the table is or was a human being."

I take it to be a hopeful sign that medical schools are now aware of such problems and are trying, at last, to help students deal with them.

CHAPTER SIX

MEN, LOVE AND MARRIAGE

Syllogism

All successful men are obsessive compulsives
All obsessive compulsives are lousy lovers
Therefore . . . .

No matter what they say about marriage, it's still popular; 92 percent of the U.S. population is married or will marry. By contrast, only 60 percent own cars, 80 percent use alcoholic beverages and 85 percent watch TV.

Indeed, marriage is *more* popular than it used to be. In 1967, a full 87 percent of women in their late twenties were married, an increase of 13 percent over 1940.[1]

But—is marriage happy? Certainly, it's convenient, and apparently, it's healthy as well. Married persons, especially married men, live longer than do single and divorced persons. At every age level, the unmarried die at a higher rate than their married or remarried counterparts. The unmarried suffer more from general illness, alcoholism and mental illness, and their suicide rate is at least three times higher.[2]

Still, many people, *most* people, are disappointed in their marriages. They don't admit it to strangers, of

[1] "Family Development in a Changing World," paper delivered by Alice Rossi at the American Psychiatric Association meeting, Washington, D.C., May 5, 1971.
[2] Figures from California Department of Health.

course. (Recently, the National Opinion Research Center polled a random sampling of couples in the United States. Sixty percent rated themselves "very happy," 36 percent "pretty happy" and only 3 percent conceded that they were "not so happy.")

When a closer look is assayed, the results are very different. To my mind, the most important and believable marriage research of the 1960's was that performed by John F. Cuber and Peggy B. Harroff (Mrs. Cuber in private life) and known as the Cuber report.[3]

Dr. Cuber is a former marriage counselor turned sociologist. He and his wife interviewed 437 highly successful Americans in depth, to discern the real quality of their marriages. Fewer than 1 in 4 had unions that could be described as intimate and loving and that in any way resembled the ideal which most young people hope to attain.

This is not to say that all of the others were actively unhappy. In many of these enduring marriages a *modus vivendi*—sometimes comfortable and sometimes not—had been achieved. Husbands and wives made their own lives and went their own ways, often avoiding each other, devoting their real attention to work, to children and (sometimes) to other sex partners. The Cubers describe these marriages as "utilitarian."

Some of the utilitarian marriage partners expressed contentment, if not happiness. A physician said: "I don't know why everyone seems to make so much fuss about men and women and marriage. . . . If anything happened to my wife I'd get married again. I think it's the proper way to live. It's convenient, orderly and solves a lot of problems. But there are other things in life. . . . The biggest thing to me is the practice of my profession. . . ."

[3] *The Significant Americans,* a book based on their findings, was published by Doubleday in 1965. It is out of print, but the Penguin paperback version is still available, retitled *Sex and the Significant Americans,* John F. Cuber and Peggy B. Harroff (New York, Penguin Books, 1966). A long article by Morton Hunt summarized their research for *Redbook* readers in September, 1965.

Most of the disappointed wives and husbands were less complacent. Their remarks were tinged with sadness and unfulfillment:

> . . . We don't sleep together except now and then when we get plastered or sentimental, or it's an anniversary. Since we don't fight and really sort of like each other, I think the kids assume that they have an ordinary father and mother. . . . My wife [is] a pretty decent gal any way you look at her—well, not *any* way—she's really kind of dull, she's preoccupied with her menopause. . . . But then, of course, there's the business which is half hers. . . . It all sort of adds up that it's sometimes better to make your peace with things as they are.

The Cuber report was a study of marriage among the successful and affluent. There is no reason to suppose that marriage among the less privileged is any better, and plenty of reason to fear that it may be worse.[4]

However, successful males in our society do labor under an awesome impediment to happy marriage.

For example, most of the men who will review this book—indeed, most of the men who will read it—are neurotic; not only neurotic, but neurotic in a way which poses very special sex problems.

If the psychiatrists are right, to become a successful and important male in our culture (*i.e.*, a book reviewer or even a book buyer) you almost have to be an "obsessive-compulsive."

The obsessive-compulsive, as described by Dr. Joseph Barnett, of the William Alanson White Institute, is:

> Over-organized, over-structured, and preoccupied with details. He places great importance on logic and intellect

---

[4]See various studies of lower-class marriages by investigators such as Lee Rainwater (*And the Poor Get Children* [Chicago, Quadrangle Books, 1960]) and Mirra Komarovsky (*Blue Collar Marriage* [New York, Vintage, 1967]).

and underestimates the role of emotion in living. He is often stubborn and pedantic. Withdrawn and aloof, he appears devoid of vitality, warmth, and spontaneous feeling. While he may be successful in many areas, and indeed this personality type includes many of our most successful business and professional people, his personal relations may suffer from his style of living, and to the degree that he is obsessional he denies himself the gratifications of intimacy. Indeed, his greatest difficulty is in forming intimate and meaningful interpersonal relations.[5]

The gentleman you have just met is the virtual model of the successful American male. Older concepts of masculinity (big biceps, physical courage) seem increasingly obsolete in our technological age. If you are smart enough to build the biggest bomb or fly the fastest plane, you don't even need muscles to be a good soldier.

What you need today for success in almost any field is, well, obsessive-compulsiveness. The obsessive-compulsive gets ahead because he is so careful about details. He knows his figures and facts, and he presents them in a confident manner. He is the *man,* the leader, for a technological age.[6] Our colleges and graduate schools know

[5]Joseph Barnett, MD, "Sex and the Obsessive Compulsive Person," *Medical Aspects of Human Sexuality* (February, 1971), pp. 35–45.

Barnett's conclusions about the connection between obsessive-compulsiveness and success in our society are not merely theoretical, but are based on the work of many investigators. Dr. Harold Lief, for example, has outlined the character traits of the medical student. Perfectionism, rigidity, overconscientiousness and other compulsive traits make up the typical personality profile. Lief points out that these very same characteristics exist in the members of the admissions committee, who select medical students "in their own images."

Investigators at the Mount Sinai School of Medicine have determined that much the same profile applies to engineers and scientists.

[6]And in accordance, the arguments for male supremacy have shifted. Before the technological age we women were kept dependent on the grounds that we were less willing fighters (having less aggression) and less able fighters (having less physical

this, and many of their entrance exams are actually tests for obsessive-compulsiveness, as are some of the personnel tests employers use.

Everyone has problems and limitations. The intelligent obsessive-compulsive male American may be sweet and gentle and in his own way very sincere. He is responsible, and he tries to keep his word, which is certainly important.

---

strength). Now we are kept dependent on the entirely specious ground that our natural endowment makes us less able to master the "technology." For example, in a scholarly monograph entitled "Sex Differences in Mental and Behavioral Traits" which was written by Joseph E. Garai and Amram Scheinfeld and published in the very prestigious *Genetic Psychology Monographs* as recently as May, 1968, the authors first acknowledge, more or less in passing, that the male is "biologically defective" compared to the female:

"From conception on, the male organism is more vulnerable to physiological and psychological stress, disease, and unfavorable environmental conditions than the female organism. Prenatal death rates and death rates throughout the life span are higher for males from almost all causes. Males are also more prone to suffer from so-called 'sex-linked' conditions resulting from deficiencies in the x-chromosome, such as hemophilia, color blindness, and blindness. The greater incidence of speech defects and hardness of hearing, infantile autism, the prevalence of 'idiots savants,' and mental defectiveness debilitate far more males than females throughout life." (p. 249)

But then, in comparing male and female talent, Garai and Scheinfeld go on to make this sexist statement:

"From early childhood on, girls are ahead of boys in manual dexterity, characterized by swift hand and wrist movements. Their greater manual skills enable them to perform manipulative tasks in industry better and more efficiently than men. It has led to their assignment to assembly line work and similar operations, and promises success in occupations requiring manual dexterity, such as sewing, knitting, dental laboratory work. . . ." (p. 254, *op. cit.*)

I do not know Mr. Garai but I do know Mr. Scheinfeld, and he is a kindly, humanistic gentleman, as well as a careful scholar, who, I believe, would never consciously set out to keep an oppressed group "in place." Yet, he suggests—without thinking, I am sure—that the greater manual dexterity of females makes them fit for "dental laboratory work," as well as sewing and knitting. It doesn't occur to him or to most of the industrial psychologists who rely on such studies, that this marvelous manual dexterity might fit women more than men for dentistry itself which is a high-paying and prestigious profession.

There are worse types to live with—the playboy, for example.

However, the obsessive-compulsive is not very likely to be what Martin Buber calls a "true" lover. For, to continue Dr. Barnett's observations:

> the sexual life and difficulties of the obsessive-compulsive person include a range of behaviors such as the mechanization of sex, impotence, premature ejaculation, retarded orgasm, and compulsive genital activities. These sexual difficulties are inseparable from his personality problems and his problems in relating to people. . . .
>
> His dependent cravings, his infantile narcissism, his anger and power needs—human feelings that every adult must be aware of in order to outgrow them—to the obsessional verify his fears of his unacceptability, exemplify his emotional vulnerability, and intensify his sense of shame and his fears of exposure.
>
> . . . *A solution often used by the obsessional is to separate sexual and emotional needs, and to employ guards against feeling or expressing his emotions while he pursues a largely ritualized and stereotyped sexual behavior pattern that can safely be adapted to an intimate situation.*
>
> *His sexual performance is a mechanized one, that is, competent, stereotyped, unspontaneous, and unimaginative. Due to the inhibition and restriction of action he uses to minimize the risks of shame and self-exposure, it fails precisely because it is so mechanical and so irrelevant to the needs and feelings of the situation of intimacy. Unaware of his impact on his partner, he cannot understand her responses to him and is confused about any dissatisfaction she may express about his performance. His innocence extends even into being in the dark about his own intentions, and he seems forever bemused about the obvious gulf between his stated intent and the negative effect he seems to have on others.* [Italics mine]

Certain very sad little marriage studies have appeared

from time to time in the past decade, especially from the University of Pennsylvania. For example, Dr. William Kephart asked 1,000 college students, "Would you marry a person you did not love if he had all the other qualities you desired?" Most of the men said no. Most of the women said maybe. One woman explained, "If a boy had all the other qualities I desired and I was not in love with him—well, I think I could talk myself into falling in love." Kephart concludes that girls are practical in their choice of a mate, while boys feel freer to follow their fancy.[7] Even an age difference, in the "wrong" direction, inhibits a man less than a woman. Only one-third of the women had ever been in love with a younger man, while two-thirds of the men had loved an older woman.

The Kephart study and others reveal that American girls are trained to approach marriage with an eminently sober turn of mind. College men marry entirely for love, without any "practical" considerations at all. College women cannot afford the luxury of genuinely free choice because, according to the studies, they *know* that their status in life will depend almost entirely on their husband's

---

[7]Writing in a recent issue of *Social Problems* (Spring, 1971, p. 551), Rose Laub Coser and Gerald Rokoff summed up the messages that go out to young people like this: "In modern American society, men are to get occupational status, and women are to get men who will get such status."

And, in an article entitled "Conjectures of the Female Culture Question," in the August, 1971, issue of the *Journal of Marriage and the Family,* Ann Battle-Sister observes: "Adolescent female cliques train members for service. Encouraged by teachers and parents, cliques stamp each girl with the marks of subordinance. The rules of such groups are rigid, and disobedience can mean ostracisim. Under community tutelage, each girl ensures her peers' compliance, like a concentration-camp *capo*. Then, welded together by common standards, all contend for boys. *The most prestigious catch is the boy who can reward subservience most highly.*" (p. 415) [Italics mine.]

Perhaps Gore Vidal summed it all up most incisively in the *New York Review of Books* (July 22, 1971, p. 10): "Most men buy their wives, though neither party would admit to the nature of the transaction, preferring such euphemisms as Marvin is a good provider and Marion is built."

status. Perhaps a certain carpenter or manqué poet is warm, congenial, intelligent and sexy. The typical (educated) young woman hardly allows herself to take such a fellow seriously, because chances are, he will not be able to support her comfortably or buy orthodontia for their children.

Thus, the obsessive-compulsive male, who is generally not a satisfactory lover, but who *is* a promising husband (financially), has been carrying off the fariest maidens, more often than not.

But from now on, thanks to the feminists, the status and security of a family will not depend on the husband exclusively. As women start to think of themselves in new ways, as competent persons who can look after themselves financially, they will become freer to marry for love.

In two-income families women will be freer to select men who are more spontaneous and less ambitious, and the sexual content of their marriages will probably improve.

In short, the economic liberation of women will probably make for better sex, for all. (For a male sociologist's unsentimental view of the current situation, see footnote 4 in the introduction of this book.)

Furthermore, our predominant obsessive-compulsive male will be virtually forced to go to the mat with himself sexually *and change,* however painful such a process may be. Up until now he has been able to attract desirable women, simply because he is successful, and women are economically and socially dependent.[8] In the future, he

[8]Perhaps Freud and other observers confused "dependency" with passivity and masochism. As Maccoby says: "What human beings did at every moment, in every setting, used to be primarily a function of what sex they were . . . for almost all their adult lives women were involved in caring for young children, and were limited in the kinds of other activities they could engage in while doing so. They were necessarily dependent upon men for protection and economic support. But," she goes on, "this is no longer true. To paraphrase a bit of terminology from clinical psychology, our 'sex-role free ego space' is expanding. Our analysis of sex differences

will not have this advantage. As he is forced to become less rigid sexually, perhaps he will also become less rigid on his job. Our society might benefit in many ways.[9]

If obsessive-compulsives are rarely "true lovers," what men are? What human qualities make intimacy possible?

Freud and the Freudians view sex as a biological urge, an irrational instinctive force which is quite independent of relationships. Existentialist psychologists and philosophers hold a rather different view. To them sex is—first and foremost—a profound expression of one's relationship to the self and others.

The sexual history of woman indicates that, for her, at least, the existentialist view is more applicable. If sex were a blind force, existing quite outside relationships, how then could female sexuality have been stamped out in so many places and cultures?

Anyone who has enjoyed sex at its finest will recognize that it can be, and is, an almost mystical experience of re-

---

has led us to the conclusion that women and girls are just as likely as boys and men to be energetic, independent and exploratory, and that boys are just as capable as girls of close attachment to other human beings. Therefore we believe that the inherent differences between the sexes place few constraints upon the development of those portions of our personalities that are simply human rather than male or female." (From paper entitled "Sex Differences and Their Implications for Sex Roles," by Eleanor Maccoby and Carol Nagy Jacklin, delivered at 1971 American Psychological Association meeting).

[9]Why are men in positions of authority so resistant to giving women an economic break? Most of them are husbands, and it would be in the interest of their joint family income if their wives could at least get equal pay for equal work. (Considering the large percentage of married women who are actually in the labor force today—or will be when their children are older—bachelors are the only group to profit financially from unequal pay for equal work.) We must consider the possibility that our patriarchs, our government and business and professional leaders, must sense, on some level that if their wives could earn a fair wage for their labors, many might choose to stop being their wives. These men will have to change in some drastic ways if they wish to retain their mating advantages. In the long run, the change should be good for them, but at present they are probably scared.

newal, where body and soul seem to be perfectly integrated, existence is given meaning and immortality is somehow affirmed. Needless to say, *all* sexual experiences are not of this caliber, not for any couple, however close and loving. *But* once an individual has experienced transcendent sex, even once, it seems to change her (or him) for a lifetime, making her (or him) more spontaneous, more open, more confident, more loving, more purposeful and more peaceful. Naturally enough, the desire to repeat such an experience becomes very strong. Many "promiscuous" persons are idealists in drag (lambs in wolves' clothing?) who are searching—futilely, as a rule—for a replay of some transcendent sexual experience they once enjoyed.

All the women we interviewed who had ever had transcendent sex expressed their agreement (in their own words of course) with the philosophies of Martin Buber, Viktor Frankl and other existentialists; in peak moments, one lover enters fully into the heart and understanding of the other, affirming him as the particular person he is, saying yes to him.

But this must be a two-way process. When monologue masquerades as dialogue, when we try to appear what we are not, or when we treat the other as an "it," we are not true lovers. We deceive and are deceived, and sex becomes, at best, a rather enjoyable indoor sport, at worst, a travesty and an evil.

When female sexuality is stamped out, nobody has good sex, for the act can hardly be transcendent for one partner unless it is transcendent for both.

As Buber observes in his (unfortunately titled) *Between Man and Man:*[10]

> Many years I have wandered through the land of men, and have not yet reached an end of studying the varieties of the "erotic man." . . . There a lover stamps around and is in love only with his passion. There one is wearing

[10]Martin Buber, *Between Man and Man* (New York, Macmillan, 1948), pp. 29–30.

his differentiated feelings like medal-ribbons. There one is enjoying the adventures of his own fascinating effect. There one is gazing enraptured at the spectacle of his own supposed surrender. There one is collecting excitement. There one is displaying his "power." There one is preening himself with borrowed vitality. There one is delighting to exist simultaneously as himself and as an idol very unlike himself. There one is warming himself at the blaze of what has fallen to his lot. There one is experimenting. And so on and on—all the manifold monologists with their mirrors, in the apartment of the most intimate dialogue! . . . They are all beating the air.

In any profound and creative sexual relationship, one meets one's partner in his "real otherness" and affirms him as the particular person he is. Sex cannot be much good if it is founded on playacting, exploitation, ego tripping or insincerity. (Awareness of the other has certain limits, of course, especially as orgasm approaches and occurs. Franz Alexander suggested that many women have poor sex experiences because they are too worried over the impression they are making, too aware of the other in the *wrong* sort of way. The existentialists would answer that individuals with this sort of inhibition are too hung up on themselves, not the other, and are tripping over their own self-images and egos.)

Does good sex occur only within the framework of a lifelong commitment? Erich Fromm, among other profound and convincing modern thinkers, has argued that this may be so. Fromm seems to believe that there must be a durable and dependable contract between two persons before good sex even becomes possible. And Buber, defending marriage, has stated that there is scarcely a substitute for it, since "otherness" is many-faced, and it is difficult for one lover to comprehend all the complexity of the other—his different ways of thinking and feeling, his unique convictions and attitudes—in any other framework.

And yet the experience of the women we surveyed did not bear this out. Yes, a certain level of trust and intimacy was necessary for all but a few before a great sexual episode could occur. But many of their most significant experiences had taken place outside marriage. Indeed, a large percentage of the happiest wives had chosen their husbands *because* premarital sex with them had been so successful.

"I am not you, but I accept you as you are." Let us assume that "little marriages" are possible and do, in fact, occur. By a "little marriage" I mean a truly intimate and nonexploitive sex relationship, which does not necessarily last for a lifetime or rest on legal contracts.

As women come into their own sexually and economically, good marriages will undoubtedly get better, while bad marriages will more readily dissolve. A happy forty-one-year-old woman who participated in our survey told us:

There is no sex as good as the sex in a good marriage, and no sex as bad as the sex in a bad marriage. Once my husband and I were so in love—our daughter was conceived in great love—but then we hurt each other. It was just little things, but the mistrust grew and sprouted, and we couldn't be spontaneous with each other. For a while I devoured marriage manuals and advice columns, but they were totally useless. Mostly they told me to persevere, and I couldn't. Persevering isn't what sex is about. I couldn't be free and spontaneous because I couldn't trust him and I couldn't let myself go. Perhaps I sound very selfish, and I don't think I am. At one point early in our marriage he had a major operation and consequently was very moody and difficult for months. I understood, and was tender, and I didn't even think of being unfaithful even though I need sex and we couldn't have it in all that time. You can do without sex, I have found if, when you have it, everything is open and loving and right.

But later on I was unfaithful. The sex had long since

soured and turned to acrimony and heartbreak. We nee-
dled each other constantly. We were both so withdrawn
and despondent. For ten years we were mechanical
players in a loveless marriage. What were we afraid of?
Our daughter's happiness? That's ridiculous. She wasn't
happy. She cried herself to sleep after our fights.

This woman had no need to hang onto her empty marriage for fear that she or her daughter would starve. She
accepts no alimony from her husband, and only minimal
child support. (He pays the school tuition because he
wanted to; she was willing to take *all* responsibility and
could have done so.) Furthermore, she lives and works in
a world where little social stigma attaches to being a
woman alone. She is probably a model for the future. As
increasing numbers of women gain social and economic
independence, they will, of course, be freer to examine the
content of their marriages and to leave if the marriages are
loveless or oppressive.

In the long run, although divorces may also increase,
the sexual liberation of women can only increase the
number of *authentic* relationships, for a woman who is
frightened, economically dependent, or otherwise anxious
about her own survival is hardly in a position to reveal her
true sexual self to a husband or lover. Or even if she is not
frightened, the burden of too many preconceived ideas
about "appropriate" feminine sex behavior can create almost insurmountable roadblocks to spontaneity and genuine passion. When we sweep away the male-created myths
about the passive or even masochistic nature of feminine
sexuality, we encounter the commonsense *fact* that great
sex is far more likely to occur when two healthy, joyful
and equally enthusiastic persons (neither of whom has any
extraneous motives) come together.[11]

[11] But if psychologist Judith Bardwick is correct, large numbers of
today's sexually active young women still approach sex with neither
autonomy nor joy. After testing and interviewing more than 200
women (many of them students at the University of Michigan), Dr.

The sexual suppression of women has been almost as destructive to men as to women themselves, for a peak sexual experience can occur only between two partners who accept each other as they really are.

Students of sexual pathology tell us that there are all kinds of common perversions which prevent a lover from accepting a partner as she really is and create a singular need for playacting. (Take, for example, the shoe fetishist, who is aroused only by women in high heels or, more precisely, by the shoes themselves.) These fetishes are extremely rare in women. If a woman wants to consort with men who have them, that is her taste and her privilege, but I, for one, resent the "swinging" modern marriage manuals which imply that such fetishes are all in good fun, and nothing to worry about. I would not feel sanguine if my daughter became sexually involved with a man who fancied her shoe, rather than her.

Bardwick reported, "Few of the women whom we studied had reached orgasm, for instance. Some admitted as much; others described the experience as 'pleasant' (which means no orgasm), or said, 'I don't know' (which also means no orgasm). When we asked them why they made love very few replied that sex was a pleasure for themselves. More frequently they said they did it 'because it makes him happy. . . .' Notice that it is the male who defines the situation; sex is important because the male says it is. In previous generations a woman abstained from sex because she feared the man would end the relationship if she did so. Now a woman may give in because she fears the man will end the relationship if she refuses to do so. The behavior is different but the motives are the same."

The psychological tests of many of these women were "shocking," Dr. Bardwick adds. "Some of the major themes (in their TAT stories) were fear of abandonment; resentment of being used as sex objects; mistrust of men and hostility toward them; guilt about sex and a need to expiate it; prostitution anxieties, and feelings of degradation." (From the article "Her Body, the Battleground," *Psychology Today* [February, 1972].)

WILL YOU HAVE A HAPPY MARRIAGE?

We know that it is difficult for people with certain kinds of neuroses to work out a good life together. Perhaps an inherent masochism leads waifs and losers to find one another. When, for example, gamblers and alcoholics "reform," their spouses are more likely than not to start developing symptoms.[12]

On the other hand, our marriage laws, customs and beliefs all contribute to an extraordinarily sexist—and vapid—view of happy marriage. The woman without identity and—perhaps above all—without *sexuality* is continually brought forward and pressed on us as the only model of a contented wife and "nurturant" mother.

—Consider our compensation laws. In 1965 a thirty-seven-year-old husband was completely paralyzed from the waist down as the result of an elevator accident. Just recently, the New York Court of Appeals ruled that his wife is entitled to damages for the loss of his sexual companionship. That was legal news because it made New York the twentieth state to recognize that wives have equal sexual rights in a marriage. In thirty remaining states—even today—a husband can recover damages for the loss of his wife's sexual services, but *the reverse is not true.*

Equalitarian marriage is bound to be difficult, if not im-

[12]Coining the phrase "rotating depression," Dr. Leonard Siegel of the Maimonides Medical Center in New York has pointed out that when a chronically depressed wife who has been married to a "well-adjusted" husband gets better, he is apt to plunge into depression a few months later. In Los Angeles, Drs. William Boyd and Darrell Bolen, who have been studying compulsive gamblers, find that when the compulsive gambler is cured, it often marks the end of his marriage, for his wife has so "enjoyed" her martyr role. It is difficult to believe that those of us who choose seriously disturbed husbands or wives are always totally innocent or naïve.

possible, in a society where the laws are all stacked against it:

> . . . The husband can legally force his wife to have sexual intercourse with him against her will, an act which if committed against any other woman would constitute the crime of rape. By definition, a husband cannot be guilty of raping his own wife, for "the crime [of rape] is ordinarily that of forcing intercourse on someone other than the wife of the person accused." Women are well aware of the "right" of the husband to "insist" and the "duty" of the wife to submit to sexual intercourse. The compulsory nature of sex in marriage operates to the advantage of the male, for though the husband theoretically has the duty to have intercourse with his wife, this normally cannot occur against his will. (Both partners are protected in that a marriage can be annulled by either party if the marriage has not been consummated.)

Women believe that we are voluntarily giving our household services, but the courts hold that the husband is legally entitled to his wife's services, and further, that *she cannot be paid for her work*. In *Your Marriage and the Law*, Pilpel and Zavin state: "As part of the rights of consortium, the husband is entitled to the services of his wife. If the wife works outside the home for strangers, she is usually entitled to her own earnings. But domestic services or assistances which she gives her husband are generally considered part of her wifely duties. The wife's services and society are so essential a part of what the law considers the husband is entitled to as part of the marriage that it will not recognize any agreement between spouses which provides that the husband pay for such services or society.

"In a Texas case David promised his wife, Fannie, that he would give her $5,000 if she would stay with him while he lived and continue taking care of the house and farm accounts, selling his butter and doing all the other tasks which she had done since their marriage. After David's death, Fannie sued his estate for the money which had been promised her. The court held that the contract was unenforceable since Fannie had agreed to do nothing which she was not already legally and morally bound to do as David's wife."

The legal responsibilities of a wife are to live in the home established by her husband, to perform the domestic chores (cleaning, cooking, washing, etc.) necessary to help maintain that home, and to care for her husband and children. The husband, in return, is obligated to provide her with basic maintenance which includes "necessities" such as food, clothing, medical care, and a place to live, in accordance with his income. She has no legal right to any part of his cash income, nor any legal voice in spending it. Were he to employ a live-in servant in place of a wife, he would have to pay the servant a salary, provide her with her own room (as opposed to "bed"), food, and the necessary equipment for doing her job. She would get at least one day a week off and probably would be required to do considerably less work than a wife and would not be required to provide sexual service.

Thus, being a wife is a full-time job for which one is not entitled to pay. (Chase Manhattan Bank estimates a woman's over-all work week is 99.6 hours.) Furthermore, the wife is not entitled to freedom of movement. The husband has the right to decide where the family will live. If he decides to move, his wife is obliged to go with him. If she refuses, he can charge her with desertion. This has been upheld by the courts even in cases where the wife could be required to change her citizenship. In states where desertion is grounds for divorce (47 states plus the District of Columbia), the wife would be the "guilty party" and would therefore be entitled to no monetary settlement.

Leo Kanowitz in *Women and the Law* found that the change in a woman's name upon marriage is not only consistent with social custom; it also appears to be generally required by law. "The probable effects of this unilateral name change upon the relations between the sexes, though subtle in character, are profound. In a very real sense, the loss of a woman's surname represents the destruction of an important part of her personality and its submersion in that of her husband. . . . This name change is consistent with the characterization of coverture as "the old common-law fiction that the husband and wife are one . . . [which] has worked out in reality to mean that the one is the husband."[13]

—Consider our distorted view of "the good women who built this country": our Puritan great-great-grandmothers. These strong, noble women who took marriage and family commitments seriously were far more disciplined about premarital sex than we are, right? Wrong!

Church records in Groton, Connecticut, show that one-third of the babies baptized between 1761 and 1775 were conceived before the marriage of their parents. That is, one-third of *all babies* baptized in the parish, mind you, not one-third of the eldest children. So we can only conclude that in Puritan America, as in Scandinavia today, marriages were usually formalized when pregnancy occurred.

—Consider the oft-repeated statement that modern appliances *(man's* technology again) have made housework a snap. Running a home is not a snap if it's done properly, and although any woman who has ever tried to run one knows this, we have been so brainwashed that some of us willingly parrot this male conclusion. (The point, supposedly, is that the discontents of modern woman stem from the fact that she has too little to do. She has plenty to do, but most of it is boring, unvalued and unpaid.) If your are a housewife, you can advise your husband to stop wondering what you do all day long. Definitive research at the University of Michigan reveals that while the average American bachelor spends only 408 hours on housework annually, the average wife *still spends* 2,053 hours.

[13]Dair L. Gillespie, "Who Has the Power? The Marital Struggle," *Journal of Marriage and the Family,* Vol. 33, No. 3 (August, 1971), pp. 449–50.

—Consider the way that American mothers are usually stereotyped as loving and nurturant—or rejecting. (As if we weren't all a little of each.) Consider the fact that in 1971 the New York *Times* should see fit to lament the current "flight from children" of American women.[14]

The ironic fact is that there is no known primitive society where mothers spend *as much time* with their children as they do in America today. Over a period of many years, researchers at Harvard, Yale and Cornell teamed up to compare a group of New England mothers with mothers in Mexico, the Philippines, Okinawa, India and Africa. These scientists report that in the primitive cultures child care is much less the exclusive responsibility of the mother. In less complex societies the job is shared by father, mother, grandmother, aunt, big sister and women "too old for heavy work" who perform as general baby-sitters.

These investigators are now trying to resolve whether "mothers become emotionally unstable when forced to spend long periods of time without help in caring for their children." There is some evidence of this. Only the Gusii of Africa spend nearly as much time with their children as the American mothers. And both Gusii and Americans are characterized by the researchers as "variable and unpredictable" in their handling of youngsters.

Consider the sly way in which our men put us down by contrasting us to the "real" women of Europe. These "real" women, we are assured, are far less competitive and more loving. (If *our* husbands don't make satisfactory love, it's because, in contrast with the women of Europe, we don't know how to make a man feel like a man.) The producers of television talk shows just love to trot out European actresses (and other intellectuals) to assure us that we lack something.

Well, what is it we lack? A woman sociologist decided to find out and reported her conclusions in the *Journal of Marriage and the Family,* where they made no impact

[14]Editorial by William Shannon, New York *Times,* July 15, 1971.

whatsoever. What she did was compare a sampling of Detroit married women with similar women living in Paris and Athens.

The Detroit woman likes to be with her husband. Once his income reaches $7,000 a year, she often complains that he works too hard and that he does not spend enough time with her. She would do without material possessions if she could see him more. The Parisian woman, in contrast, loves money. The higher her husband's income, the happier she is. French women in modest circumstances say that they have bad marriages, while rich women say that they have good marriages. Rich French women never complain that they don't see enough of their hard-working husbands.

The Detroit woman wants a 50-50 marriage, according to the *Journal of Marriage and the Family*. She is most content when she and her husband *share* important decisions. The woman of Athens wants to be boss. Only 4 percent of Athenian women still allow their husbands to dominate. Far more frequently, the woman rules the roost. She —and she alone—decides how money is spent and how children are reared. At the same time, she is discontented while her children are little, because she cannot get out much at night. The woman of Athens measures her "marital satisfaction" in terms of how much time she can spend out of the house.

Who is the "head of your household"? The Census Bureau and indeed most sociologists and pollsters assume that if you are a married woman, your husband is.

Two male sociologists—Ernest Barth of the University of Washington and Walter Watson of the University of Alberta—have finally raised their voices in protest. They point out that the average working wife contributes about one-third of her family's income. The extra money she earns and the social contacts she makes may definitely upgrade the status of her family. (No, her job *isn't* just "busywork" or a way of getting mother out of the house before she beats her brains out against the four walls of it. She is contributing, to her family, as well as to society.)

What is more, *some* wives have higher-status occupations than their husbands. Many "blue-collar men" are married to "white-collar women," especially secretaries, nurses and schoolteachers. In such marriages, the wife determines the actual social status of the family, and the family usually leads a "white-collar life." And yet when the census taker comes around. . . .

American customs make it very difficult for a *wife* to view herself (comfortably) as an independent, competent and fully sexual person.[15] This, I suppose, explains why many spinsters are more sound emotionally than married women, while the same is far from being true of bachelors vis-à-vis married men.[16]

However, to my mind the most offensive antiwoman propaganda of all is probably contained in the pages of the marriage and family texts that young women (and men, of course) are forced to read in college.

These texts purport to tell you how to have a happy marriage, but without so much as a blush or a by-your-

[15]The brainwashing starts almost in the cradle, according to a recent analysis of award-winning children's literature. Sociologist Lenore Weitzman, who studied several hundred children's picture and story books, found that the girls and women in these books were almost always depicted in roles and situations which were secondary to those of the boys and men. Women were characterized as being passive stay-at-homes, while men were described as active achievement-oriented persons.

Children, during their most impressionable early days, are thus strongly influenced to believe that men and women are not equal. *Behavior Today*, Vol. 2, No. 35 (August 30, 1971).

[16]A recent study of aging people in Kansas City provides, I think, a most eloquent testimonial to the effects of marriage, as it has been constituted, on women. The wives over sixty-five who were not widowed *envied* the widows for their freedom, independence and fun in life. They were inclined to feel that they were unfortunate, in contrast with the widows, in being stuck in the house at the beck and call of a usually temperamental and demanding retired husband. The widows, they pointed out, were free to socialize, have fun and travel at their will.

leave they continually use "happy" and "durable" interchangeably.

According to these, conventional people have more durable marriages.[17] Your outlook is favorable if you had a happy childhood, a good education, were not too young when you married, knew your husband for at least a year, had a formal engagement, go to church, like sports and music, met your husband in a "respectable" place, come from similar backgrounds, had a religious wedding, belong to one or more organizations and *did not engage in premarital sex.*[18]

In short, if you are a shiny-faced wholesome couple, just like the pictures in the bridal magazines, your marriage has an excellent chance to last. The boy and girl who not only attend the same church, but actually met there, have all the odds on their side.

The trouble with all these concepts is that there is too much subtler research which simply invalidates them. They apply only in a world where the woman is a zero, a faceless-and-formless wife-mother-servant with no needs and striving and identity of her own—that she dares express.[19] And yet these are the naïve and outdated marriage

[17]Gerald Albert, "A Handbook to Awareness Among Non-Professionals of Psychological and Related Factors in the Determination of Marital Success and Failure" (Ann Arbor, University Microfilms, Inc., 1965).

[18]Many high school sex education courses are also constituted for the purpose of encouraging premarital chastity in females, according to Dr. Harry Martin, a University of Texas sociologist. Dr. Martin has been observing sex educators, and, as he told the American Psychiatric Association, he is "not impressed. . . . They have no right or basis to tell teenagers that their old morality of total chastity is better than their new morality of freer sexual expression, emphasizing love and fidelity."

[19]Marriage prediction tests make little effort to distinguish between quantity (in years endured) and quality. Judith Long Laws of Cornell University has pointed out that women who have few other "options" are probably most hesitant to admit that their marriage is a disaster. (See footnote, page 256.) The woman who feels like a person in her own right and who *has* other options can afford to be more critical and can leave if she is dissatisfied.

concepts that are still being foisted on our high school and college students.

Women who were premaritally chaste have "better" marriages. How can that be when we know from Kinsey and other good sources that women who were premaritally chaste have a difficult time reaching orgasm within marriage? What *kind* of marriage are these textbooks promoting?[21]

And what kind of motherhood? Psychosomaticists at Stanford studied 156 pregnant women. They found that women who enjoy sex are less anxious during pregnancy. They have fewer fears for themselves and their unborn babies. They enjoy stronger *maternal feelings* and are less depressed. They even have fewer physical complications.

American women are still being asked to perform a nearly impossible turnabout—to eschew sex and sexuality during their premarital years and then, following a ceremony and a contract, to jump in and love it. The illogic, the untenability, of this approach has become so apparent that a distinguished study group of adolescent psychiatrists has finally worked up the courage to comment, *"The union of tender and sexual love in relationships with the marriage partner is difficult to attain without sexual experience and experimentation during the years of late adolescence."*[22]

[20]Paper entitled "Feminist Perspectives on Marital Happiness" presented at the annual meeting of the American Sociological Association, September, 1971.

[21]What kind of marriages indeed? Sex can be fun, but the marriage manuals make it sound like work. Dr. Lionel Lewis, a Buffalo sociologist, has analyzed fifteen popular sex guides and reports that they overemphasize efficiency, scheduling and fear of "job dismissal."

[22]The Group for the Advancement of Psychiatry (GAP), *Normal Adolescence* (New York, Scribner's 1968). The GAP Committee emphasizes that there are no easy answers and that what is right for one young person might be all wrong for a less mature one of the same age. By eighteen or nineteen, this study group concludes, most persons are probably mature enough to behave responsibly toward their partners and to manage birth control. Some are ready a good

Today, according to Dr. Ira Reiss, it is, by and large, the best educated and most intelligent young women who do not deem it important to maintain their virginity until marriage.[23] Nonetheless, sex-is-for-men values are still being pressed on young women, from many quarters.[24] Even if these women do not observe them, their very prevalence is apt to make them feel needlessly guilty. As we shall see in the next chapter, guilt over personal morality is usually a useless and destructive emotion.

In a chilling analysis—unlike any that has hitherto been attempted—Carol Ehrlich, of the University of Iowa, explores woman's place in the currently influential marriage and family texts.[25] All these books were written by estab-

---

deal sooner, and some not until later. The person herself is usually the best judge.

[23]In a national study Reiss found that girls with "permissive" attitudes are apt to be the daughters of professionals—doctors, lawyers, teachers and even clergymen. They are likely to come from cities outside the South, with populations over 100,000. They may be Protestant, Catholic or Jewish but are not very orthodox and are unlikely to attend religious services more than once a month. The parents of these young women are relatively liberal also, especially if they are under forty-five.

Among college students, Reiss found great variation from one campus to another. At a well-known college in New York State—where most of the students do come from big-city professional families—80 percent felt that premarital sexual intercourse was perfectly acceptable. At a Midwestern university—where many more of the students came from small towns and from lower-status families—only 34 percent hold this belief.

[24]The popular lovelorn columnists tend to be highly negative toward premarital sex. One said to Patrick M. McGrady, Jr., "If a girl has to write to *me* to ask whether she should sleep with her boyfriend, I guess she's not ready and she wants to be told 'no.' " The columnist could be right.

[25]Carol Ehrlich, "The Male Sociologist's Burden: The Place of Women in Marriage and Family Texts," *Journal of Marriage and the Family,* Vol. 33, No. 3, August, 1971, pp. 421–30.

The six tests examined in Ms. Ehrlich's article are:

1. William J. Goode, *The Family* (Englewood Cliffs, New Jersey, Prentice-Hall, 1964).

2. William M. Kephart, *The Family, Society, and the Individual* (Boston, Houghton Mifflin, 1961, 1966).

lished scholars, are recent, or recently revised, and are considered among the most sophisticated in their field.

The most widely read author (Kephart) makes a great issue of woman's sexual inferiority. He sounds almost Victorian in stating, "It would be an exceptional case, indeed, where a woman assessed a man in terms of his potentiality as a sex partner. . . ." Kephart goes on to warn that if wives ever take the sexual initiative, they are almost doomed to fail, for such unseemly behavior might have "adverse repercussions" on their husbands. Kephart expresses regret that polygyny has passed out of fashion, since males have a natural desire for both variety and exclusivity. In addition, polygyny "permits superior males to contribute to a larger share of the population."

Another author, Kenkel, cites Freud's theory of penis envy as if it were established and irrevocable fact. Frigid women are those who have "a desire to emulate the male and to assume the masculine role." If a girl does not resolve her penis envy, she may attempt, "through her choice of occupation . . . to be as much like a man as she possibly can," and she will never find sexual fulfillment. If wives must work, they are well advised to continue thinking of themselves as wives, *not* co-breadwinners, because "the phenomenon of the successful career woman cast aside by her husband for a less able but more dependent woman is far from unknown."

Saxton, a third author, sheds some crocodile tears for the lot of modern American housewives. But then he warns, if husbands fail to provide income and material security, and wives fail to fulfill their nurturant and household duties, if through some awful circumstance these tra-

3. William F. Kenkel, *The Family in Perspective* (New York, Appleton-Century-Crofts, 1960, 1966).

4. J. Richard Udry, *The Social Context of Marriage* (Philadelphia, Lippincott, 1966).

5. Gerald R. Leslie, *The Family in Social Context* (New York, Oxford, 1967).

6. Lloyd Saxton, *The Individual, Marriage, and the Family* (Belmont, California, Wadsworth, 1968).

ditional roles should be shared or switched, the family is "disrupted" and the children will become "disturbed."

All told, as Ehrlich concludes, *the female as viewed by the American male sociologist belongs at home, ministering to her husband and children and forswearing all other interests. . . . Areas where major questions remain unanswered (and sometimes unasked) are treated by all these influential writers as if folklore were fact. . . . With respect to the female, all the textbooks are, primarily, collections of folklore and myth, not compilations of social science.*

Let us hope that we are entering an era where all women (and men, too) will be freer to find themselves in love and marriage. Those who wish to remain single will do so, without social pressure.[26] Those who wish to experiment with communal living and other new life-styles will be equally free. The sexual morality of an individual is and should be a private matter, for it has no bearing on the general welfare if she conducts herself responsibly.

As for the question of whether you will find a man with whom you'll want to stay for a lifetime. . . . Forget your sociological scales and your marriage prediction texts, for they speak only of averages and do not in any way take the intimate measure of a relationship.

Emily Dickinson said it all when she wrote: "The soul selects her own society."

[26] A sad observation was made recently by Dr. Robert Berns, Student Health Service psychiatrist at UCLA. According to Berns, the majority of middle-class parents still seem to believe, incorrectly, that there is a contradiction between "femininity" and academic success. Berns urges parents, especially fathers, to take a more active interest in the academic progress of their daughters. "Some of our healthiest and most attractive honor students develop doubts about themselves—they even think they need psychiatric help— just because their families, and many of their professors as well, are indifferent or worse." While putting pressure on their sons toward "success," parents subtly pressure their daughters against it and toward marriage. The independent, academically gifted woman is still treated as a "second-class citizen," according to Berns.

CHAPTER SEVEN

A SKEPTICAL GUIDE TO VD
AND CONTRACEPTION

A divorced man of my acquaintance is somewhat disappointed in the outcome of his vasectomy. He had hoped and expected that it would increase his popularity, but it didn't. "I've stopped telling women about it," Steve confided recently. "It makes some of them think that I'm really odd. Even when they say they believe me, they go right on taking their pills or using their diaphragm. The surgeon who did it should have provided me with a tattoo saying, 'This model inoperable.'"

At first I suspected Steve might be exaggerating, but as I've had more and more experience rapping with young women about birth control, I'm starting to think not. Men, some men, are willing to share the responsibility, and when they are, a great many women decline to trust them.

I remember one young woman who commented—at a National Student Association Convention—that she didn't see much point in pouring money into male contraceptive research. "A guy might tell you he's taking a pill or something, but what proof would you have?"

What proof! "Why on earth," I replied to the student,

"would you want to have sex with a man you don't even trust that far?"

Today, it seems to me, a great many young women are merely swapping the old-fashioned sex-is-for-men sexual masochism of their mothers for a new type of self-punitive behavior. They are trying to copy the *worst* sexual behaviors of men, the promiscuity and exploitation. Sometimes they bed down with people who hardly attract them at all, merely to add another conquest to the "list." (Indeed, I know of one high school sorority where the girls are actually keeping such lists. The "champ," a pretty seventeen-year-old, has 121 entries on it.[1]

Fortunately, most young women who engage in such behavior outgrow it as time passes. They recognize that it is self-destructive.

A psychiatrist who has worked extensively with such young women tells me that many of them emerge from this stage remarkably undamaged psychologically. That is to say, they seem quite capable of settling down and enjoying more wholesome relations with men whom they care about.

[1] This illustrates how social pressure can be a powerful prod toward self-damaging promiscuity. However, social pressure in itself is rarely a complete and sufficient explanation. Most of our important decisions are probably "over-determined." They are influenced by current social factors *and* by past experiences. Like a river which is fed by diverse tributaries, past and present images all seem to join in the same direction.

Many young women today are eager to rid themselves of the sexual masochism and passivity of their mothers. So they set out to act differently. However, it is quite likely that if they love and admire their mothers at all, they feel guilty about going off in an entirely new direction. Hence, they may feel a need to punish themselves, and this could help explain why, instead of sexual freedom and autonomy, they are finding their ways into new kinds of traps.

It has long been argued that it takes "three generations" to make a natural gentleman. Perhaps by the same token, it will take three generations to make a naturally liberated woman. Some of the girls who discover sexual freedom are a bit like *nouveau riche* males, at first, expending their wealth unwisely and with very questionable taste.

Physical damage is quite another question. Dangerous birth control methods, back room abortions and, above all, VD often lead to permanent sterility or other serious problems.

VD

In 1964, I wrote an article for a women's magazine advising mothers not to rear their daughters on "scare talk about VD." I recant. Young women have plenty of reason to be frightened of it, as I learned, recently, when we interviewed a group of students at a highly prestigious Eastern women's college.[2]

VD has reached epidemic proportions in the United States and is now thought to be the second most common infectious illness, after the cold. In 1969 there were more than 600,000 cases of gonorrhea reported, an increase of 130 percent over the reported cases of 1963.[3]

But, you may ask, isn't VD easy to clear up with penicillin or other drugs? So what if you get it? You have a shot, and it goes away.

The answer is yes; in its early stages VD usually *is* easy to cure. (Uusually, but not always. Some strains of VD are developing considerable resistance to the antibiotics used for treatment.) But nature has played a nasty little trick on women, for, unlike men, we *cannot usually tell that we have it in the early stages.* Our symptoms are not

[2]The interviews were conducted by Carolyn Kone. She found that "VD information" was high on the list of sex questions these very "advantaged" and intellectual young women wanted answered. Several classmates had been infected with gonorrhea and had not suspected it until their conditions became acute.

[3]And reported cases are just the tip of the iceberg, for most physicians still hesitate to "embarrass" their private patients by notifying local health departments. It is estimated that more than 4,000,000 Americans contracted VD last year, and that at least half a million have undiagnosed cases of syphilis.

obvious most of the time, and the conventional laboratory tests for it are not reliable either.[4]

Apparently a new and more complicated laboratory procedure has improved the chances for accurate physician diagnosis of gonorrhea in females. But going to a doctor is the second stage, so the question remains, how will a woman know that she's been exposed to VD in the first place? She won't unless her lover or "contact"—whose early symptoms are much more obvious than hers—tells her that she has been exposed. She can protect herself only if, like one young acquaintance of mine, she has the courage to carry condoms in her purse. Whenever Rachel has sex with a stranger, she whips one out and orders, "Wear it."

Which brings us back to the college student mentioned earlier, who would not trust her lovers to use birth control.

[4]On October 4, 1971, Dr. Hollis S. Ingraham, the commissioner of health for the State of New York, sent a letter to New York physicians which contained the following statements:

"Effective immediately, the New York State Department of Health will provide both transport media for the culture of gonorrhea and laboratory processing of the specimens without charge to either physicians or patients. *As you are aware, gonorrhea in the male is usually symptomatic and easy to diagnose by gram stain. In women, on the other hand, about 80 percent of those infected will have no symptoms whatsoever. Examination of gram stained smear is not a reliable diagnostic tool in women and we must rely on culture to make the diagnosis.*

"The recent introduction of 'Transgrow' medium has made it possible for physicians to take gonorrhea cultures in their offices and mail the specimens to the laboratory. *This was not previously possible due to the fragility of the organism.* Although the organism will grow in Transgrow at room temperature, yield is increased by incubation for 16–18 hours at 35–37 degrees Centigrade before mailing. Our laboratory is working in conjunction with others to improve 'Transgrow' and develop new media which will have an even higher yield.

". . . I encourage you to take routine screening cultures for gonorrhea from sexually active female patients, especially those between the ages of 15 and 29. This group includes 90 percent of infected women. Specific details regarding how to take the culture and how to inoculate the medium are enclosed. . . ."

She can protect herself against pregnancy, but not against VD, so she still risks serious bodily damage by consorting with untrustworthy men.

Syphilis is transmitted by having sex relations with an infectious person, of the same or opposite sex, and occasionally by kissing *if* the infected person has the sores of syphilis on his lips or in his mouth.

It has three stages. In the first or primary stage a sore appears at the point of contact ten to ninety days after infection. It can be small enough to go unnoticed. It does not hurt or itch and disappears even without treatment. The victim does not have any other side effects.

Three to six weeks later the symptoms of the secondary stage begin. These symptoms are confusing, and for this reason syphilis is called "the great imitator." Sore throat and rashes on various parts of the body, particularly the palms of the hands, may occur. Hair may fall out in patches, and there is an overall sick feeling, as with flu or perhaps mononucleosis.

Stage three lasts for many years. During this time syphilis is no longer infectious and, initially, the victim may feel perfectly well. However, the syphilis spirochetes are quietly attacking many vital organs of the body, such as the brain, eyes, bones, kidney and liver. Ultimately, the victim may be permanently crippled.

Gonorrhea, which is vastly less serious than syphilis, is also more common. As with syphilis, where the early sore is all too apt to be hidden within the body of a woman, the initial symptoms are very likely to go unnoticed.

As with the syphilis spirochete, the gonococcus is transmitted through sexual relations. A few days after infection, a man usually experiences a burning sensation while urinating and a pus discharge from the penis. Chances are that these symptoms will be alarming enough so that he will want to see a doctor.

But women have so many vaginal discharges anyway that their early symptoms, which tend to be more subdued, are very likely to pass unnoticed. There may be some discomfort during urination, but a majority of infected females do not feel or notice anything unusual.

The complications of gonorrhea are not as severe as the complications of syphilis, but they too are tragic. If gonorrhea advances untreated, sterility is a frequent outcome. Scar tissue forms in the reproductive organs and makes conception impossible. This can happen to men, as well as women. In women the scar tissue forms in the fallopian tubes; in men it forms in the tubules of the testicles. But it doesn't seem to happen to men as often, since most men know they have been infected early on and seek treatment in time. If gonorrhea is allowed to reach advanced stages, it can also be excruciatingly painful.

Should a woman infected with VD become pregnant, the outcome may be dreadful for her baby. If a mother has untreated syphilis, her baby may be born deformed or dead, which is why forty-three states require that pregnant women take a blood test for syphilis. Untreated gonorrhea can cause blindness in babies, who come in contact with the infection as they exit from the mother's body during childbirth. This used to be a common problem, but public health measures have greatly reduced it. In most hospitals a newborn's eyes are routinely treated with a preventative such as silver nitrate or antibiotic drops.

To put it all bluntly, the woman who consorts promiscuously with men she does not know—and who cannot be relied on to tell her if they are VD carriers—runs a grave risk of making herself sterile and a smaller but nonetheless real risk of getting the horrible degenerative diseases associated with advanced syphilis. Furthermore, she endangers the health of any future wanted children that she might be lucky enough to conceive. Men can usually get VD treatment in time to prevent serious damage; women cannot, unless the men who gave them the illness can be trusted to warn them.

Thus, in one sense, at least, the widsom of our grandmothers still holds. Despite modern birth control and abortion reform, the physical risks of promiscuity remain greater for a woman today than for a man.

The typical propaganda against VD which is put out by government and voluntary agencies constitutes yet another dismal example of unconscious male chauvinism. Some of these booklets or films fail to mention at all that it is much harder for women than for men to notice VD in the early stages.[5] Others mention sex differences, but they talk about the woman as "a carrier." Because VD is so hard to detect and diagnose in women, the usual commentary goes: "A woman can be unaware that she is *a carrier* of a venereal disease."[6] Few of these booklets are addressed to the real concerns of self-respecting women—*their* bodies and *their* health.

The fact that a woman with gonorrhea is far more likely than a man to neglect it until *she becomes sterile* doesn't appear to be a significant point to the public-health-minded males who are (sincerely) trying to help curb the spread of VD.

However fastidious, no sexually active woman can be certain of escaping VD, for, as Robert Lugar, an adviser to the Los Angeles County Health Department, likes to observe:

"If you pose this question, 'Where is V.D.?' the answer is: 'Everywhere.' My God, if there's anything in this world today we can't stop it's VD. It's no more possible to restrict the spread of venereal disease than it is to keep the flies in one room of your house.'"[7]

[5]Some of the publications which do not mention sex differences, imply or even state that the only *women* who would risk VD must be prostitutes. Professional prostitutes, presumably, know enough to get regular medical checkups.

[6]The publications that describe women as unwitting carriers seem to assume that the fear of getting a "bad reputation" should be enough to send a teenager scurrying to her doctor. Boys will stay away if rumors get around.

[7]Cokie and Steven V. Roberts "The Venereal Disease Pandemic," *New York Times Magazine,* November 7, 1971, p. 64.

BIRTH CONTROL

The Bible tells us that God said to "Go forth and multiply." Apparently, She meant it. For a healthy young couple, fertility is a good deal more troublesome to curb than most modern birth control propaganda would lead you to believe.

On the other hand, the effective curbing of fertility is far from being an exclusive miracle of modern technology, and our current birth control technologists do not deserve quite the measure of undiluted gratitude that they ask and usually receive.

Historians tell us that Cleopatra had *some* effective method of birth control, probably crocodile dung which is highly spermacidal, if equally unappetizing. They also tell us that during the Middle Ages in Europe, the upper classes were so successful in curbing their fertility that population growth and the encouragement of babies became serious matters of royal concern. It may be that educated men became highly skilled at the practice of withdrawal. No historian or demographer has offered a better explanation, but all agree that few unwanted babies were conceived.

The point about birth control, ancient and modern, is that you don't get something for nothing. There are always certain drawbacks, either inconveniences or medical risks.

The older methods tend to be inconvenient; the newer ones risky. The perfect birth control method is safe, simple, totally reliable, very convenient and completely without risk. It hasn't been invented yet, and what's more, there is little reason to believe that it is about to come down the pike.

A lot of people with good intentions have been feeding you upbeat propaganda about birth control. They are concerned about the population explosion. They are concerned about teen-aged pregnancies and unsavory abortions and unwanted babies. They believe that it's in your interest to "have faith" in birth control, and they believe that you are too stupid or too selfish to use it consistently if you know that there are problems attached. So they lie to you.

They tell you that every method is marvelous, and you have merely to choose. They could better put it—"Every method has drawbacks: which troubles you the least? Which can *you* live with if you want to control your fertility?"

Every experienced woman knows that no birth control method is as safe and simple as proponents make it sound. Diaphragms are a nuisance to put in and take out. IUD's can hurt a lot when they are inserted and make your period heavier. Sterilization, even in men, is often a lot more painful than the propaganda says, and it may leave you feeling depressed and mutilated. Rhythm requires enormous self-discipline. The pill, that great sexual liberator, has more than fifty different side effects, some of them fatal, and the majority of users stop within a few years because of side effects. Condoms diminish sexual pleasure for many people. Foam diminishes sexual pleasure for some and may not be a sufficiently reliable method. Abortion, as an occasional backup, has much to recommend it, but at best it is not a pleasant experience, nor is it entirely safe, even when legal. You surely wouldn't want to have one every month.

The entire birth control situation is not unlike Dorothy Parker's famous discussion of suicide.[8] You almost feel

[8]From *Enough Rope,* by Dorothy Parker (New York, Boni & Liveright, 1926).

> ### Resume
> Razors pain you;
> Rivers are damp;
> Acids stain you;
> And drugs cause cramp.
> Guns aren't lawful;

like saying, "To hell with it all," and that is what many people do, to their regret usually.

On the other hand, people are always hoping for something better, some new miracle. If you have been keeping up with the birth control stories in magazines and newspapers, you know that we have long since been promised:

—A pill for men.
—Reversible sterilization.
—A permanent diaphragm.
—A safe morning-after pill.
—A safe once-a-month pill.

A Jane Brody story in a recent New York *Times* described a reversible vasectomy for men, involving a "tiny valve placed in the sperm duct that can be turned on and off like a faucet."[9] The urologists behind it estimate that the device will be ready for large-scale clinical trials within a few years.

Other stories of just-around-the-corner reversible vasectomies go back a decade or more. It's possible, of course, that sooner or later one of these new birth control wonders actually will prove out. But I'll believe it when I see it. The only thing new and available in mid-twentieth century is the pill.[10]

The pill has been widely promoted as a sexual liberator, almost, indeed, an aphrodisiac. For some women, it is. To *Time*'s Latin-American edition, a woman wrote, "To the pill I can credit harmony, communication, fulfillment, satisfaction, happiness, stability, understanding, acceptance, relaxation, achievement, compatibility, courage, love, peace, and Christ."

Nonetheless, sooner or later most of the women who

Nooses give;
Gas smells awful;
You might as well live.

[9]New York *Times*, October 2, 1971.
[10]The IUD is *not* a new method, as we shall see later. Vasectomy has been used on men since the nineteenth century to prevent those with hereditary defects from fathering children.

take the pill do develop adverse symptoms, and most stop because of them. The latest study—reported at the 1971 annual meeting of the American Fertility Society—revealed that out of 2,000 women who had started on the pill in 1962, only 34 percent were still using it, at the end of six years.[11]

In 1960, the pill was approved for contraceptive use after having been tested for a full year or longer, continuously, on only 132 women.[12] And even among these women, the main thing being monitored was *effectiveness*. Several women died and were not even autopsied. At the time, their deaths were attributed to "heart attacks," but in retrospect it appears that pulmonary embolism was a more likely cause.[13]

It is not surprising that the undesirable side effects of the pill began to emerge only after it was in general use. The synthetic hormones in these powerful drugs act through the pituitary, which has been called the "master gland" and even "the conductor of the endocrine symphony." There is no organ or tissue which is not affected by the pill to some degree, and the longer a woman stays on the pill, the more her organs and all her metabolic functions are apt to be subtly altered.[14] The 20,000,000 women who take the pill—and the doctors who prescribe it—are engaged in a massive and unprecedented human experiment. We delude ourselves if we believe that a similar experiment on *males* would have been allowed. One of the cornerstones of medical ethics is "First, do no harm." Until the pill—and except for the pill—it would be unthinkable to prescribe, for continuous long-term use by healthy persons, a powerful drug of which the side effects,

[11]*Medical Tribune*, July 21, 1971.
[12]Revealed in a 1963 investigation of the FDA by the Senate Committee on Government Operations.
[13]Herbert Ratner, MD, *Child and Family* (Oak Park, Illinois, December, 1969).
[14]Hilton Salhanick, ed., *Effects of Gonadal Hormones and Contraceptive Steroids* (New York, Plenum Press, 1969).

and even the mechanisms of action, are imperfectly known.

If you doubt that there has been sex discrimination in the development of the pill, try to answer this question: Why *isn't* there a pill for men? Studies of the male reproductive system are well advanced, and a man's organs, being handily placed outside the body, are easier to work with than a woman's.

There are only a handful of researchers in male contraception, and they have a difficult time getting money, but most of them are inclined to believe that it could be easier and safer to interrupt the sperm production of men chemically than the egg production of women. It might be possible, for example, to interfere at the stage where the sperm are mixed with the seminal fluid instead of at the more dangerous level of the pituitary.

The British government has specifically rejected a proposal to channel research funds toward a pill for men. When the matter came up in the House of Lords, a Labour peer—to the accompaniment of much laughter—urged the government not to take too much notice of "those do-gooders who take all the fun out of life."

But women have always had to bear most of the risks associated with sex and reproduction. Therefore, governments and scientists reasoned, it would be all right to substitute one risk for another. One still hears this argument from certain doctors, such as Planned Parenthood's Malcolm Potts, who like to point out that the risks connected with the pill are less than the risks of pregnancy.

The trouble is, there are at least three reasons why it's not true.

One: You can't compare a known risk with an unknown risk, and the long-range dangers connected with the pill are still totally unknown. For example, close to 80 percent of the women who take the pill experience diabetic-like changes in their sugar metabolism. Some 15 percent actually test out as chemical diabetics. Will these women eventually come down with overt, clinical diabetes? Nobody can say yet, but the handful of diabetes specialists around the world who are studying the pill are extremely worried.[15]

The prospect of cancer is even more alarming. Estrogens can cause cancer in laboratory animals and can speed up the course of an existing cancer in humans. But cancer in humans takes many years to develop, so we will not know for some time whether the pill can actually *cause* it.

A new research report out of Harvard is not reassuring.[16] A synthetic estrogen given women during their pregnancy has caused a rare vaginal cancer in their daughters fifteen to twenty-two years later. The drug was administered between 1945 and 1951 to prevent miscarriages. A grown woman may not be as susceptible as a fetus, of course, but, as it happens, through the pill we are now giving these artificial estrogens to nursing babies. When their mothers take the pill, estrogens go right into the milk.

Two: The argument that the risks of pregnancy "outweigh" the risks of the pill rests on the absurd supposition that if you don't take the pill, you are going to be pregnant every year. A diaphragm—properly fitted and conscientiously used—is a 99 percent effective birth control method.[17] The newer IUD's are in the same range.[18] In fact, the leading biostatisticians of birth control, such as Dr. Christopher Tietze of the Population Council, have demonstrated repeatedly that the pill is *not* the best guardian of maternal health. The safest choice for women—in terms

[15]See testimony of Drs. Victor Wynn and William Spellacy at hearings before the Subcommittee on Monopoly of the Select Committee on Small Business ("Nelson" Hearings). (May be ordered from the Government Printing Office.)

See also Paul Vaughan, *The Pill on Trial* (New York, Coward-McCann, 1970), or Barbara Seaman, *The Doctors' Case Against the Pill* (New York, Wyden, 1969; Avon, 1970).

[16]*New England Journal of Medicine,* 284:878 (1971).

[17]See various papers of Charles Westoff (Princeton University).

[18]Hugh Davis, *Intrauterine Devices for Contraception* (Baltimore, Williams and Wilkins Co., 1971).

of mortality and morbidity statistics—is a local harmless method of contraception, backed up by readily available medical abortion.[19]

And haven't men grown a little spoiled? When I was in high school, even the virginal (*especially* the virginal) boys used to carry condoms in their wallets. Now, I understand, high school boys have become so delicate that even *they* complain that condoms are "too much like raincoats." We know, of course, that if unmarried persons were still using condoms, VD would not have enjoyed its current renaissance.[20] We also know that a good brand of fresh condom is a reliable method, and we know that in Japan, where condoms come in many colors and some even glow in the dark, couples use them as part of their

[19]Suppose 100,000 women are at risk of pregnancy for one year:

—Under condition one, these women use no contraceptive and have no abortions. 40,000 to 60,000 will become pregnant, and there will be 8 to 12 maternal deaths.

—Under condition two, the women use no contraception and all who become pregnant have illegal abortions. There will be an average of 1 pregnancy per woman, with 100 deaths.

—Under condition three, the women use no contraception, but all who become pregnant have legal abortions. There will be 3 deaths.

—Under condition four, the women use oral contraceptives. There will be 3 deaths from the contraceptives, as well as 50 hospitalizations for nonfatal blood clots.

—Under condition five, the women use local contraception, such as the diaphragm or condom and have no abortions. There will be 2.5 deaths.

—Under condition six, the women use local contraception and have illegal abortions when the contraception fails. There will be 14.3 deaths.

—Under condition seven, the women use local contraception, backed up by legal abortions. There will be only 0.4 deaths, which, in Tietze's words, is "a whole different ball park."

[20]Condoms were originally designed to prevent VD, and they remain an almost 100 percent safeguard against it. Furthermore, many investigators believe that the pill actually changes the chemical milieu of the vagina, from acidic, which tends to kill germs, to alkaline, which does not. If a woman who is not taking the pill is exposed to VD, her chances of getting it are estimated to be 20 to 30 percent. If she is taking the pill, her chances of getting VD approach 100 percent.

sex play, and the men rarely complain that their potency or pleasure is affected.

Do you know what the safest and simplest immediate solution to the population explosion might be? Vasectomize all boys at sixteen or eighteen, after having taken a sample of their sperm and frozen it. When they are ready for children, their wives could be artificially inseminated. It sounds repulsive, doesn't it? But it may be equally outrageous to encourage 20,000,000 women to play biological roulette with their own bodies and those of their unborn babies.

Now here is flaw number three in Dr. Potts' argument. The pill has not been at all widely accepted in underdeveloped countries, where, indeed, the pregnancy risks are substantial. Instead, it is used as a middle-class method in developed countries. Among middle-class women, receiving good health care, the risks of pregnancy are not so grave as Dr. Potts makes out. Furthermore, an important cause of maternal complications are blood clots, which are most apt to occur in the postpartum period.

In recent years, the personnel at maternity hospitals in Wales and Scotland have finally asked an important question. Which new methods get these blood clots?[21]

Their answers, which have been reported in bits and pieces in *Lancet* and the *British Medical Journal*, add to the case *against* the pill. Women who decline to breastfeed their babies are often given the pill itself or artificial estrogens in other form, to help suppress lactation. Postpartum blood clots are rare in women who do not take

[21]A woman with O type blood who is taking a low-estrogen birth control pill (under 50 micrograms per tablet) has less reason to fear blood clots than A, B or AB women or any woman taking a high-estrogen pill. In 1970 it was finally established that the incidence of clotting disorders is directly associated with the estrogen content of the various tablets. It was also learned that women of other blood types run a clotting risk nearly three times greater than that faced by type O women.

these drugs and several times more common in new mothers who take them. In other words, when pill defenders feed you statistics about women in civilized countries who die in connection with childbirth, a substantial number of the casualties they cite are women who *should* be grouped with the estrogen casualties but who, instead, are being used to dramatize the dangers of childbearing.

In Dr. Potts' recent and highly regarded book on contraceptive practice, he makes the following statement:[22]

"Contraception is not merely a medical procedure. It is also a social convenience, and if a technique carried a mortality several hundreds of times greater than that now believed to be associated with the pill, its use might still be justified on social if not medical grounds."

A mortality several hundreds of times greater! Healthy young women would be crippled or dying all over the place. As things stand, 1 to 2,000 pill users per year develops a clotting condition severe enough to warrant hospitalization. If this figure were multiplied by "several hundreds of times," 1 pill user in 7 would be hospitalized each year. One in 100 would die. One cannot but ask *whose* social convenience does Dr. Potts have in mind?

There are two general areas of research concerning the pill and sex. First, there are the studies which explore the frequency of libido change. Second, there are studies which explore the reasons.

Perhaps half the women on the pill report that their sex drive is unchanged or that their sex life is improved owing to an increased feeling of security. In fact, when couples go on the pill, they make love more often at first. But Drs. David Rodgers and Frederick Ziegler of the Cleveland Clinic report that this increase is deceiving because it just brings the couple up to the cultural norm. In other words, before starting the pill, many couples were having inter-

[22]Malcolm Potts and John Peel, *Textbook of Contraceptive Practice* (Cambridge, England, University Press, 1969).

course less frequently than the average American husband and wife of the same age. These researchers also report that noncoital methods of stimulation to orgasm—mutual masturbation or oral stimulation—increase appreciably when couples go on the pill. In a group of women who had used the pill for four years, 86 percent reported that their husbands used manual or oral techniques to bring them to orgasm. There is no evidence that the pill increases promiscuity among married women. Oddly enough, women on the pill had fewer extramarital affairs than the wives of men who had undergone vasectomies.

While some women report an improvement in their sex drives after starting the pill, and many others report no change, a large number—from 25 to 60 percent depending on the study—report a noticeable loss of sex drive. Studies have now been performed at the University of North Carolina School of Medicine in Chapel Hill, at the University of Lund in Sweden, and by the Council for the Investigation of Fertility Control in England. The principal American investigator has been Dr. Francis J. Kane, formerly of the Chapel Hill Psychiatry Department and now a professor at Tulane. He estimates that for every woman who experiences an increased sex drive on the pill, ten or more experience a decrease.

Dr. Michael Grounds of Australia reports that a loss of sex drive is the most frequent reason women in his country give for going off the pill. And in *Lancet,* two doctors from the Aberdeen Maternity Hospital wrote: "At present, it is probably true to say that depression and reduced libido associated with the administration of estrogen-progestogen mixtures caused more women to discontinue oral contraception than any other single cause." Dr. William Masters has not made any systematic study of libido loss in pill users, but as long ago as 1966 he commented, "The first question we ask about frigidity patients who were previously responsive is 'Has she been taking the pill?' "

Some pill users report that they lose their ability to reach orgasm. Others require more "effort" than previously and reach it less frequently. Still others become apathetic to sex. In some cases, there is an anatomical explanation. For example, 2 to 3 percent of women experience dyspareunia on the pill, owing to the drying up of natural secretions. For these women, intercourse becomes painful. A still larger group of women develop frequent or intractable vaginal infections while taking the pill, and others develop intractable bladder infections. Still others are troubled by breakthrough bleeding.

With time, an experienced woman whose sex drive declines on the pill is usually able to figure out why, and she stops taking it. Inexperienced women have no base level of comparison. Dr. Phillip Ball, an Indiana internist, has said, "The worst offense in my book is to give the pill to a bride. She gets married and goes to live in a different city. She doesn't like the city. She doesn't like married life, doesn't like the apartment, and doesn't like *him*. I've seen women who thought it was the wrong city and the wrong husband, but when they stopped taking the pill, everything was rosy."

Dr. Ball is referring to the fact that, in addition to libido loss, *one pill user in three* experiences mild to severe depressive changes in her personality.[23] In many cases, these depressive changes are hard to separate from libido loss; a lowering of sex drive is one of the most frequent and reliable clinical signs of depression.[24]

It should be noted that the hormones in the pill affect each woman's body in a highly personalized manner and that, furthermore, there are many different pills with dif-

[23]Anne Lewis and Masud Hoghugi, "An Evaluation of Depression as a Side Effect of Oral Contraceptives," *British Journal of Psychiatry* (1969), Vol. 115, pp. 697–701.

[24]This is not the case for some post-menopausal women, according to a recent report from the Mayo Clinic. In certain older women, depression is accompanied by an "almost insatiable" sex drive.

ferent combinations of hormones. Dr. Kane reports that 1 to 2 percent of pill users experience an increase in sex drive and a new ability to reach climax. He has reported one case of outright nymphomania, which terminated when the pill was discontinued.

A small percentage of pill users become severely depressed or psychotic.[25] Suicides have been reported to the FDA as a pill side effect. Much more commonly, however, pill users who experience adverse emotional effects describe them in one or two ways. Some women feel as if they were "pregnant all the time," slower, sleepier, more clumsy. Other women say that their symptoms mimic premenstrual tension. They are tense and irritable, and they cry easily. It now appears, although there is still a great deal of contradictory evidence, that pills with larger amounts of estrogen in proportion to the progestin are likely to produce the pregnancy type of mood change, while pills with relatively more progestin are associated with menstrual-like syndromes. It also appears that the higher progestin pills have a less discernible effect on sex drive per se, but are more commonly associated with severe depression.

Dr. Steffan Nordgvist of the University of Lund has noted an important distinction between pregnancy malaise and the apparently similar condition which afflicts many pill users. In pregnancy, symptoms usually do not last beyond the early months. In pill users, they tend to accumulate and grow more marked as time progresses.

From a biochemical standpoint, Drs. Ellen Grant and

[25]Lewis, *op. cit.*

See also various papers of Francis J. Kane, *e.g.,* "Psychiatric Problems Associated with Oral Contraceptives," *Transactions New England Obstetrics and Gynecology Society* (April, 1970); "Psychoendocrine Study of Oral Contraceptive Agents," *American Journal of Psychiatry* (October, 1970); "Emotional Change Associated with Oral Contraceptives in Female Psychiatric Patients," *Comparative Psychiatry* (January, 1969); "Psychosis Associated with the Use of a Sequential Oral Contraceptive," *Lancet* (August 26, 1967), (and other papers).

John Pryse-Davis in Great Britain have discovered that higher progestin pills produce more MAO[26] activity in the cells of the womb than do pills with relatively more estrogen. MAO is known to have some influence on mental states, and substances which curb its activity are often used as antidepressants.

It has also been discovered that some women who take the pill excrete in their urine lower amounts of certain breakdown products than non-pill users—including one derived from androgen. It is known that androgen will stimulate sex drive in a woman, so perhaps the pill interfered with the normal secretion of androgen, thus causing normal sexual interest to decline.

Those who hate to hear a word said against the pill are apt to suggest that the unpleasant emotional reactions some women have must be "all in the mind." Obviously, it would be naïve to assume that all the sexual problems associated with the pill are due entirely to biochemistry. Dr. Roger Pluvinage, a Paris neuropsychiatrist, has been studying women who develop migraine headaches on the pill. His patients confided a variety of secret fears, which sometimes express themselves as headaches and migraine. They felt anxiety over what the pill might do to subsequent pregnancy and guilt feelings over what their friends or the priest might say. Often the wife felt repressed anger at her husband for allowing her to use a contraceptive method which might be dangerous.

It has also been pointed out that some women enjoy sex

[26]MAO (monoamine oxidase) is an enzyme that breaks down certain chemicals, the monoamines. With increased MAO activity, the monoamines may be broken down too fast.

One theory of depression is that, for some reason, there are inadequate amounts of monoamines in certain parts of the brain. With a better monoamine supply, the patient comes out of his depression.

Some of the most effective chemicals used as antidepressants are MAO inhibitors. What they do is the reverse of what the pill seems to do; they slow down the activity of MAO, so monoamine levels increase. The pill increases MAO activity, at least in the womb.

most when there is a risk of pregnancy and that many women have "magical expectations" of the pill. Dr. Natalie Shainess suggests that the pill has led many couples to realize that they just don't care for each other sexually. It was not just an old-fashioned pre-pill contraceptive or fear of pregnancy that kept them apart, as each had pretended, or hoped.

At this point, it seems safe enough to say that some of the sexual problems associated with the pill are strictly chemical or physical, some are largely emotional, and a great many are both. There is no question that hormone fluctuations in women can cause or contribute to emotional disorders.

Observers have noted that the pill also makes some husbands nervous. Rare cases of impotence have been reported. Other husbands have become resentful because their wives are taking charge or fearful of too many sexual demands. Drs. Rodgers and Ziegler have an interesting finding. In marriages where the husband dominates, he is apt to insist that his wife stop taking the pill as soon as any symptoms appear. In marriages where the wife is strong and the husband weak, she is apt to continue the pill longer, despite her symptoms.

However, investigators at the Primate Research Center in Beckenham, England, have come up with a fascinating bit of information. When female rhesus monkeys are given the pill, the sexual interest of their gentlemen friends is considerably dampened. They groom the females less, mount them less often and generally work harder to obtain fewer ejaculations. Nobody knows why this happens, but it has been suggested that the synthetic steroids might somehow upset olfactory messages between the sexes. People aren't monkeys, of course, and I relate this reseach only to remind you that we can't be positive that even a husband's adverse reactions to the pill are entirely in the mind. Just possibly, an obscure biochemical disharmony lies at the bottom of it. Perhaps some people—like animals and insects—still respond to pheromones.[27]

In conclusion, I would like to remind you of a sad fact of life about the pill. Many of the prominent doctors who are still sanguine about these synthetic hormones have a long-standing commercial relationship with them. Take Dr. Robert Kistner, an assistant professor at Harvard, who writes books and articles defending the pill. Dr. Kistner has performed research for the following companies: William Merrell, Mead Johnson, Cutter, Squibb, Searle, Parke Davis, Upjohn, Wyeth and Lilly. In the past he has worked for Organon; he is still working for all the others.

A couple of years ago Dr. Kistner wrote an article for *Glamour* magazine in which he urged the pill on young girls who have menstrual difficulties.[28] To my astonishment, it won a major journalism prize. I cannot believe that the editors of *Glamour* or the judges connected with the Penny-Missouri women's journalism awards were aware of Dr. Kistner's commercial relationships. In any case, they certainly failed to mention them.[29]

---

[27]See earlier footnote about pheromones in Chapters Three and Four.

[28]Dr. Robert Kistner, "What Women Won't Ask and Doctors Don't Tell Them About Menstruation," *Glamour*, July, 1969.

[29]It is hoped the judges who lauded him for his contribution to women's better understanding of their own bodies were not aware either of the astonishing testimony he had given at Senator Nelson's pill hearings.

On January 15, 1970, Dr. Kistner was asked: "Doctor, do you regularly inform a woman of . . . potential side effects?"

Kistner: ". . . Of course, this is good medical practice."

(At this point the transcript of a trial where, a few months earlier, Dr. Kistner had testified on behalf of the Searle Company was read. At the trial, Dr. Kistner was asked whether he ever tells the pill patient that there is a risk of blood clots. His answer was, "No, I do not.")

Kistner explained, "I don't believe it is good medical practice with any medication to go through the list of possible complica-

Glamour is hardly the only magazine which has brought you pill doctors, as if they were objective experts. On June 30, 1970, *Look* carried an article entitled "The Pill Is Safe," an interview with Dr. Edward T. Tyler. Dr. Tyler was identified to *Look* readers as having "played a major role in developing and testing the pill. An associate clinical professor of obstetrics and gynecology at U.C.L.A., he is also medical director of the Family Planning Centers of Greater Los Angeles." But he was *not* identified as a researcher, consultant and promoter for: Merck, Sharpe & Dohme, Cutter Laboratories, Searle & Company, and the Upjohn Company.[30]

Redbook has recently hired Dr. Elizabeth Connell as an obstetrics and gynecology columnist. She has had commercial connections with the following pharmaceutical firms: Lilly & Co., Syntex Laboratories, Mead Johnson Laboratories, Organon, Inc., Ortho Pharmaceutical Corporation and Searle & Company.[31]

---

tions." Kistner was then asked to distinguish between a "side effect" and a "complication."

Dr. Kistner: "A side effect of a drug is one that is generally accepted as occurring in some individuals as an undesirable effect other than that for which the drug is given. If one takes estrogen, one frequently becomes nauseated, estrogen 'pulls in' sodium and some women don't excrete the excess fluid and they become edematous and 'blow up.' These are side effects; but if a woman takes estrogen and gets a blood clot and dies that is a complication." (P. 6082 of the *Hearings Before the Subcommittee on Monopoly of the Select Committee on Small Business,* United States Senate, January 14, 15, 21, 22, 23, 1970, reprinted in *Competitive Problems in the Drug Industry.*)

[30]Dr. Taylor is also a former gag writer for Groucho Marx, so perhaps "The Pill Is Safe" is just another one of his jokes.

[31]On February 24, 1971, five weeks after Senator Nelson first began hearings on the pill, Dr. Connell stated before his committee:

"We are already unfortunately beginning to reap the rewards of the publicity coming out of the January hearings. Most reporting, happily, has been both objective and accurate, but even so, it has created vast uneasiness and unhappiness. This was clearly foreseen and predicted by all physicians working closely with family planning at the grassroots level. I can speak most accurately about the results as I have seen them in New York City, but I know from

When Dr. Kistner and the others decry "scare talk" about the pill, they are identified only by their university affiliations. I feel that this is misleading, and I am proposing to my fellow science writers that in our news stories, we identify medical researchers by their commercial connections, as well as their academic ones. Some—although not all—of the present confusion about the pill sorts itself out when you get to know your way around the pill doctors.[32]

---

many personal contacts that this experience is being mirrored throughout this country and abroad.

"We are just now beginning to see the first of the pregnancies of women who panicked in January, stopped their pills and did not seek or use another means of birth control. These women will not be here to testify, but they now bear within their bodies mute testimony to the effectiveness of induced fear." (P. 6509.)

Of course, Dr. Connell's predictions were not borne out. There was no special increase in births nine months after the Nelson hearings.

Furthermore, it is difficult to believe that she even thought *she* was speaking "objectively and accurately." Suppose a woman did quit the pill on January 14, the day the hearings opened, and became pregnant within the next few weeks. Women do not go to a doctor to confirm a suspected pregnancy until they have skipped at least one period.

Connell's logistics just don't work out. February 24 was too soon for doctors to be seeing an increase in pregnancies, even if one had existed.

[32]And some of the present confusion about the morality of the pill may sort itself out when you ponder the following vignette from Graham Greene's perceptive novel *Travels with My Aunt* (New York, Viking [Bantam], 1971), pp. 115 and 131:

" 'Haven't you anywhere you call home?' I asked her.

" 'Julian and me felt like home, but then he got angry about my forgetting the pill. He's very quick-tempered. "If I have to remind you all the time," he said, "it takes away my spontaneity, don't you understand that?" He's got a theory women want to castrate their men, and one way is to take away their spontaneity.' . . .

" 'It's Julian's fault as much as yours.'

" 'But it isn't any longer, not with the pill. It's all the girl's fault now.' "

WHAT YOU SHOULD KNOW ABOUT THE PILL

In the spring of 1970, the FDA commissioner, recognizing that the pill is unique among prescription drugs in that it is given to healthy people and makes some of them sick, announced that he was ordering a long warning to the consumer, to be included in every pill package.[33]

Drug industry and AMA lobbyists[34] rushed to oppose the measure. After long delay a compromise was agreed upon. A short consumer warning would be included with every pill package. A longer warning, also in lay language,

[33]This was to be the first and only time that the detailed warning to consumers was to be included in any prescription drug. In explaining the reasons behind the decision, FDA Commissioner Charles Edwards stated:

"I think one of the responsibilities of the Food and Drug Administration is to bring the facts to bear so that they are available to the patient. I think that there have been more women taking the pill than perhaps should have been taking the pill.

"I am not sure that this number is absolute, but I think it does indicate there is a need to better inform the patient of the potential dangers of the pill and the risks involved.

". . . I think that the Food and Drug Administration has a responsibility to make sure that these individuals taking the oral contraceptives have received this information, and this is what we are going to propose.

". . . We are going to publish in the Federal Register a patient information sheet that we are proposing to place in all containers of oral contraceptives."

[34]In a meeting of the AMA house of delegates on June 23, 1970, a resolution opposing the warning was issued. The resolution cited this objection:

"The proposal to supply information on side effects . . . intrudes on the patient-physician relationship and compromises individual medical evaluation. . . . The proposed statement would confuse and alarm many patients. The package insert is an inappropriate means of providing a patient with information regarding any prescription drug; the most effective way to inform the patient is through the physician."

The resolution also stressed "the importance of making certain this FDA requirement not be extended to other prescription drugs."

would be distributed to doctors to hand out *personally to their patients*.[85] (The theory was that the patient's understanding would be clearer if the doctor were available to answer any questions the pamphlet might raise.)

These pamphlets, entitled *What You Should Know About the Pill*, were distributed to United States physicians in the summer of 1970. Rarely has so much postage —and paper—been wasted on what amounts to a bad joke on women. A year and a half later, I have failed to locate *one* pill user whose doctor has actually given her the pamphlet.

For this reason, both versions of the elusive warning are reproduced here.

The warning as originally composed by an FDA committie in the winter of 1970:[36]

WHAT YOU SHOULD KNOW ABOUT BIRTH CONTROL PILLS (ORAL CONTRACEPTIVE PRODUCTS)

All of the oral contraceptive pills are highly effective for preventing pregnancy, when taken according to the approved directions. Your doctor has taken your medical history and has given you a careful physical examination. He has discussed with you the risks of oral contraceptives, and has decided that you can take this drug safely.

This leaflet is your reminder of what your doctor has told you. Keep it handy and talk to him if you think you

---

[85]There were a number of consumer protests when the FDA went back on its initial promise. The Center for the Study of Responsive Law (Ralph Nader's organization) attempted court action to force the FDA to use the longer version. A delegation from D.C. Women's Liberation not only held a sit-in at HEW Secretary Robert Finch's office, but also arrived uninvited at a "top-secret" FDA meeting on the pill and stayed for the entire meeting, insisting, "It's our health and our bodies you're talking about. What will you be saying that we're not supposed to hear?"

[36]"Nelson Hearings," March 4, 1970, *op. cit.* pp. 6800–1.

are experiencing any of the conditions you find described.

A WARNING ABOUT "BLOOD CLOTS"

There is a definite association between blood-clotting disorders and the use of oral contraceptives. The risk of this complication is six times higher for users than for non-users. The majority of blood-clotting disorders are not fatal. The estimated death rate from blood-clotting in women *not* taking the pill is one in 200,000 each year; for users, the death rate is about six in 200,000. Women who have or who have had blood clots in the legs, lung, or brain should not take this drug. You should stop taking it and call your doctor immediately if you develop severe leg or chest pain, if you cough up blood, if you experience sudden and severe headaches, or if you cannot see clearly.

WHO SHOULD NOT TAKE BIRTH CONTROL PILLS

Besides women who have or who have had blood clots, other women who should not use oral contraceptives are those who have serious liver disease, cancer of the breast, or certain other cancers, and vaginal bleeding of unknown cause.

SPECIAL PROBLEMS

If you have heart or kidney disease, asthma, high blood pressure, diabetes, epilepsy, fibroids of the uterus, migraine headaches, or if you have had any problems with mental depression, your doctor has indicated you need special supervision while taking oral contraceptives. Even if you don't have special problems, he will want to see you regularly to check your blood pressure, examine your breasts, and make certain other tests.

When you take the pill as directed, you should have your period each month. If you miss a period, and if you are sure you have been taking the pill as directed, continue your schedule. If you have not been taking the pill as directed and if you miss one period, stop taking it and call your doctor. If you miss two periods see your doctor even though you have been taking the pill as directed. When you stop taking the pill, your periods may be irregular for some time. During this time you may have trouble becoming pregnant.

If you have had a baby which you are breast feeding, you should know that if you start taking the pill its hormones are in your milk. The pill may also cause a decrease in your milk flow. After you have had a baby, check with your doctor before starting to take oral contraceptives again.

WHAT TO EXPECT

Oral contraceptives normally produce certain reactions which are more frequent the first few weeks after you start taking them. You may notice unexpected bleeding or spotting and experience changes in your period. Your breasts may feel tender, look larger, and discharge slightly. Some women gain weight while others lose it. You may also have episodes of nausea and vomiting. You may notice a darkening of the skin in certain areas.

OTHER REACTIONS TO ORAL CONTRACEPTIVES

In addition to blood clots, other reactions produced by the pill may be serious. These include mental depression, swelling, skin rash, jaundice or yellow pigment in your eyes, increase in blood pressure, and increase in the sugar content of your blood similar to that seen in diabetes.

POSSIBLE REACTIONS

Women taking the pill have reported headaches, nervousness, dizziness, fatigue, and backache. Changes in appetite and sex drive, pain when urinating, growth of more body hair, loss of scalp hair, and nervousness and irritability before the period also have been reported. These reactions may or may not be directly related to the pill.

NOTE ABOUT CANCER

Scientists know the hormones in the pill (estrogen and progesterone) have caused cancer in animals, but they have no proof that the pill causes cancer in humans. Because your doctor knows this, he will want to examine you regularly.

REMEMBER

While you are taking——, call your doctor promptly if you notice any unusual change in your health. Have regular checkups and your doctor's approval for a new prescription.

The revised version, softened by AMA and drug industry representatives, and mailed to doctors (for alleged distribution to their pill patients) about six months later:[37]

WHAT YOU SHOULD KNOW ABOUT "THE PILL"

Several kinds of oral contraceptives are now available and your physician has prescribed for you the one he believes will best meet your individual needs. All types of oral contraceptives contain female sex hormones (estrogens and progestogens) and are designed to prevent the release of an egg from a woman's ovaries during the cycle in which the pills are taken. They are almost completely effective in preventing pregnancy.

"The Pill" is the most effective of all contraceptives if you follow the directions for its use and are careful not to skip doses or take it irregularly.

Oral contraceptives, like all potent drugs, have some side effects. Fortunately, serious side effects are relatively rare. Periodic examinations, as recommended by your doctor, are essential to provide the early detection which may prevent serious complications. Report any special problems to your doctor.

[37] I have not been able to determine if the AMA actually distributed the pamphlets as widely as it said it would. My husband, a psychiatrist, never received them, although the AMA claimed that it was sending them to psychiatrists, presumably because depression is one of the more serious pill side effects. Several gynecologists have also told me that they never received them.

COMMON REACTIONS

A few women experience unpleasant side effects from the pill which are not dangerous and are not likely to damage their health. Some of these side effects are similar to symptoms women experience in early pregnancy and may be temporary. Your breasts may feel tender, nausea and vomiting may occur, and you may gain or lose weight. A spotty darkening of the skin, particularly of the face, is possible and may persist. You may notice unexpected vaginal bleeding or changes in your menstrual period which should be reported to your physician.

Your physician may find that the levels of sugar and fatty substances in the blood are elevated. The long-term effect of these changes is under study.

Other reactions, although not proved to be caused by the pill, are occasionally reported: nervousness, dizziness, some loss of scalp hair, increase in body hair, an increase or decrease in sex drive, or appetite changes.

After a woman stops using the pill, there may be a delay before she is able to become pregnant. After childbirth there is special need to consult your physician before resuming use of the pill. This is especially true if you plan to nurse your baby because the drugs in the pill are known to appear in the milk and the long-range effect on the infant is not known at this time. Furthermore, the pill may cause a decrease in your milk supply.

ABOUT BLOOD CLOTS

Blood clots occasionally form in the blood vessels of the legs and pelvis of apparently healthy people and may threaten life if the clots break loose and then lodge in the lung or if they form in other vital organs, such as the brain. It has been estimated that about one woman in 2,000 on the pill each year suffers a blood clotting disorder severe enough to require hospitalization. The estimated death rate from abnormal blood clotting in healthy women under 35 not taking the pill is 1 in 500,000; whereas for the same group taking the pill it is 1 in 66,000. For healthy women over 35 not taking the pill, the rate is 1 in 200,000 compared to 1 in 25,000 for pill users. Blood clots are about three times more likely to develop in women over the age of 34. For these reasons it is important that women who have had blood clots in the legs, lung, or brain not use oral contraceptives. Anyone using the pill who has severe leg or chest pains, coughs up blood, has difficulty in breathing, sudden severe headache or vomiting, dizziness or fainting, disturbances of vision or speech, weakness or numbness of an arm or leg, should call her doctor immediately and stop taking the pill.

OTHER CONSIDERATIONS

If you miss one menstrual period and are following your dose schedule, you should continue taking the pill as directed. If you miss two periods, you should stop taking the pill and see your doctor, even though you think you have followed the prescribed schedule.

There is no proof at the present time that oral contraceptives can cause cancer in humans. However, the possibility that they may continues to be studied, based on observations that large doses of female sex hormones have produced cancer in some experimental animals.

SPECIAL NEEDS

If you have or have had a special health problem, such as migraine, mental depression, fibroids of the uterus, heart or kidney disease, asthma, high blood pressure, diabetes, or epilepsy inform your physician. He may wish to make sure that it is suitable for you to take the pill by doing special tests if necessary. All these conditions may be made worse by the use of oral contraceptives.

You should report to your doctor any unusual swelling, skin rash, yellowing of the skin or eyes, or severe depression.

There are some women, in addition to those with tendencies toward blood clotting disorders, who should not use oral contraceptives. These include women who have cancer of the breast or womb, serious liver conditions or undiagnosed vaginal bleeding when cancer has not been ruled out. It is comforting to know that, in such cases, your doctor can recommend other methods of birth control.

SUMMARY

Oral contraceptives, when taken as directed, are drugs of extraordinary effectiveness. As with other medicine, side effects are possible. The most serious side effect is abnormal blood clotting. The fact is that serious problems are relatively rare, and the majority of women who would like to use the pill can do so safely and effectively.

See your physican regularly, ask him any questions you may have about the use of the pill, and report to him any special problems that may arise.

The label that appears on birth control packages reads as follows:

This Label is required by the Food and Drug Administration.

ORAL CONTRACEPTIVES (Birth Control Pills)

Do not take this drug without your doctor's continued supervision.

The oral contraceptives are powerful and effective drugs which can cause side effects in some users and should not be used at all by some women. The most serious known side effect is abnormal blood clotting which can be fatal.

Safe use of this drug requires a careful discussion with your doctor. To assist him in providing you with the necessary information, a booklet has been prepared that is written in a style understandable to you as the drug user. This provides information on the effectiveness and known hazards of the drug, including warnings, side effects and who should not use it. Your doctor will give you this booklet if you ask for it and he can answer any questions you may have about the use of this drug.

Notify your doctor if you notice any unusual physical disturbance or discomfort.

THE IUD

The IUD is a small plastic insert—some no bigger than a nickel—which prevents pregnancy inside the uterus. The device does not interfere with sex, and unlike the pill, it does not change the hormones or the rest of the body. These effective little gadgets are gaining rapidly in popularity—3,000,000 women have used them in the United States in recent years and more than 14,000,000 have been inserted around the world.

And yet, the IUD continues to lag behind the pill in popularity. Dr. George Langmyhr, medical director of Planned Parenthood-World Population, suggests that there are at least two reasons. First, there are, as yet, relatively few physicians who have been thoroughly trained in using this method. (And inserting an IUD properly does take skill. Studies at various clinics reveal that many of the serious problems associated with IUD's can be traced back to one or two inept doctors. In other words, some doctors have an excellent success record with them, while others have a poor one.[33] Experience seems to be essential. If your doctor reluctantly agrees to give you an IUD and then has to blow the dust off the box in which he keeps them, jump into your pantyhose and run.)

Second, as Dr. Langmyhr points out, the IUD has suffered from a "relative lack of commercial promotion." The pill is a somewhat expensive method, and the user must keep on buying it—to the profit of the drug compa-

[33]This may, in part at least, depend on a doctor's attitude. In one New York clinic, doctors remove intrauterine devices from 3½ percent of the patients in the morning clinic—and 15 percent in the evening clinic. The reason for the variation: Removal of the IUD takes only a minute, but examining and reassuring a worried patient takes much longer. The doctors staffing the evening clinic had already put in a full day's work and were evidently just too tired to make the extra effort.

nies. (And others, as we have seen.) The IUD costs only a few cents to manufacture, sells for very little and lasts a long time.

Rumor and mystery surround the IUD, perhaps because it seems too simple to be true, and its exact mechanism of action has only come to be understood very recently. Here is how Dr. Hugh Davis explains it:[39]

> In the presence of the IUD, natural body defense cells —the white cells—are attracted to form a thin coating on the device. These are the same cells which protect against bacteria or any other foreign material. The white cells are not usually present inside the uterus at the time of fertilization. But when the IUD is present, the protective white cells form a delicate natural barrier which prevents pregnancy.

Insertion of an IUD takes only a couple of minutes, according to Davis:

> The IUD comes loaded in a sterile package with a special inserter. The device of soft plastic folds to pass through the mouth of the womb, opening to its original shape inside the uterus. Most devices have a threadlike tail which the doctor can later see at the cervix to make sure it is correctly positioned, or to remove the IUD when further pregnancies are desired. Once in place, the device stays high inside the uterus, where it is not touched or felt during intercourse.

While IUDs are inserted most frequently in women who have had one or more children, the modern devices can be worn by women who have never been pregnant. A drawback of some of the older devices was their tendency to produce cramps and excessive menstrual bleeding, especially in younger women with sensitive tissues. Some of the older devices could also be expelled by the uterus easily, making the method unreliable. Better IUD

[39]Dr. Davis, of the Johns Hopkins University School of Medicine in Baltimore, is author of the recent medical book *Intrauterine Devices for Contraception* (Baltimore, Williams & Wilkins, 1971).

designs have eliminated most of such drawbacks. The improved modern devices not only provide a better protection against pregnancy, but also are smaller and more flexible, and therefore cause fewer side-effects. When fitted properly, the modern devices are retained almost perfectly. They can be used by practically all women and are well retained even by women with sensitive uteri.

Admittedly, the IUD has some disadvantages. Davis continues:

Local effects such as cramping or bleeding due to the device stretching the uterus are experienced by some women. It is natural to have bleeding for a few days after insertion, hardly noticeable if the device is put in at the time of menstruation. The modern devices eliminate most such complaints, and can be successfully used by many women. With most devices, any minor bleeding from insertion clears up in a few days. A few women do experience pain or persistent prolonged periods after being fitted, and need to switch to a smaller device or use another method.

Dr. Davis is a developer of the Dalkon Shield, a new intrauterine device which has been tried with good results at Hopkins and elsewhere.[40] He points out that IUD's go back to the turn of the century or earlier. What was probably the first device was invented by Dr. Richard Richter, a practitioner in the village of Waldenberg, in present-day Poland. After that, they were used almost in secret by a few skilled gynecologists serving wealthy patients. Some women have worn them for as long as 20 years.

Fertility is not impaired among women who discontinue the IUD in order to become pregnant. However, if pregnancy occurs soon after removal of the IUD, there may be an increase in the frequency of spontaneous abortion.

[40] 604 were inserted at Hopkins during the first six months of 1970. One year later 23 had been removed because of side effects and 4 pregnancies had occurred.

Have any deaths been caused by the IUD? The answer, unfortunately, is yes, although fatalities are much rarer than with the pill.

First, there is some question concerning the wisdom of giving an IUD to a woman who has PID, or pelvic inflammatory disease. (PID occurs when bacteria invade the upper genital tract. The uterus and tubes are usually involved, and sometimes other organs as well. Gonorrhea is the most common cause of PID, but streptococcus or staphylococcus may sometimes cause it, following childbirth or an abortion. Very occasionally, the tubercle bacillus is responsible.)

When a patient has *acute* PID, she becomes extremely ill, experiencing acute pain and high fever, among other symptoms. She is most unlikely, at this stage, to be seeking a new birth control method. However, even a single attack of acute PID is apt to leave some residue of *chronic* inflammation.

One drawback to IUD's is that their insertion may reactivate chronic or subchronic PID. Usually, the infection is mild and can be successfully controlled with antibiotics. The IUD stays in place. However, complications may become serious on occasion. Ten deaths attributed to PID and associated with IUD use are known to have occurred in the United States. The case histories of these unfortunate women suggest that in four instances "the insertion of the IUD may have been the precipitating cause of the fatal illness."[41]

It is not known for certain whether IUD insertion can *cause* PID in a woman who has not had it previously. At present, it appears that women who have never suffered from PID need not fear this complication.

A few PID deaths have also been associated with perforation of the uterus at the time of insertion. This accident

[41]Drs. Sheldon Segal and Christopher Tietze, "Contraceptive Technology: Current and Prospective Methods," *Reports on Population/Family Planning*, No. 1, July 1971, New York, The Population Council, page 9.

is most unlikely to occur if, as noted previously, the physician is experienced with IUD's. Overall, counting skilled technicians and poor ones, the accident occurs once in 2,500 insertions.[42] Strangely enough, this sounds worse than it really is, for even when it happens, the patient is usually asymptomatic. She does not become seriously or evenly slightly ill. But very occasionally, and only with certain kinds of devices (the use of which has now, largely, been discontinued), the device may cause fatal obstruction of the intestines.

Some women fear that as "foreign bodies" the IUD's might cause cancer. They have been in use a good deal longer than the pill, and so far there is no evidence which links them to malignancy. On the other hand, no really good studies exploring the matter have yet been performed. Dr. Davis points out that the portion of the uterus which comes in contact with the IUD is precisely the portion which is sloughed off and renewed with each menstrual cycle, so this would prevent long-term irritations from occurring.

The IUD has its drawbacks and its dangers, but most *objective* experts would probably agree with Tietze, who says: "The virtue of the IUD is that it is in the uterus, minding its own business. Its mischief is confined to the female organs."

GREASY KID STUFF

The diaphragm does not prevent pregnancy when it is applied to the night table drawer. Neither do condoms or spermacidal foams. But all these methods can serve a woman well,[43] for, as Dr. Tietze likes to remind us, "The

[42]Segal and Tietze, *ibid.,* p. 9.

[43]There is no question that a properly fitted and carefully used diaphragm is a 98 to 99 percent reliable method. A good-quality fresh condom is almost as dependable. Vaginal creams, suppositories and tablets are less reliable than foams, and even foams are

main reason for contraceptive failure is failure to use the contraceptive."

Unless the scientists come up with something new and amazing, I suspect that greasy kid stuff may enjoy a renaissance among the sexually liberated. Many people make more of a negative fuss over these methods than the actual amount of nuisance would seem to justify. Yet by and large these methods are both reliable and safe. The lowest birth rate we have ever had in the United States occurred during the Depression of the 1930's, when diaphragms and condoms were the only good methods available. People simply couldn't afford children so they were willing to take the trouble. (And in recent years four nations—Japan, Hungary, Bulgaria and Czechoslovakia—have reduced their population growth rate to below zero. The citizens are not even reproducing themselves. In all these countries the method used was simply to make safe abortion widely available, as a backup to old-fashioned contraceptives.)

Perhaps our masturbation taboos explain why so many women are loath to insert their fingers in their vaginas. As we grow more comfortable with our bodies[44] and as we

---

surprisingly controversial. According to some studies, foams are a 97 percent method in conscientious users. According to other studies, they are far less reliable than that.

A good thing to be said for foam is that it is readily available at drugstores, without a prescription. In combination with a condom (also available in drugstores without prescription), protection is virtually surefire.

Tips on foam: It may be that one brand (Delfen) has a more potent spermacide than others. It may also be that the standard applicatorful does not afford as much protection as a double dose. If price is no object, use two applicatorsful. As time passes, foam loses its punch. If foreplay is apt to last for more than 45 minutes, delay using foam until just before intercourse.

There *is* an underground of experienced women who say they have been using foam successfully for a decade or longer. They prefer it to the diaphragm because it is somewhat less complicated to use. For some women, at least, it does seem to work very well.

[44]Whether or not we are getting more enlightened in our attitudes toward masturbation is still questionable. Children in grades

learn to respect our bodies more, perhaps we will return to the old-fashioned methods that are reliable and free of side effects.[45]

The vaginal diaphragm, invented by Wilhelm P. J. Mensinga, a German physician, sometime before 1882, is still in use with minor modifications. The diaphragm is a mechanical device which acts as a simple physical barrier between sperm and egg. It entails no more side effects than one can expect from wearing a raincoat or carrying an umbrella. (In rare cases allergic reactions to one of the components of the contraceptive jelly or cream that is used with the diaphragm have been reported. A change of brands often takes care of the problem. Yet more rarely, an individual may be allergic to the diaphragm's rubber itself.) In England, people refer to it as "the cap," perhaps a more descriptive name. A diaphragm is a dome of soft rubber or latex with a springy rim that pinches together for insertion. It is designed to lie diagonally across the vaginal canal and cover the cervix. It cannot be felt when it is in place.

Diaphragms must be fitted by a doctor or other trained

7–12 still regard masturbation as a very serious problem, even though it's now deemed nothing of the kind, according to a survey reported in the *Journal of Consulting Psychology*. The only "behaviors" the students consider worse are stealing, destroying school property and untruthfulness.

[45]Another argument in favor of the pill, IUD and sterilization—those methods which require no special effort at the time of coitus—is that they do not interfere with "spontaneity," as the so-called coitus-connected methods do. However, the need for "spontaneity" is sometimes an expression of lack of confidence in one's ability to reach orgasm. If the orgasm seems chancy or precarious, an interruption may spell the difference between success and failure. By contrast, if the orgasm habit is well ingrained, an interruption is not usually such an important drawback, and it may even enhance the pleasure, on some occasions.

Sexual power games may also signify. One woman told me, "I have complete confidence in the diaphragm, but it used to kill me to put it in [at bedtime] and then have my husband roll over and go to sleep. I felt rejected. With the pill I just take it along with my vitamins. I don't even connect it with sex."

person. They are manufactured in various sizes. Very precise measurements are taken before prescribing a particular size for an individual. A new user must be instructed on exact methods of insertion. Most women get accustomed to it very quickly.

When a woman seems awkward or nervous, a doctor may advise that she practice inserting the diaphragm at home without having intercourse. He will ask her to return after a few days so he can make a final check to be sure that she is inserting it correctly. At the Margaret Sanger birth control center in New York women are routinely told to practice for a week at home and then come back to show that they have mastered the procedure. Once they have, there is usually no more cause for nervousness because the technique is like dealing with any simple appliance. Once one learns, one never forgets.

Before inserting the diaphragm, the equivalent of about a teaspoon of contraceptive cream or jelly is applied evenly around the spongy rim and inside the dome. This lubricant makes insertion easier. It is also a vital part of contraceptive protection because these creams and jellies contain a spermacide. If, by chance, the diaphragm should be inserted incorrectly or become slightly dislodged during lovemaking, the spermacide is usually enough to prevent conception. (Masters and Johnson report that diaphragms are sometimes displaced during the orgastic expansion of the inner two-thirds of the vaginal barrel.)

Doctors advise that the diaphragm can be inserted up to six hours before intercourse; in practice, it is more reassuring, especially for a new user, to insert it about half an hour to an hour before, so that she will have no doubts that the spermacides are active and doing their job. The diaphragm may be removed anywhere from six to twenty-four hours after intercourse.

Women are also counseled to make a habit of regularly holding the diaphragm up to the light to make sure that no tiny imperfections have developed. Many women find it convenient to have two diaphragms available just in case one should develop a tiny hole or tear. It is necessary to be refitted after the birth of a baby, and it is also advisable to have the size rechecked every year or so.

The diaphragm is not always the ideal contraceptive for sexual beginners. Doctors sometimes advise that they wait for two weeks to two months before being fitted with a diaphragm. And of course, a virgin with an intact hymen cannot be fitted. (For sexual beginners, the drugstore methods, condoms and foams, are probably most suitable, and certainly the easiest to obtain. . . . Any woman who has mastered tampons should be able to cope with spermacidal foam, which rests on similar methods of insertion. . . . Is there anything yet for the virgin-on-the-brink, the young woman who wishes to carry some feminine equivalent of condoms in her purse, just in case? There might be. The Ortho Pharmaceutical Company has a new nonprescription product called Conceptrol birth control cream, which comes in a disposable prefilled tamponlike applicator and costs about forty cents, the same as a good condom. The effectiveness of Conceptrol is not yet known although Ortho, as always, has high claims for it.)

A well-fitted diaphragm in a conscientious user is an extremely reliable contraceptive. Only one or two pregnancies a year occur in each 100 conscientious diaphragm users, which compares favorably with pregnancies among pill users. Most "diaphragm babies" are babies whose mothers failed to use it one night, or failed to take adequate care of it, or were not given full instructions by the doctor who fitted it.

Humans have long sensed that female fertility must vary with the menstrual cycle, so rhythm (based on incorrect premises as often as not) is an age-old method of birth control. At the present time, two varieties are practiced: calendar rhythm and temperature rhythm.

Calendar rhythm, the easier version, was developed in the 1920's. Proponents claim that the day of ovulation can be estimated by means of a formula based on menstrual history, recorded over a number of months. Abstinence must be practiced for several days before and after the estimated day of ovulation.

As one tired joke goes, there is a word for women who practice calendar rhythm—*mothers*.

A group of doctors at the Georgetown University School of Medicine studied the menstrual cycles of more than 2,300 women. Not a single woman maintained a "classic" twenty-eight-day cycle for a full year. Most of them showed variations of five days or longer. For 87 percent the difference between the shortest and the longest cycle was more than six days. Only women who have exceptionally regular cycles would do well with calendar-based rhythm—even if the safe period is carefully calculated under supervision—and would be entitled to have any degree of confidence in this method. Researchers are working on new, simple tests to help women determine their time of ovulation each month, but these are not yet perfected.

Temperature rhythm is a different story. It probably works quite well, but it requires enormous self-control and discipline. To practice it, a woman must take her basal body temperature every morning, during the first part of her menstrual cycle. Intercourse is permitted only *after* her thermometer indicates that ovulation has occurred.

Thus, the period when sexual intercourse is permissible is severely limited. However, it is wrong to downgrade the *effectiveness* of temperature rhythm to women whose religious convictions call for it. Correctly taught, correctly understood and consistently practiced, temperature rhythm may serve a woman very well.

The co-eds at Oberlin College have some of the highest IQ's of co-eds at any college in the United States. But even these very bright and sophisticated young women are quite naïve about birth control. A recent study of their practices revealed that a large percentage of those who were sexually active relied on "some vague notion of rhythm."[46] These women were not taking their basal temperatures every day or even tracking their menstrual cycles carefully on a calendar. However controversial foam may be, it is surely more dependable than the nonmethod they were actually using—and they could have purchased it easily enough at a pharmacy, without any doctor hassles.

A particularly unreliable form of contraceptive is the post-coital douche. It is supposed to wash the sperm out of the vagina. In fact, about all that may be said of it is that it is slightly better than nothing at all—if taken within five minutes after intercourse.

The condom has been used effectively by men for more than 400 years. It is made of rubber or of animal tissue. Animal tissue condoms are more expensive—and thinner. Some men who find that rubber condoms diminish the sensation of the sex act prefer the "skin" condoms.

The condom should be drawn on when the penis is in full erection and before it has made any contact with the woman's genitals. The uncircumcised male should be sure that his foreskin is fully retracted. About an inch should be left free to provide room for the male ejaculate and to prevent possible leakage.

Following intercourse and before the penis has lost its erection, the condom should be grasped against the base of the penis and removed carefully to avoid spillage. Good-quality condoms, if purchased at a drugstore and not from a machine, are usually fresh and should be reliable. The condom is even more reliable if a bit of spermacidal jelly is applied to the outside after it has been drawn on. The effectiveness of foams used in combination with a condom has been discussed earlier. The condom, as most people know, not only prevents pregnancy by retaining the

[46]Alan Wachtel and Barbara Taylor, "Sexual Behavior and Related Health Needs of 1300 College Women," *Advances in Planned Parenthood*, Vol. 5 (Amsterdam and New York, Excerpta Medica Foundation, 1970).

seminal discharge, but also prevents the spread of venereal disease.

Condoms, or "contraceptive sheaths," first made their appearance in England during the eighteenth century. They were made from intestines of sheep and other animals. In the United States, these devices are under the jurisdiction of the Food and Drug Administration. Nine hundred and ninety-seven out of every 1,000 sold are free from defect demonstrable by current tests. Very rarely, an individual cannot use them because he is sensitive to rubber.

Withdrawal of the penis prior to ejaculation is probably the oldest birth control method of all. It is referred to in the Old Testament and has been noted by anthropologists among diverse tribes throughout the world. The effectiveness of coitus interruptus, as it is technically called, has been traditionally underestimated by the medical profession.

Drs. Tietze and Segal report that "careful studies in the United States and the United Kingdom have revealed pregnancy rates only slightly higher than those achieved by the same populations using mechanical and chemical contraceptives."[47] However, the man must be sufficiently skilled and self-controlled to defer his own orgasm until the woman has reached hers, and he must then be willing to withdraw before a single drop of semen is deposited in the vagina. Withdrawal has been criticized for placing a heavy "psychological burden" on the male. Yet some men maintain they do not find it burdensome. The method is most suitable for those mature experienced males who have developed such excellent control that neither they nor their women find it tension-producing. Its contraceptive value should never be underestimated for occasions when any couple may be caught unprepared.

[47] Segal and Tietze, *op. cit.*, p. 2.

STERILIZATION

Sterilization is a surgical means of contraception. The female operation—tying off the fallopian tubes—is called tubal ligation; the male procedure—closing the sperm ducts—is called vasectomy.

In both sexes the operation is drastic, but in the female it is major surgery, with a significant mortality rate attached. The risks occur not only at the time of surgery, but for many years afterward. Sperm and ova are both very tiny. In some female sterilization procedures, the fallopian tubes may be imperfectly closed. After sterilization, sperm may wind its way up and fertilize an egg, but there is generally not enough room, in the damaged fallopian tube, for the conceptus to make its way to the uterus. Tubal pregnancy, a frequently fatal condition, may be the outcome. Sterilized women have died of surprise tubal pregnancies as long as twelve years after their operation.

Sterilization is more or less permanent. Until recently, population controllers who were interested in promoting these procedures claimed in many newspaper and magazine articles, that tubal ligation was "up to 50 percent reversible," while vasectomy was "up to 75 percent reversible." Promoters tried to make these operations sound as if they were not necessarily permanent at all . . . in case circumstances should change and you would want to change your mind. However, the surgeons to whom it sometimes fell to reverse these operations have, in self-defense, become more and more outspoken in denying the propaganda. In women the chances for reversal are tiny; in men they are somewhat better, *perhaps* 20 or 25 percent, but there is never any guarantee, the surgeons are quick to add. Even the staunchest promoters of sterilization now concede that any person contemplating it should be counseled to regard it as permanent.

A woman must be hospitalized for a tubal ligature. A vasectomy can be performed in a doctor's office, although the healing process is often more painful than the propagandists would have you believe. One man in five experiences post-operative swelling of the testicles.[48]

Vasectomies are not 100 percent safe in terms of contraceptive results. There have been a significant number of cases where the sperm's normal pathway re-formed, as part of a long-term healing process. The figure is no more than 2 or 3 percent, but still this makes vasectomy no more reliable than a conscientiously used condom. (Tubal pathways can also re-form after ligation, but this happens less frequently. In women, as noted earlier, a re-formed tubal pathway—which is usually incomplete—is apt to result in tubal pregnancy.)

A couple who attempted to sue their surgeon after a post-vasectomy pregnancy were told by the judge that "the birth of a normal baby" could not be regarded as a catastrophic event. They lost.

Vasectomy does not impair potency or orgasmic response, but is it sound and sensible? To put it another way, how *does* a normal male respond to sex organ surgery?

The literature on vasectomy could fill a psychology book. Perhaps Arthur Godfrey summed it all up pretty well when he told me, "It was great for me, but bear in mind that I'm a wealthy older man who pilots his own plane. I don't need to get a woman pregnant to prove my masculinity. . . . Any guy who has any doubts, I wouldn't recommend it."

Consider the findings of Merlin Johnson, a Seattle psychiatrist at a VA hospital. A few years ago Johnson reviewed the precipitating causes for *all* the psychiatric hos-

[48]Andrew S. Ferber, MD, Christopher Tietze, MD, and Sarah Lewitt, "Men with Vasectomies: A Study of Medical, Sexual and Psychosocial Changes," reprinted from *Psychosomatic Medicine*, Vol. XXIX, No. 4 (July–August 1967), Hoeber Medical Division, Harper & Row, © 1967 by American Psychosomatic Society, Inc.

pitalizations on his service during a certain period. In a startling number, a recent vasectomy appeared to be the precipitating cause of the breakdown.

These men were probably troubled and vulnerable to start with, but in a very good study of healthier men[49] it was found that *most* who have vasectomies become more domineering in subtle ways, as if to compensate.

Vasectomy beckons as a most attractive birth control solution for population-conscious couples who are certain that their marriage is permanent and that they have all the children they want. And as a feminist, I cannot help admiring the men who are willing to put themselves on the surgeon's block in order to spare their wives. Yet as Godfrey says, this is clearly not a method for "every guy." No man should enter into it without very patient self-inspection.

John Gagnon, a former Kinsey Institute researcher, suggests that there are six questions which every man contemplating a vasectomy should ask:

1. Do you want more children?

[49]See David A. Rodgers, Frederick J. Ziegler, Sali Ann Kriegsman, "Effect of Vasectomy on Psychological Functioning," reprinted from *Psychosomatic Medicine*, Vol. XXVIII, No. 1 (January–February, 1966), Hoeber Medical Div., Harper & Row, © 1966 American Psychosomatic Society, Inc.; Rodgers and Ziegler, "Vasectomy, Ovulation Suppressors and Sexual Behavior," *The Journal of Sex Research*, Vol. 4, No. 3, pages 169–93, August, 1968; Rodgers and Ziegler, "Social Role Theory, the Marital Relationship, and Use of Ovulation Suppressors," *Journal of Marriage and the Family*, Vol. xxx, No. 4, November, 1968; Rodgers, Ziegler, and Nissim Levy, "Prevailing Cultural Attitudes About Vasectomy: A Possible Explanation of Post-Operative Psychological Response," *Psychosomatic Medicine*, Vol. 29, No. 4, July–August, 1967, Hoeber Medical Division, Harper & Row, © 1967 by American Psychosomatic Society, Inc.; Rodgers, Ziegler, Levy, and John Altrocchi, "A Longitudinal Study of the Psycho-social Effects of Vasectomy," *Journal of Marriage and the Family*, February, 1965, Vol. 27, No. 1; Rodgers, Ziegler, Kriegsman, and Purvis L. Martin, "Ovulation Suppressors, Psychological Functioning and Marital Adjustment," *Journal of the American Medical Association*, June 3, 1968, Vol. 204, pages 849–53, © 1968, AMA.

2. If one of your children died, would you want another child?

3. If you got married again, would you want children by another woman?

4. Do you fear that it's going to affect your erections and your potency, or your masculinity in any way?

5. Are you afraid of someone with a surgical instrument—a sharp knife—around your testicles?

6. Do you derive most of your gratification from children and breeding and family life?

If the answer to all these is no, conditions are psychologically favorable for a vasectomy, Gagnon believes.

About half of all sterilized women adjust well to their operations. But first they go through a troubled period, which Dr. Peter Barglow, of Chicago's Michael Reese Hospital, likens to the successful "working through" of the loss of the childbearing function at menopause.

Some women show long-term effects. They become unrealistically attached to their pets or overprotect the children they already have. Some grow very disturbed and may, for example, begin to wander through hospital obstetrics wards, "looking for a baby."

THE HUMAN FACTOR

There are gimmicks and gadgets and pills. There are jams and jellies. What most people want in a birth control device is *reliability*. And here we come to one of the most obvious—but least understood—facets of modern birth control.

Once we reach the higher ranges of reliability—say 97 percent and up—the differences hardly matter. With any of the better methods, the chances of pregnancy should be very slight, and the need for abortion quite remote. However, as Dr. Tietze pointed out in an interview, "our hang-up about abortion probably helps explain the popularity of the pill. People are willing to run the risks of serious over-medication with hormones in order to approach absolute protection. They pay a high price to get that extra, almost insignificant wedge against abortion."

Furthermore, the reliability statistics we laypeople usually see deal with "theoretical" effectiveness, not "use" effectiveness.

Consider the pill, which, *in theory,* is 99.9 percent reliable. (Certain formulations are more reliable than others, but all fail occasionally, even when taken as directed. Under ideal conditions, only 1 woman out of every 1,000 who is taking the "combined" type of pill will get pregnant each year. Three out of every 1,000 who are taking "sequential" pills will get pregnant.)

In actual practice however—*in use*—even the pill is not so near-perfect as it sounds. Many women skip pills from time to time, especially when they are distracted or off their normal routines. With each missed pill the chance of pregnancy increases, so that even in a well-motivated population of emotionally stable pill users there are apt to be several accidental pregnancies a year. In less stable populations the pregnancy rate is much higher. Women who lead chaotic edge-of-desperation lives cannot easily get back to clinics for their checkups or their refills. You have to *do* something to use the pill effectively, just as you have to *do* something to get good results with a diaphragm, condoms, foam or rhythm.

There are only two available methods which free the user from all obligation: sterilization and the IUD. With these methods, and these methods only, "use" effectiveness and "theoretical" effectiveness are the same. With all the others some effort is required, and human laziness or inertia—or perhaps an unconscious wish for pregnancy—can thwart them.[50]

[50]The fact that birth control works for couples who *will it* was demonstrated ingeniously by Dr. Charles Westoff, a Princeton University demographer. Westoff queried a large number of couples about their birth control practices. He found that in the early years of marriage, when "desired family size" has not yet been achieved, many couples use birth control rather haphazardly. Many pregnancies are thus *unplanned, but not unwanted.* (American families, Westoff notes, are, or used to be, much less concerned about the spacing of their children than the total number.) However, when desired family size is reached, stable, well-motivated couples appear to buckle down and use birth control much more consistently and cautiously. The *same* methods (very often) with which they had experienced earlier failures start to prove highly reliable.

Dr. Hans Lehfeldt of New York University-Bellevue Medical Center, who has made a study of accidental pregnancies, tells of one forty-three-year-old woman who had five sons. Her husband, who was sixteen years older than she, had high blood pressure and symptoms of heart disease. With his health precarious and her menopause approaching, it was certainly impractical for them to assume any new family responsibilities. Yet she stopped taking birth control precautions because, as she later told her doctor, "I was sure I was too old to get pregnant."

It is easy to guess the rest. She had a change-of-life child, the baby girl she had always longed for. In this case, the woman was profoundly happy about the birth, even though she had had a difficult delivery complicated by hemorrhaging, and even though she may find herself a middle-aged widow with a young child.

Dr. Lehfeldt's study of what he calls "willful exposure to unplanned pregnancy" (WEUP) reveals some distressing instances of "emotional desire for pregnancy that is neither conscious nor rationally sound." Most of the persons he studied were under some severe stress because of marital infidelity, premenopausal panic, fear of sterility, religious conflicts about contraception or the threat implied in severe illness. In each case, pregnancy was not an ideal solution to the problem. But for most of the persons it changed the terms of their stress or perhaps helped them to bury it temporarily.

Many accidental pregnancies happen when couples are in turmoil, particularly when a divorce, separation or drifting-apart process has begun but is regretted, at least partially, by one or both partners. One of Dr. Lehfeldt's patients was a woman who discovered that her husband was having a homosexual affair with a young man. She was so horrified and grief-stricken that she went to

For the commercial reasons mentioned earlier, the pill has been overpromoted during the past decade as *the reliable method*. I recall reading an article in the *New York Times Magazine* in which the reliability figures for the diaphragm were given as 80 percent. No doubt this is an accurate "use" figure for certain clinic populations—populations which, as a rule, do not use the pill very much more successfully. However, the average reader of the *Times* is probably educated enough and motivated enough to use the diaphragm with something approaching the "theoretical" effectiveness. It is difficult to understand why the *Times* would want to shake readers' faith in their diaphragms.

Birth control experts have yet another way of dealing with these issues. They talk about "method failure" and "human failure." By this measure, only a tiny percent of the women who get pregnant on the diaphragm do so because the method itself is inadequate to the job. The others get pregnant owing to human error, on the part of either their doctors or themselves.

So the real word about the diaphragm—and most other contraceptives—is contained in the lyrics of a popular song: "It's what you do with what you got." Fertility is never *easy* to curb, but any one of a number of methods can do it effectively, if the *motivation* is there. . . . And alas, all methods have drawbacks. Anyone who tells you otherwise may just be trying to sell you something.

a lawyer to start divorce proceedings. Yet she still loved her husband, and unconsciously, she did not really want to end the marriage. She evaded her agonizing conflict by a pregnancy that she called accidental. Thus she tipped the scales toward the side of continuing the marriage.

CHAPTER EIGHT

THE CHILDREN OF LIBERATED WOMEN

The research evidence . . . strongly suggests that the best arrangement for the development of the young child is one in which his mother is free to work part-time. As we have seen, the establishment of an effective reciprocal relationship does require a substantial amount of time, probably more than can easily be combined with full-time work outside the home. But, in order to be able to function effectively as a parent, the mother must also have the opportunity of being a total person. Moreover, as we have noted, the young child does not require care by the same person all the time, and indeed profits from the intercession of others, notably his father. It was in the light of these considerations that the . . . Report to the White House Conference urged business, industry, and government as employer to increase the number and status of part-time positions. . . .

Urie Bronfenbrenner,
"Developmental Research and Public Policy" (1971)

In this chapter, we return to the first. Western women have been deprived of sexual fulfillment for a long, long time. Our bodies have been vessels not for our own pleasure, but for other people.

This charge is not strictly true because when most of us were mainly mothers, we derived great physical comfort and even sexual pleasure from our babies and children.

In Chapter Four I quoted a remarkable woman who, having had successful natural childbirth, ventured that this was the "great orgasm" of her life. Perhaps she was exceptional, although I do not doubt that if childbirth practices were arranged by women (sexually healthy women) instead of by men, a much larger number of mothers would look back on childbirth as a peak experience, instead of as an agony.

Breast-feeding is often presented in a pious light—as a sacrifice (of her figure and her freedom) that a conscientious mother makes for baby. Nothing could be further from the truth. Longitudinal studies of breast- versus bottle-fed babies show that the latter do just as well except, perhaps, that they may develop more allergies and digestive upsets in their early months. Psychologically, bottle-fed babies grow up just as secure.

Nobody admits it, but it is the *mother* who loses when she declines to breast-feed. Breast-feeding (not in the first few weeks, but once it is comfortably established) is a sensual and sensuous experience unlike any other, somewhat related to and yet different from good sex. As noted in Chapter Three some women experience orgasms while nursing. Even those who don't often report intense sexual pleasure.[1]

Feminists who are *not* mothers tend to underrate the gratifications of child rearing. A friend of mine who is active in the women's liberation movement had some doubts about having children at all. Recently she had a baby—and a boy at that—and she wrote to me, "He's an adorable baby and now he's beginning to smile—each time he does it's like the world beginning again."

Margaret Mead maintains that men are terribly jealous of our childbearing capacity, and all their drumbeating and culture are merely compensation for it:

In every known human society, the male's need for achievement can be recognized. Men may cook or weave or dress dolls or hunt hummingbirds, but if such activities are appropriated occupations of men, then the whole society, men and women alike, votes them as important. When the same occupations are performed by women, they are regarded as less important. In a great number of human societies men's sureness of their sex role is tied up

[1] In the early 1960's I wrote a women's magazine article in which I mentioned that breast-feeding was possibly of greater benefit to mothers than to babies. La Leche League, an organization devoted to the promotion of breast-feeding, organized an angry write-in campaign. I received several hundred pieces of nearly identical hate mail from women who claimed that they had not got any physical pleasure out of nursing, but had done it strictly for their babies' sake. Apparently, the sexual joys of breast-feeding is a rather taboo and threatening topic in our society.

with their right, or ability, to practice some activity that women are not allowed to practice. Their maleness, in fact, has to be underwritten by preventing women from entering some field or performing some feat. Here may be found the relationship between maleness and pride; *that is, a need for prestige that will out-strip the prestige which is accorded to any woman.* There seems no evidence that it is necessary for men to surpass women in any specific way, but rather that men do need to find reassurance in achievement, and because of this connection, cultures frequently phrase achievement as something that women do not or cannot do, rather than directly as something which men do well.

The recurrent problem of civilization is to define the male role satisfactorily enough—whether it be to build gardens or raise cattle, kill game or kill enemies, build bridges or handle bank-shares—so that the male may in the course of his life reach a solid sense of irreversible achievement, of *which his childhood knowledge of the satisfactions of childbearing have given him a glimpse.*[2] [Italics mine.]

However, it has been apparent for some time that most of us are *not* mainly mothers anymore. One hundred years ago the average American woman gave birth to eight or nine children. Now she has only two or three. Lacking other creative expression, she is apt to poke and prod and hover over her small brood to such an extent it is a wonder that any grow up sane. Kenneth Keniston and Edgar Z. Friedenberg are only two of the adolescent specialists who have pointed out that many of today's unhappiest youth are the victims of smother love. And as Betty Friedan has stated so eloquently, "It's the child who supports life in the mother . . . and he is virtually destroyed in the process."

It is not in the interest of modern women to be kept de-

---

[2]Margaret Mead, *Male and Female* (New York, William Morrow & Co., 1949), pp. 159-160.

pendent and housebound. It is not in the interest of their children for, as Bronfenbrenner concedes, in his aforementioned paper, "in order to be able to function effectively as a parent the mother must also have the opportunity of being a total person." Hence, it is difficult not to conclude that the current model of a "normal" family, where the wife-mother stays home for a lifetime just to raise two children, is highly abnormal after all. It has been perpetuated by adult men because it serves their ego needs and also, I think, because it places the responsibility for housework squarely on their wives' shoulders.

Cooking, sewing and gardening may be fun, but only a mental defective could take genuine pride in Joy-clean dishes and aromatic-blue toilet bowls. There are few jobs as unrewarding as housework, for it is lonely, dirty, repetitive and tiresome, and it immediately gets undone.

Given our modern technologies and the small size of our average families, there is little question that to serve the interests of women and children better, what we need now is a great increase in part-time jobs—for young mothers, principally, but for young fathers, too.

In 1970 experts convened at the White House Conference on Children made a strong recommendation to this effect. Naturally, it has been ignored.

As noted in Chapter Six American mothers spend too much time in the exclusive company of their young children, more than in any known primitive society. This abnormal situation often makes the mothers behave in a neurotic and rejecting fashion.

When the children grow older, the mother often attempts to pick up the threads of her career. She usually fails. It is extremely difficult to enter a profession in the late thirties or forties and still amount to anything. Furthermore, the family is now well trained at letting mother do all the housework, so unlike her husband, she does not have free time for extra career-enhancing activities on evenings and weekends.

And yet most young mothers do not really desire to be away from home all day, every day, when their children are very small. Growth and change during the early years of life are rapid and exciting. Most of the working mothers who must be away full time feel sad about it.

But what is a professional woman to do? Our customs and our culture are most unkind to the woman who wishes to combine career and motherhood. We writers are relatively fortunate. Provided that we have started to establish ourselves before the first baby arrives, sometimes we can successfully free-lance from our homes afterward. A woman physician can have a part-time practice *if* she has finished her training, but she cannot take training part-time. She is twenty-six when she completes medical school, twenty-seven when she completes internship and anywhere from thirty to thirty-five when she completes her residency. That is rather long to wait for a first child. For years, women physicians have been imploring the men in charge of their training programs to allow them to make part-time arrangements so that a psychiatric residency, for example, could be spread out over six or seven years instead of being concentrated in the usual three. With only a few exceptions, even the heads of *psychiatry* departments have been unresponsive.[3]

If a woman lawyer hopes to amount to anything, she must get off to a running start during her twenties and thirties. As far as I know there are almost no provisions for such women to take long maternity leaves or to work

[3]The Stanford University School of Medicine has adopted a new program designed to attract women. The curriculum has been made completely elective, with no fixed timetable for the completion of the MD degree.

Female students may take fewer courses than their classmates and may also take pregnancy leave without any penalty. Explaining the program in the *New England Journal of Medicine,* Dr. John Bunker said, "We must make sure that young women know that the gates of the medical schools are open to them, and we must assure them that becoming a physician is an appropriate and realistic goal."

part-time. College teachers face a very tight job market. Young women who take a two- or three-year maternity leave rarely get their jobs back, unless they have tenure.

The Newtime Employment Agency in New York City is to be congratulated for its efforts to find twenty-five-hour-a-week jobs for mothers who are professional women. (One of their recent ads: "If Madame Curie were alive and only able to work from 9:30 to 3:15, would you hire her?") Twenty-five-hour-a-week jobs are a marvelous idea for mothers of school-age children, but many mothers of children who are still younger would jump at the chance to work even shorter hours. And it could be done. A lawyer could work on one case; a teacher could take one class. A newspaper reporter could work from home and, perhaps, share her beat with one or two other reporter-mothers.

Educated women are bitter because they are forced to make a cruel and unnecessary choice: Rock the cradle, *or* keep a foot in the door to their profession.

Our employers and our government are not going to hand us good day care, good part-time jobs or reasonable tax deductions for working mothers.[4] We are going to

[4]The insanity of our tax laws is illustrated by the following item from the April, 1971, issue of *Family Health:* "The latest *official* IRS guide for taxpayers gives the unbelievable information that bribes and kickbacks constitute a legitimate deduction from income tax! . . ."

The IRS has also ruled that a traveling salesman who is made nervous by sexual deprivation and cannot consequently perform his job to his satisfaction can deduct the price of a call girl as a legitimate business expense. But only in 1971 did Congress finally address itself to the problem of including deductions for child care in tax legislation.

However, also in 1971 an almost unbelievable new tax law went into effect. Single taxpayers and married couples where the wife *earns no income at all* are given preferential treatment, at the expense of two-income families.

If a husband and wife each earn $7,000 a year, their joint federal taxes are about $56 more than if they lived in sin, as it used to be called. If each earns $15,000, marriage increases their joint taxes by $1,045. If man and wife each earns $25,000, divorce becomes very attractive, for it would save them $2,940 in annual taxes.

have to organize and agitate for these things, as labor unions did a generation ago. It is most important for women to get together with other women and try to work out sensible solutions. In some cities, women are starting to have success with share-a-job programs. Two nurses, for example, may offer to cover a certain hospital shift jointly, one of them working three days a week and the other two, or each working half a day. Needless to say, in fields where there are employee shortages, employers are especially apt to be flexible. In any field, however, shared jobs reduce absenteeism, for should one employee have an emergency, the other can take over.

I have made the assumption that most mothers would prefer not to work full-time when their children are very small. However, there are many women who have to work, and others who prefer to do so. Are their babies damaged?

Apparently not. One of the best-kept secrets (from American women) is that even preschoolers whose mothers work shape up just as well as the children of full-time homemakers. True, there are many *theories* which posit that the children of working mothers should be lonely and maladjusted, but when such children are actually compared to the children of full-time homemakers, the differences are negligible or nonexistent. Sometimes, when differences *are* found, they favor the children of working mothers!

This is most apt to be true when a mother does not feel guilty about working. If she does experience guilt—or fear that she may be neglecting her child—then her efforts to overcomepensate may do some psychological harm.

In a recent summary of all the studies in this area, Dr. Lois Hoffman wrote:

It seems clear that our tax laws are still premised on the belief that a married woman's place is in the home. For further details, see Professor George Cooper's "Working Wives and the Tax Law," which appeared in the *Rutgers Law Review* (Fall, 1970).

The research, on the whole, does not support the dire predictions of disaster for the working mother's child. Maternal employment does not appear to be a major or uniform factor in its effects on the child. Most of the studies found no effects; none found very strong relationships; the findings were not completely negative. (Several studies indicate a positive effect of maternal employment on girls. The daughters of working mothers are more likely to choose their mothers as models and as the person they most admire.)

The research should be reassuring to working mothers.

Dr. Hoffman, who teaches at the University of Michigan, is co-author of a standard academic work, *The Employed Mother in America*. Last year, the editors of *Child Craft Encyclopedia,* a division of the World Book Encyclopedia, asked her to contribute an article on "maternal employment." The paragraphs just cited are from her article, which was never published. The following letter explains why:

David L. Murray   February 11, 1971
Senior Editor
Childcraft—The How and Why Library

DEAR DR. MURRAY:

The manuscript I received from your office is so completely changed from the original in content that I could not possibly allow my name to be connected with it. The major thrust of the present article is diametrically opposed to the existing research findings. While the article is filled with dire warnings to the potential working mother, there is not one shred of evidence to justify this approach. . . .

. . . whatever the personal view of your writers, 51% of the mothers of school aged children now work and the percentage will increase. Those women need more than the personal and highly fallacious views of whoever authored this article. Page 6 is the only part of the current version that is in any way related to my original piece.

The article is quite beyond correction. Under no circumstances is it to carry my name nor to in any way imply that I am in agreement with it.

I also consider the article a social disservice and would urge you to delete it. It is precisely such materials that have made working mothers fearful that their employment will lead to their child's neglect, when in fact there is no study—none at all—in countless attempts—that has shown the working mother's child neglected. The only negative effect clearly shown has been the attempt to overcompensate as a result of these fears. There are many positive effects mentioned in the original article but deleted in this one. To publish an article of this sort is to support ignorance and fears.

Yours truly,
LOIS WLADIS HOFFMAN, PH.D.

But—you may be wondering—isn't there conclusive evidence that if a *baby*, at least, fails to get lots of attention from his mother, then both his IQ and his personality will be seriously damaged?

The answer is no, although in college courses and in women's magazines (as well as certain encyclopedias), Americans are still being led to believe that such evidence exists.

In the October, 1971, issue of the *American Journal of Orthopsychiatry*, Dr. Rochelle Paul Wortis presents an objective review of the research:[5]

The principal argument used to encourage women to devote their constant attention to newborns is based on

[5]Rochelle Paul Wortis, "The Acceptance of the Concept of the Maternal Role by Behavorial Scientists: Its Effects on Women," *American Journal of Orthopsychiatry*, Vol. 41, No. 5 (October, 1971), pp. 733–46.

the suggested deleterious effects of mother-child separation (the "Bowlby-" or "Spitz-hypothesis"). Most of the
studies of mother-child separation have been based, however, not on normal separation of infants from their
parents, but on institutionalized children. Because of the
physical and social sterility of many hospitals and or-
phanages, these children often suffered from inadequate
environmental and human stimulation.

. . . In fact, there seems to have occurred a dangerously unscientific extrapolation of assumptions from studies
of institutionalized infants to the much more common
situation in which infants leave their homes for part of
the day, are cared for by other responsible individuals,
and are returned again to their homes. As a result,
women are taught to believe that infants require their un-
divided attention during the first two or three years of
life, at least. The way our society is structured, this attitude functions to confine the woman physically (to her
home) and socially (to her family unit).

Years earlier, writing in the same journal, Margaret
Mead made a similar point:[6]

At present, the specific biological situation of the continuing relationship of the child to its biological mother
and its need for care by human beings are being hopelessly confused in the growing insistence that child and
biological mother, or mother surrogate, must never be
separated, that all separation, even for a few days, is inevitably damaging, and that if long enough it does irreversible damage. This . . . is the new and subtle form of
antifeminism in which men—under the guise of exalting
the importance of maternity—are tying women more
tightly to their children than has been thought necessary
since the invention of bottle feeding and baby carriages.
Actually, anthropological evidence gives no support at

[6]Margaret Mead, "Some Theoretical Considerations on the Problem of Mother-Child Separation," *American Journal of Orthopsychiatry*, Vol. 24 (1954), pp. 471-83.

present to the value of such an accentuation of the tie
between mother and child. . . . On the contrary, cross-
cultural studies suggest that adjustment is most facilitated
if the child is cared for by many warm friendly people.

On the basis of no evidence at all, or even in the face of
evidence pointing in the opposite direction, American
women have been encouraged to believe that it would be
extremely negligent to allow others to share in the rearing
of their young. They have also been urged to think that it
would be "abnormal" to forgo having children altogether
and folly to attempt to raise a child outside of a conventional marriage arrangement. Hence, even women who do
not desire marriage or motherhood are pressured into
seeking both.

There is no natural law that children and marriage must
go together. Any woman has or should have four basic options:

> She can not marry and not have children.
> She can not marry and have children.
> She can marry and not have children.
> She can marry and have children.

Most women who want children opt for marriage as
well. Economically—and socially—it is probably easier to
raise a child when there are two concerned parents. However, two parents are *not* absolutely necessary for the welfare of the child. Some of the most commanding figures in
human history were out-of-wedlock children who were
reared by their mothers.

Nor is it necessary for a parent to be the *biological*
mother of a child. It is true that many pregnant women
feel extremely close and loving toward the fetus who is
growing and moving within them. However, other pregnant
women do not harbor such emotions. In any case there is
not (insofar as modern science has been able to deter-

mine) any special maternal instinct which is exclusively connected with hormones or pregnancy or reserved unto females. Maternal behavior emerges *after* the birth of a baby.[7] In humans and other mammals, there appears to be a "critical period" during which close contact with an infant has the effect of arousing caretaking behavior. These responses, stimulated by the sight and sounds and touch and odors of a baby, can be fully aroused in women who have not given birth, as well as in males. The key issue *seems to be frequency and intensity of contact.* Unless a mother is absent, a father or other adult is unlikely to have a very high frequency of contact with an infant. But when he does have it—in the animal as well as the human world—he often rises to the occasion. In some species of animals, he builds the nest or shelter which, ordinarily, the mother would have built. There are even some scattered reports of human males who have succeeded in nursing their babies when no other source of nourishment was available. The baby is put to the breast and suckles. In a few days' time—if these reports are true—lactation begins. (At the 1971 meeting of the American Association for the Advancement of Science, Margaret Mead summed it up like this: "We have some instances of male lactation, but lactation on the whole is a female trait.")

Strictly speaking then, while children need love and attention, they do not need the constant love and attention of their biological mothers. Their caretakers can be other women—or men. A recent study of the families of Harvard graduate students showed that toddlers can become just as attached to their fathers as their mothers, provided that they spend sufficient *time* with them.[8]

We now know from psychological and animal studies

[7]Eleanor E. Maccoby and Carol Nagy Jacklin, "Sex Differences and Their Implications for Sex Roles," paper delivered at 1971 Annual Meeting of American Psychological Association.

[8]M. Kotelchack, unpublished Harvard University doctoral thesis, 1971.

that there is probably no such thing as a maternal instinct. At least, there is more concrete evidence against it than for it. We also know from anthropology that there is no primitive culture where mothers are expected to spend as much time in the exclusive company of their babies and young children as they are expected to spend in the United States (see previous chapter). And we surmise from our studies of history and biographies of great men and women that a perhaps disproportionately large number were raised in one-parent families or under other "unconventional" circumstances.

Women, then, should feel freer to select their own lifestyles than many of them do. The old argments that

> we-cannot-be-happy-unless-we-have-children
> and
> we-cannot-raise-normal-children-unless-we-stay-home-
> with-them

are simply invalid, no more than wishful thinking on the part of males. The factors which are important for healthy infant and child development are:[9]

> Consistent care; sensitivity of the caretaking adult(s) in responding to the infant's needs; a stable environment, the characteristics of which the growing infant can learn to identify; continuity of experience within the infant's environment; and physical and intellectual stimulation, love and affection. There is no clear evidence that multiple mothering, without associated deprivation or stress, results in personality damage.

Knowing what we now know, we can strive, with a clear conscience, for day-care centers, equal pay for equal work, abortion and tax reform, legal redress, and opportunities for part-time work. We will not damage our children

[9]Rochelle Paul Wortis, *op. cit.,* p. 739.

and we may benefit them greatly, for as one young mother recently confessed:[10]

"I feel it should be more widely recognized that it is in the very nature of a mother's position, in our society, to avenge her own frustrations on a small, helpless child; whether this takes the form of tyranny, or of a smothering affection that asks the child to be a substitute for all she has missed."

However, as the women in Scandinavian countries and Eastern Europe have learned—and as our black women in the United States have always known—it is not enough for women to become fully human unless men become human, too. Women in these other countries have gone far ahead of us in winning the rights to careers.[11] Yet, even the busiest and most successful complain that they continue to be solely responsible for child care and housework—with little help from their husbands. They have "won" two demanding jobs instead of one, and they frequently state that they have little time for enjoying their children or anything else.

In Sweden, where women have achieved most of the goals feminists are seeking here, the *rehumanization of men* has become the new societal objective.[12] Paid paternity leaves and greater opportunities for fathers to participate in the care of the newborn have been recognized as essential. The legal status of house-husbands (*hemmaman*)

[10]Wortis, *op. cit.*, p. 739.

[11]But the recent experience of Russian women gives strong support to Mead's thesis that as soon as women are deemed suitable for a certain job, that job is downgraded. Today a majority of Russian physicians are women, but they do not enjoy nearly the same high status which physicians enjoy in the United States. The Russians now believe that the "best" scientific brains (generally male) should be encouraged to go into physics, chemistry, etc. or medical research, but not practice. . . .

[12]Birgitta Linner, "What Does Equality Between the Sexes Imply?," *American Journal of Orthopsychiatry*, Vol. 41, No. 5 (October, 1971), pp. 747–56.

has been upgraded. Husbands and wives have been deeemed equally responsible for the guardianship of their children, so that couples may voluntarily agree to divorce, without guilt being assigned to either partner. Sex-role stereotyping in children's books and in advertising has been ended, and ever since 1962, when a new public school system was introduced, boys have been taught traditionally feminine subjects such as home economics, sewing and child care, while girls learn manual handicraft and other "masculine" skills.

In Sweden, Group 8, a prominent women's liberation organization, appears to have advanced far beyond our own feminist groups in the United States. The Group 8 manifesto states that "even if women manage to gain equality with men, they will not be free . . . before men are also free." Two of Group 8's most interesting current goals are:

—Laws protecting part-time personnel, men as well as women.

—The assignment of one-quarter of all new housing to collectives. (The Swedes are experimenting with new marriage forms, trial marriages, "loyalty" marriages, weekend marriages, one-parent families. Communal family life, however, is the new form that seems to have evoked the most enthusiasm. Swedes have been complaining that they are hard pressed to find *housing* which is suitable for the establishment of communes.)

In general, most Swedish women have started to agree with Eva Moberg, a feminist leader who pointed out in 1961 that "as long as society demands a double role (work outside and inside the house) from women, a single role from men, equality can never be achieved. Responsibility for home and children must be shared by mother, father, and society."

I, for one, do not want my daughters to grow up as joyless and overburdened as the women of Eastern Europe. I hope that American feminists will learn early to keep their eye on the real prize—the rehumanization of men.

CHAPTER NINE

THE MIDDLE-CLASS MALE
AS MIGHTY JOE YOUNG,
OR CAN MEN BE REHUMANIZED?

A psychiatrist I know has long declared himself "a feminist." He'd like his own daughters to be psychiatrists, too, not social workers or psychiatric nurses. (Freud's daughter, Anna, the inheritor of her father's mantle, never did get to medical school. She is a lay analyst, practically the only one in the world who can charge as high fees as analysts with medical diplomas.) Our modern psychiatrist likes to warn his students that a woman "must be her own person. . . . If she fuses her life-style into that of her husband, she is apt to develop emotional illness or 'social dysfunction' such as drinking."

Naturally, he has allowed his wife to do her own thing. He let her go back to work as an interior designer when their daughters were still in nursery school.

"Ginny is a damn good designer," he once boasted to me. "She commands a high salary and she's worth it. . . . Let me show you how she decorated my office. Isn't it sensational? Would have cost me ten thou if I hadn't had her in the family.

"To tell the truth, though, she's not such a great cook or

disciplinarian. Like anyone else, she has some talents and not others. When she went back to work, our whole operation smoothed out. Her paycheck bought us a splendid cook and a fine nurse-housekeeper for our children.

"As I tell all my students, my life is really enriched by having a career-woman wife. I've gotten to meet such interesting people in business and the arts, because Ginny gets invited to all these openings and cocktail parties. And—I might as well admit it—a lot of my celebrity patients come to me through *her* social connections."

Last year Ginny divorced her psychiatrist-husband, refusing alimony. Fortyish, she suddenly looked fifteen years younger:

"We'd worked out an arrangement, or adjustment, and we were both so busy that we thought things were OK. The sex wasn't much, but we blamed it on the fact that we were both so tired.

"Then everything disintegrated over, what appeared on the surface, to be one silly issue. Years before, when the girls were small and I went back to work, I agreed to turn all my paychecks and commissions over to my husband. He was the one deciding our budget, and he had a bookkeeper-secretary paying the bills. I was glad to be relieved of the responsibility. I had my own little checking account for personal expenses, and each month, when I got my bank statement, his bookkeeper would write me out a large enough check to bring my balance to five hundred dollars.

"Last year a friend of mine who is in the women's liberation movement persuaded me to write a hundred-dollar check toward bail money for Joan Bird, a black revolutionary who was in jail and whom the black men were not helping. On the way home I realized that I had overdrawn my account and the check would bounce. I asked my husband to give me a check to cover it. He got very mad, and he said he wouldn't because giving money to Joan Bird should have been a mutual decision. He wasn't sure that he approved of her. I said that I didn't agree with her politics either, but that wasn't the point. She was a woman who had to turn to other women for help because the men in her own movement had let her down.

"I couldn't believe my husband's anger. He doesn't consult me before writing out a donation. He gives the AMA lots of money every year, and in my opinion they are little better than the Mafia.

"After that I stopped turning my money over to him. I put it in my own account. One day he tried to grab a check from me, and I ran back to my desk and put it in the drawer that locks. I hid the key. Suddenly, my psychiatrist-husband turned into Mighty Joe Young. He picked up chairs and lamps and end tables and crashed them down on the floor. He threw a cup of scalding coffee on me. Then he broke my nose.

"Maybe I could have forgiven him if we'd been alone, but my daughters witnessed the performance. I don't want them to grow up to be women who would take that kind of treatment. I had to leave."

Is this an unusual story? There is no reason to think so. As women awaken to their autonomy and their rights, men—the most civilized men—seem to be taking it all quite badly.

As Gore Vidal has suggested:[1]

There has been from Henry Miller to Norman Mailer to Charles Manson a logical procession. The Miller-Mailer-Manson man (or M3 for short) has been conditioned to think of women as, at best, breeders of sons; at worst, objects to be poked, humiliated, killed. Needless to say, M3's reaction to Women's Liberation has been one of panic. He believes that if women are allowed parity with men they will treat men the way men have treated women and that, even M3 will agree, has not been very well. . . . Women are not going to make it until M3

[1]Gore Vidal, "In Another Country," *New York Review of Books* (July 22, 1971), p. 8.

is reformed and that is going to take a long time. . . .
M3's counterattack is only now gathering momentum.
. . . Miller-Mailer-Manson. Woman, beware. Righteous
murder stalks the land. . . . M3 has every reason to be
fearful of woman's revenge should she achieve equality.
He is also faced with the nightmare (for him) of being
used as a sexual object or worse, being ignored. (The
menacing cloud in the middle distance is presently no
larger than a vibrator.) He is fighting back on every
front. . . .

Today we are witnessing the breakup of patterns thousands of years old. M3's response is predictable: if man
on top of woman has been the pattern for all our known
history, it must be right. This of course was the same argument he made when the institution of slavery was
challenged. . . . M3's roar is that of our tribal past, quite
unsuitable, as the old Stalinists used to say, to new necessities.

On first reading these thoughts, I found them amusing
but exaggerated. Manson is, after all, a mass murderer,
and Mailer once stabbed and almost killed his wife. The
civilized men we know can't all be M3's. Now I am not
so sure. For as the women in my circle are becoming more
outspoken, their husbands and lovers are reacting with
curses and violence, genuine physical violence on occasion.

These are the husbands and lovers who, in the comfortable past, prided themselves on their egalitarianism.

But what manner of egalitarianism was it, actually?

In the Midwest, sociologists Margaret Poloma and T.
Neal Garland have completed a study of fifty-three couples
where the wife is a practicing physician, college professor
or attorney.[2]

Only *one* couple—out of fifty-three—could be classi-
led as "truly egalitarian" in the view of the researchers:

[2]Margaret M. Poloma and T. Neal Garland, "The Married Professional Woman: A Study in Tolerance of Domestication," *Journal
of Marriage and the Family*, Vol. 33, No. 3 (August, 1971), pp.
531–40.

This case consisted of two professors who made a conscious effort to *share* (not merely *help*) in both traditional male and female role tasks. Both considered it their *responsibility* to cook, clean and care for the children. More important, both considered it their responsibility to provide for the family's economic needs; and under no circumstance was the husband's career deemed more important than the wife's. In all the other couples, the wife was *responsible* for the traditional feminine tasks (although usually the husband did "help" in varying degrees). . . .

Most of these women, Poloma and Garland report, accepted things as they were and even took pride in their ability to perform as superwomen. Some pointed out that they had one great advantage over their husbands—more job freedom. They considered themselves the last of the "genteel professionals"—able to accept positions when they found the work challenging, exciting or philanthropic—without worry about pay.

Other sociologists, such as William Goode, have noted that educated, upper-class husbands are often, in fact, *more* domineering than their lower-class counterparts:[3]

Since at present this philosophy (of equalitarianism in the family) is most strongly held among better educated segments of the population, and among women more than among men, two interesting tensions may be seen: Lower-class men concede fewer rights *ideologically* than their women in fact *obtain,* and the more educated men are more likely to concede *more* rights ideologically than they in fact grant. . . . One partial resolution of the latter tension is to be found in the frequent assertion from families of professional men that they should not make demands which would interfere with his *work:* He takes preference as a *professional,* not as a family head or as a male; nevertheless, the precedence is his. By contrast,

[3]William Goode, *World Revolution and Family Patterns* (New York, The Free Press, 1963), p. 21.

lower-class men demand deference as *men,* as heads of families.

What has been taken for granted—in all strata of our society—is that husbands are and should be dominant, that they have the right to tell their wives what to do. Male dominance is socially approved, and expected, even in the most highly educated "liberal" families.

Married professional women have accepted subjugation, believing (as many of the Poloma-Garland subjects noted) that this is the only way to achieve "the best of both worlds"—marriage and motherhood, plus an interesting job.

Such women have been *afraid* to make any direct gestures toward marital power. When they want something important, they must get their husband's approval first (as he need not get theirs), and they nag or wheedle, bargain, manipulate or whore (exchange sexual favors) to win his compliance.

Should a woman take a direct power stand (as Ginny did when she deposited her own paycheck in her own account) her "permissive" husband flies into a rage, like an animal.

When a large animal encounters a smaller or weaker one, he may make certain dominance gestures. In return, the weaker animal makes gestures of submission.

Should the weaker animal fail to submit, the larger attacks. Ordinarily, a wife submits appropriately to her husband's dominance gestures.[4]

A husband and wife are at a party. The wife says something that the husband does not want her to say (perhaps it reveals something about him that might threaten his ranking with other men). He quickly tightens the muscles around his jaw and gives her a rapid but

[4] Lynn Connor, "Male Dominance, the Nitty-Gritty of Oppression," *It Ain't Me Babe,* Vol. 1, No. 8 (June 11–July 1, 1970), pp. 9–11.

intense direct stare. Outsiders don't notice the interaction, though they may have a vaguely uncomfortable feeling that they are intruding on something private. The wife, who is acutely sensitive to the gestures of the man on whom she is dependent, immediately stops the conversation, lowers or turns her head slightly, averts her eyes, or gives off some other gestures of submission which communicate acquiescence to her husband, and reduces his aggression. Peace is restored; the wife has been put in her place. If the wife does not respond with submission, she can expect to be punished. When gestures of dominance fail, the dominant animal usually resorts to violence. We all know stories about husbands beating up their wives after the party when they have reached the privacy of their home. Many of us have experienced at least a few blows from husbands or lovers when we refuse to submit to them. It is difficult to assess the frequency of physical attacks within so called love relationships, because women rarely tell even one another when they have taken place. By developing a complicated ethic of loyalty (described above in terms of privacy), men have protected themselves from such reports leaking out and becoming public information. Having already been punished for stepping out of role, the woman is more than a little reluctant to tell anyone of the punishment because it would mean violating the loyalty code, which is an even worse infraction of the rules and most likely would result in further and perhaps more severe punishment.

In New York City, it has long been the custom of construction workers to whistle and yell obscenities at passing females. The female is expected to smile, avert her eyes, hurry on or otherwise express submission—that is, not fight back. In recent months, some women have been taking a stand against these intrusions on their privacy and their persons, by slowing down and asking firmly, "What did you say?" or perhaps demanding, "Repeat that please."

The rage of these construction workers is terrifying to

behold. They do not apologize. They do not laugh. They
attack the passing female or threaten to attack her. Some
are now carrying water guns, which they use to squirt her.
(After such an episode, one young woman brought the
construction worker to court. The judge asked her if she
was a member of women's liberation—and then dismissed
the case.)

The same sort of problem is—apparently—plaguing
many contemporary marriages. The middle-class husband,
like the hard hat, cannot tolerate insubordination. Perhaps, as Maccoby believes (see Chapter One), the male is
truly more aggressive than the female.[5] Perhaps, as Mead
believes (see Chapter Eight), he cannot forgive her for
making babies and cannot put aside his need to compensate.

The humanization of men will not come swiftly or
easily. It will not come at all in our generation, not—
certainly—on any major scale.

Many of us are trying to rear sons who are untainted

[5]In the December, 1971, issue of *Family Circle*, Beatrice Buckler
wrote: "Maybe the only hope for peace lies with women. Women's
liberationists have claimed that it's all a matter of cultural conditioning. But researchers at the University of Wisconsin say that
there appear to be genetic differences in the behavior of males and
females—at least male and female monkeys. Studies of the primates
indicate that females act less aggressively during play than males.
The comparisons were made after isolating male monkeys for six
months after birth and then providing them with only female companions. Even when deprived of examples of their own sex to follow, the isolated monkeys behaved in the same rough-and-tumble
aggressive manner as normal males.

"Another instance of the possible difference between boys and
girls was witnessed by the wives of White House counselors Donald
Rumsfeld and Robert H. Finch, who were accompanying their husbands abroad on a special mission for President Nixon. The wives
worked on their own mission, visiting schools in Rumania, Yugo-
slavia and France. Of a nursery school in Rumania, Mrs. Rumsfeld
recalls: 'Boys and girls of toddler age were dressed alike in skirts.
But it was easy to tell the boys from the girls, because the boys
were so much more pugnacious than the girls. They were poking
and pushing, while the girls played quietly with a shovel in the
sandbox.' "

by sexism, but the culture stands against it. The books they read and TV programs they watch, the history and "psychology" they study in school and the sex-segregated classes they are forced to attend—all these turn them in a sexist direction.

The Swedes have embarked on a noble experiment in non-sexist child rearing and education. Painfully, carefully and over a period of many years, they have tried to eliminate all sex-stereotypic material to which young children might be exposed.

If boys can be reared to accept girls as true equals, if both boys and girls can be taught that they are fully human and autonomous, then the Swedes will probably know it first.

Index